CINEMA BY OTHER MEANS

CINEMA BY OTHER MEANS

Pavle Levi

OXFORD
UNIVERSITY PRESS

Oxford University Press, Inc., publishes works that further
Oxford University's objective of excellence
in research, scholarship, and education.

Oxford   New York
Auckland   Cape Town   Dar es Salaam   Hong Kong   Karachi
Kuala Lumpur   Madrid   Melbourne   Mexico City   Nairobi
New Delhi   Shanghai   Taipei   Toronto

With offices in
Argentina   Austria   Brazil   Chile   Czech Republic   France   Greece
Guatemala   Hungary   Italy   Japan   Poland   Portugal   Singapore
South Korea   Switzerland   Thailand   Turkey   Ukraine   Vietnam

Copyright © 2012 by Oxford University Press, Inc.

Published by Oxford University Press, Inc.
198 Madison Avenue, New York, New York 10016

www.oup.com

Oxford is a registered trademark of Oxford University Press

All rights reserved. No part of this publication may be reproduced,
stored in a retrieval system, or transmitted, in any form or by any means,
electronic, mechanical, photocopying, recording, or otherwise,
without the prior permission of Oxford University Press.

Library of Congress Cataloging-in-Publication Data
Levi, Pavle.
Cinema by other means / Pavle Levi.
p.   cm.
Includes bibliographical references and index.
ISBN 978-0-19-984140-0 (hardcover: alk. paper) — ISBN 978-0-19-984142-4 (pbk: alk. paper)
1. Experimental films—History and criticism. I. Title.
PN1995.9.E96L48   2012
791.43'611—dc23   2011025577

For Jelena, Luka, and Eva

TABLE OF CONTENTS

Acknowledgments	ix
Preamble	xi
1. Film, or the Vibrancy of Matter	3
2. On Re-materialization of the Cinematographic Apparatus	25
3. Written Films	46
4. Notes around General Cinefication	77
5. Whither the Imaginary Signifier?	105
6. The "Between" of Cinema	138
Notes	161
Bibliography	181
Index	191

ACKNOWLEDGMENTS

Numerous persons helped me on this journey through the theory and practice of "cinema by other means." I am indebted to Annette Michelson, Branko Vučićević, and Scott Bukatman for years of spirited guidance and most generous support of my scholarship. Sam Ishii-Gonzales and Malcolm Turvey have my gratitude for offering extensive and vital commentary on my writing at decisive points in the book's evolution. I am greatly appreciative of the strong encouragement I received from my colleagues in the Department of Art & Art History at Stanford University, especially Kristine Samuelson and Michael Marrinan.

I should particularly like to acknowledge that many ideas expressed here took form in lively and illuminating discussions with Slobodan Šijan, Miodrag Milošević, Soyoung Yoon, Kiersten Jakobsen, Hrvoje Turković, Miroslav Bata Petrović, Daniel Hackbarth, and Jamie Nisbet. I sharpened my perspective in memorable exchanges with Allen S. Weiss, Jean-Michel Frodon, P. Adams Sitney, Paul DeMarinis, Dudley Andrew, Pamela Lee, Federico Windhausen, Branislav Jakovljević, Branimir Stojanović, Milica Tomić, Jean Ma, Lazar Stojanović, Želimir Žilnik, Jean-Luc Godard, Michael Witt, Michel Giroud, and Tomislav Brčić. The study also substantially benefited from the knowledge and kind help of Diana Nenadić and Željko Radivoj (Croatian Film Association, Zagreb), Ivko Šešic (AFC-Academic Film Center, Belgrade), Dejan Sretenović

ACKNOWLEDGMENTS

(Museum of Contemporary Art, Belgrade), Marinko Sudac (Sudac Collection, Varaždin), and Miroljub Stojanović (Film Center Serbia, Belgrade).

My heartfelt thanks to all who invited me to publicly present and discuss parts of the material as it was developing: Jurij Meden, Nil Baskar, Maja Krajnc, Andrej Šprah, Dora Baras, Petar Milat, Rick Warner, Joshua Landy, Dušan Grlja, Dragana Kitanović, John Bender, Marie-Pierre Ulloa, Milanka Todić, Matthew Tiews, Nadja Rottner, Ina Blom, Svetlana Gavrilović, Borka Pavićević, Nebojša Jovanović, Zoran Saveski, Boro Kontić, and Bojana Piškur. I am grateful to David Fresko for his meticulous work during the final stages of preparing the text for publication. Valuable help in obtaining illustrations was provided by many already mentioned individuals, as well as Miroljub Todorović, Roland Sabatier, Jelena Perać (Museum of Fine Arts, Belgrade), Annika Keller (Art Resource, New York), Andrea Fisher (Artists Rights Society, New York), Werner Spies and Julia Drost. I also wish to sincerely thank Kenneth White, Jim Kent, Mark Urbanek, Jill Davis, Peter Blank, Elis Imboden, Danica Sarlya, and Zoe Luhtala for facilitating my research in a variety of ways; and, Sebastian Salvado, Amber Ruiz, and Huey-Ning Tan for making the process of image production painless.

I am indebted to Shannon McLachlan, my editor at Oxford University Press, for the enthusiasm and confidence with which she saw the project through. The expertise of Brendan O'Neill, Ryan Sarver, and Ashwin Bohra A. is also much appreciated.

Research and writing of the book were generously funded by a McNamara Faculty Grant in the Department of Art & Art History at Stanford University; a Green Faculty Fellowship at Stanford; and a Rados Grant from Stanford's Center for Russian, East European, and Eurasian Studies (CREEES). I am obliged to Nancy Troy for supporting the production of the book on behalf of the Department of Art & Art History.

Maja Levi and Božidar Levi, as well as Ljubinka Živković, have my gratitude for the years of unremitting support. Jelena Levi makes nothing seem impossible. I owe her my happiness.

PREAMBLE

Around the turn of the twentieth century, a simple invention helped define the operating character of film technology. A *loop* was added to the film's threading path in the camera/projector, thus eliminating the negative side effects of intermittent movement. A strip of film could now be safely advanced through, and paused at, the camera/projector gate without the danger of excessive tension causing it to break at the spool.

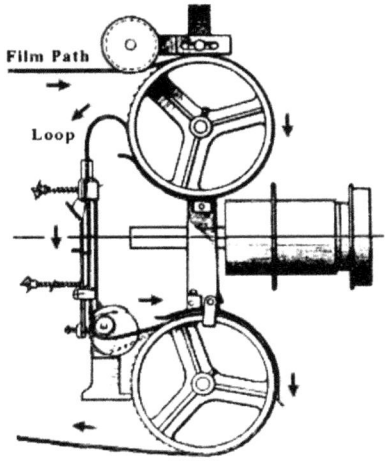

Figure 0.1

The Latham Loop (fig. 0.1), as this invention came to be known, is a relational function residing at the heart of the cinematographic machine. It is, essentially, a *curvature of space* demarcated between the spools, the gears, and the gate: a trajectory of movement made explicit and visible only once the filmstrip has been threaded into the camera/projector. The Latham Loop may thus be thought of as a friendly "ghost in the machine," bringing together thought and technology, conceptual and mechanized labor. In the realm of the cinema, the Latham Loop stands for the inseparability of idea and matter, practice and theory.

In 1902, Raoul Grimoin-Sanson and Jules Demaria created a machine capable of projecting both static and moving images.[1] Embodied in this hybrid apparatus was a historical rupture. The dual projector was a symptom of a major technological and cultural change—it signaled the end of the era of the magic lantern and the slide show and the beginning of the epoch of film. The Grimoin-Sanson and Demaria apparatus bespoke the magic lantern's "eternal dream": the dream to be, to become, the cinematograph!

At the same time, however, by upholding the difference between the magic lantern and the film projector, between the two generations of mechanical visual media, Grimoin-Sanson and Demaria's machine also forewarned future film historians and theorists of the need to resist teleological and essentialist interpretations of cinematographic technology and of its place and function in the complex entity that is the cinema. The gap that in this case literally separates stasis from movement and the singular from the serial image points toward the sort of difference that is in fact internal to every medium, figuring between the medium as a concept (as an intention and a possibility) and its practical realization. Here, specifically, this difference is the one between the idea, the dream, of a medium capable of reproducing motion, and an actual, functioning cinematographic apparatus. It is precisely in this difference and gap that the "pure" cine-desire may be said to originate: a desire subsequently sustained and perpetuated through the dialectic of film and cinema, of the two nonidentical though entirely interdependent phenomena. In this book, I hope to make the desire in question palpable, so to speak, through a twofold exploration.

First, I will consider various aspects of an incredibly rich history, stretching from the 1910s to the present, of avant-garde endeavors to practice the cinema by using the tools, the materials, the technology, and the techniques that either modify and alter, or are entirely different from those typically associated with the normative cinematographic apparatus. It is a tale of the multiple states or conditions of cinema, of a range of extraordinary, radical experiments not only with but also "around" and even without film.[2] We live in an age in which it is easy to overlook the fact that this severance of cinema from its traditional, historical base—the film apparatus—did not emerge as a possibility only with the advent of digital technologies. This book hopes to shed some light on the extent to which the separation of film and cinema—but also the multiple modalities of their imaginative re-alignment—had, in fact, already been practiced throughout the era of cinematographic normativity; during those (scarcely past) "pre-digital" days when film was still widely accepted as the material-technological foundation of the phenomenon that is the cinema.

In chapter 1, I explore the struggle waged by a number of 1910s and 1920s European avant-gardists—notably, Man Ray, Ljubomir Micić, and Dragan Aleksić—to establish film as, first and foremost, *vibrant raw matter* (at times directly opposed to, or irreconcilable with, signification/meaning) and to explicate a "corporeal-libidinal" dimension of the film machine through a series of both cinematographic and non-cinematographic interventions (such as those carried out in the register of the written word). In chapter 2, I theoretically elaborate the concept of "cinema by other means," focusing on a number of assemblages, photo-collages, drawings, and paintings, as well as theoretical writings, by artists such as Laszlo Moholy-Nagy, Raoul Hausmann, Aleksandar Vučo, Dušan Matić, and Francis Picabia. I argue that a profoundly dialectical understanding of the couple film/cinema developed in the context of the historical avant-garde's concern with medium-specificity, giving rise to a variety of experiments in *re-materialization* of the cinematographic apparatus. Chapter 3 analyzes the practice of "written cinema," which was widespread in the 1920s and the 1930s among the Dadaists, the Constructivists, the Surrealists, and their contemporaries. What is at stake here is the production of written texts *a priori* designated as films proper. The bulk of the chapter closely scrutinizes one such "written film": *Doctor Hypnison, or the Technique of Living*, produced in 1923 by the Yugoslav poet Monny de Boully. Chapter 4 addresses a multitude of ways, some more progressive than others, in which filmmakers, artists, and writers have responded to the effects of the "general cinefication" of the living reality, ever more apparent since the 1950s. Changes in the manner in which the dialectic of cinema and film came to be interpreted in this increasingly normative atmosphere of the ubiquitous moving image are at the center of my focus as I consider the theory and practice of Isidore Isou and the Letterists in the 1950s France and, moving into the 1960s, the work of Ljubiša Jocić and the Signalist movement (Yugoslavia), Pier Paolo Pasolini (Italy), and Miklós Jancsó (Hungary). Chapter 5 revisits the question of filmic materiality, particularly pronounced in the context of experimental cinema in Europe and the United States in the late 1960s and the 1970s. I explore ways in which the dynamics of cinematic projection and the "imaginary" status of the film image have been questioned by a variety of extreme (and sometimes entirely nonrepresentational) physical-materialist practices through a consideration of the works of Birgit and Wilhelm Hein, Malcolm LeGrice, Mihovil Pansini, Paul Sharits, Slobodan Šijan, and others. Finally, in chapter 6, I discuss the alignment of some variants of "cinema by other means" with an overtly political-activist approach to filmmaking advanced by Jean-Luc Godard beginning in the late 1960s. The crux of the chapter is an analysis of the epistemological functions of montage, understood as a general principle: montage as a procedure the logic of which firmly resides in the cinema, while its applications belong to the world at large.

Second, by studying a multitude of unorthodox ways in which filmmakers, artists, and writers have pondered, created, defined, performed, and transformed the "movies"—with or without directly grounding their work in the materials of film—I also hope to demonstrate the value of a strongly integrated (critics might say "insufficiently differentiated"), theoretical-practical approach to the question of the cinema's conditions of existence. Underlying nearly all works considered in this book is the conviction—sometimes explicitly stated, at other times merely implied—that the cinema is a form of praxis: that it firmly belongs in the register of the human subject's general pursuit of a unity of thought, matter, and action, of critical-theoretical thinking and practical labor. From this perspective, theory, at least insofar as its primary concern is with medium-specificity, is to be understood not only as an instrument of explaining but also of redefining, and even of reinventing its object of study. In a specific sense, then, sometimes to theorize the cinema is also to practice the cinema "by other means."

To identify the cinema as praxis is, furthermore, to invite a genuinely nondeterministic mode of thinking about the notion of the cinematographic apparatus (the relevance of which is thereby not disputed but in fact is further affirmed). Suffice it for now to illustrate this point, elaborated at greater length in chapter 2, with a single telling example taken from the realm of Yugoslav experimental cinema. (Clearly, a substantial portion of my study concerns the Yugoslav avant-garde, in both its pre- and post-World War II emanations; this is a tremendously rich subject, still largely unknown in the Western scholarship.) In 1971, two filmmakers, Milenko Avramović and Miša Jovanović, invented a device they called "Blink-O-Scope" (Trepljoskop; color plate 1). This was a homemade "alternative" to the regular cinematographic apparatus, and it consisted only of a small rectangular cardboard and a short piece of 8mm film "threaded" in it. Avramović and Jovanović's instructions for the use of their Blink-O-Scope invited the viewer to hold the apparatus (a piece of cardboard) in one hand while repeatedly moving the filmstrip up and down with the other hand "at the speed of 6.1 centimeters per second." While looking at the moving piece of film through a small hole in the cardboard, the viewer was also supposed to "blink at the rate of 16 times per second."

It has been noted that watching the "Blink-Film" in the Blink-O-Scope is only "theoretically possible."[3] The human eye is physiologically incapable of blinking sixteen times per second and thus cannot generate the same impression of synthetic movement as that produced (externally, in relation to the spectator) by the standard cinematographic machine. What, then, should one make of Avramović and Jovanović's apparatus? Does it bespeak its creators' hopelessly idealist attitude toward the cinema—an attitude according to which to desire a film, to imagine it unfold, is no less a cinematic experience than an actual cinematographic event (in which projection technology is combined with our perceptual and mental activity)? Or, is Blink-O-Scope perhaps to be understood as evidence of the fact that, despite our perceptual and mental engagement with it, film is, strictly speaking, a phenomenon dependent on the physical presence and the work of a specific technological apparatus, and that failure to properly exhibit it cannot, therefore, be compensated for with some vague evocation of the cinema mentally projected "beyond" film?

The wager of this book is that we can begin to answer these and similar questions only if we pay detailed attention to the various modalities of the dialectical interplay between film and cinema, and only if we fully endorse the principle of inseparability of theory and practice. From this perspective, the Blink-O-Scope is both more and less than an alternative to the normative cinematographic apparatus. It is an embodiment of the elementary "truth" about the cinematograph. The Blink-O-Scope is proof positive of the fact that, in Philippe Dubois' excellent formulation: *"The apparatus itself is . . . in a way always theoretical—a concept as much as a form, a machination as much as a machine."*[4]

CINEMA BY OTHER MEANS

Chapter 1

Film, or the Vibrancy of Matter

Break all the words we used to know by heart
and toss them to a wind
so that blood can flow, wine, venom, and grace
what people gave them once

—Dušan Matić

What makes Marcel Duchamp's *Bicycle Wheel* (1913) or Man Ray's *Gift* (1921) (fig. 1.1) quintessential Dada objects? What is their smallest common denominator? In an all-out attack on reason and logic and the bourgeois conceptions of ethics and aesthetics, artistic genius and good taste, Dadaists opted for randomness and chance, and for what Duchamp himself, reflecting on the manner in which he chose his *ready-mades* (*Bottlerack, Fountain,* etc.), provocatively characterized as "visual indifference." Signification itself became the ultimate target of various Dadaist practices of negation. This negation, however, persistently took place in the shadow of its own negation—against the background of a profound awareness of the impossibility of ever entirely foreclosing Meaning. Thus, Dadaist "negation of negation" frequently resulted in foregrounding the *irreducible materiality of the auto-referential signifier*. Objects like a steam iron "enriched" with a straight line of tacks (*Gift*); a bicycle fork with the front wheel attached upside-down to a wooden stool (*Bicycle Wheel*); or a coat rack nailed to the floor (Duchamp's *Trap* of 1917) sought to muddle meaning with matter, "to make the signifier constantly overflow onto the signified so that what appears in the place appointed for meaning remains completely stuck in the materiality of the word to be defined."[1]

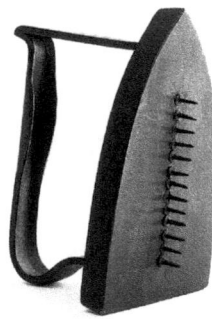

Figure 1.1 Man Ray, *Gift* (c.1958; replica of 1921 original) © 2011 Man Ray Trust / Artists Rights Society (ARS), NY / ADAGP, Paris. Digital Image © The Museum of Modern Art/Licensed by SCALA / Art Resource, NY

It is precisely because of its insistent engagement with the irreducible materiality of the cinematographic image that Man Ray's *Return to Reason* (1923) strikes one as a proper Dada film. The artist's first-ever exercise in filmmaking released onto the screen a deliberately irrational kinetic series (a barrage, really) of radically indexical and only partially decipherable moving images. To use George Bataille's fitting formulation, the film invites the viewer to "submit" his/her faculty of reason "entirely to what must be called matter," to "*that* [which] exists outside of myself and the idea"—"base matter ... external and foreign to ideal human aspirations, ... refus[ing] to allow itself to be reduced to the great ontological machines resulting from these aspirations."[2]

Return to Reason employs a variety of stylistic techniques and formal devices, the three principal ones being (a) *rayography*; (b) disorienting or de-familiarizing *close-ups*; and (c) *disjunctive montage*. Man Ray had already used all of these techniques in his non-cinematographic works—photographs, paintings, collages, and assemblages.

a. *Rayographs*. At the origin of *Return to Reason* is a well-known anecdote about Man Ray's apparent chance discovery of the "rayographic" process. Film historian Stephen Kovács relates this anecdote in his detailed account of Man Ray's involvement with the cinema:

> He discovered the [rayographic] process by accident, a circumstance which endeared the new medium all the more to its Dada

discoverer. Working in his studio, Man Ray had accidentally mixed in an unexposed sheet of photosensitive paper with exposed sheets in the developing tray. Waiting in vain for an image to appear, he placed a couple of objects on the paper and as he turned the light on, he saw the image take form right in front of his eyes. The following day Tristan Tzara, the wizard of Dada, showed up and immediately took notice of the rayographs. It was only poetic justice that the Dada leader took part in the birth of a new art form. Immediately they set to work making rayographs together, each proceeding in his own manner. Tzara took a matchbox, placed the matches on the sheet, tore up the matchbox, and even burned a hole in the paper. Thus, he proceeded systematically to utilize and violate the newly found medium simultaneously in true Dada fashion. Man Ray, on the other hand, formed cones, triangles, and wire spirals, thus exploring the possibilities of the new process in geometric terms. The results, in his words, were "startlingly new and mysterious."

"As a result of his experimentation with photography," continues Kovács, "Man Ray became sufficiently interested in moving pictures to buy a small automatic camera. His initial idea was to shoot enough footage for a 10 to 15-minute film, insert some meaningless captions, and then show it to his Dada friends. He had shot only a few scenes when Tzara, the only person who knew of these plans, dropped in one morning with an announcement of the Dada program Le Coeur a Barbe which listed Man Ray as presenting a Dada film. He protested that he would not have enough for a showing, but Tzara prevailed by suggesting the addition of rayographs to the shots he already had. And so was born the first Dada film!"[3]

In *Return to Reason*, moving images produced through the rayographic process show tacks, nails, and a stunning "field of shimmering dots" (the film's opening shot, fig. 1.2). The "dots" are, in fact, grains of salt spilled over the photosensitive surface. In all of these, indexicality inherent in the photographically based image is literally pushed to its limits. The existential link between the object and its photographic trace is granted a thus far unprecedented degree of immediacy: instead of light bouncing off the object and passing through the lens onto a strip of film, the object now

Figure 1.2 Man Ray, *Return to Reason* (1923), opening shot

directly touches the photosensitive surface. And yet, these indexical images often come across as structural abstractions. In the words of László Moholy-Nagy (Man Ray's contemporary and also a great champion of "photography without camera"), such an image is "productive rather than reproductive."[4] Like a blueprint or a template, the rayograph is by its very nature anti-reificatory. It is representationally reductive yet—for that very reason—powerfully explicative of the design patterns and the relational properties commonly concealed by the "natural," external appearance of objects, their textures and density.

b. *Close ups*. Man Ray's photographic close-ups (*Anatomies* (1929), for example), typically estrange an object by isolating it from its broader surrounding. The object's figural representation is not directly abandoned, but is charged with an intensified sense of materialness, a surplus acquired at the expense of the object's visual and perceptual familiarity. In the same vein, extreme cinematic close-ups in *Return to Reason* transform various objects into partially legible or entirely illegible dynamic matter: matter without fixed symbolic valence, moving though not charged with stable meaning; matter as it may have been before its decisive "fall" into the cycle of spectatorial consumption and interpretation.

c. *Montage*. For many Dadaists, montage was a fundamental production technique, the principle upon which innumerable visual and textual collages and assemblages were built. In one of his well-known manifestoes, Tzara offers some telling advice on how to create a Dadaist poem: "To make a Dadaist poem/Take a newspaper./Take a pair of scissors./Choose an article as long as you are planning to make your poem./Cut out the article./Then cut out each of the words that make up this article and put them in a bag./Shake it gently./Then take out the scraps one after the other in the order in which they left the bag./Copy conscientiously."[5]

Many of Man Ray's objects similarly engage dynamics of randomness, bringing together disparate, often contradictory elements. In *Gift*, as already indicated, the artist placed a line of tacks onto the surface of a steam iron, while in the kinetic *Indestructible Object* (1923), he attached a cutout photograph of an eye to the pendulum of a metronome. In *Return to Reason*, techniques of film montage also articulate a thorough commitment to the laws of discontinuity and chance. As Barbara Rose put it, the film comes across as "hardly more than an assemblage of unrelated images"[6]—nails, egg-cartons, human torsos, city lights (most of these already substantially defamiliarized through tight framing, unusual angles, night photography, and/or short on-screen duration). When the arrangement of some rather wooly pieces of film stock is left to chance, the relationships established between the consecutive images easily slip into total semantic and syntactical indeterminacy. Instead of ordered and meaningful successions, driven, as is commonly the case, by the laws of causality, the result is a series of aleatory encounters which affirm the free-floating status of each distinct cinematographic fragment. Image A is related to image B in an arbitrary and nonhierarchical manner. A sequence is built on the principle of absolute equality among all of its constitutive elements.

In a sense, *Return to Reason* may be thought of as a cinematic cousin of a construction by Kurt Schwitters (color plate 2), or of a driftwood assemblage by Hans Arp (such as *Trousse d'un Da*, from 1921–1922). In each case, some relational principle seems to be holding together the work's constitutive debris—the deformed, discarded matter collected by Schwitters and Arp; or Man Ray's randomly assembled film footage (both rayographic and camera-based) of thumbtacks, bulbs, abstract geometric shapes, spinning carousels, and so forth. But these presumed systems remain (for the spectator) systems without decipherable codes. Their laws are difficult to determine and follow. They are hardly productive (in a functionalist sense), but seem more like the hard residual evidence of some elaborate potlatch—material leftovers of a massive nonutilitarian expenditure.

Insistence on the "irreducible" raw materiality of structures comprising auto-referential signifiers (structures that may be complex or simple; cinematic or otherwise; Man Ray's, Schwitters's, Arp's . . .) thus calls attention to certain aspects of the process of artistic production—specifically, to the flow and fluctuations of energy that underwrite an artwork's coming into being. In lieu of stable symbolic values (Meaning) and determining interpretational cues, the viewer's perception and cognition of the work become aligned with the task of charting the manner in which a set of energetic currents is petrified into a particular formation of base or debased matter.

From the standpoint of psychoanalysis, this is the libidinal foundation of art. Jean-Francois Lyotard defines *libidinal apparatuses* as "ebbing intensities stabiliz[ing] themselves into configurations," as "affects distributed according to the vast matrix-*dispositifs* . . . into voluminous bodies . . . ."[7] He describes the fundamental operation governing the production of any libidinal formation thus:

> Why and how is there a capture and inscription of this wandering energy in a formation or figure? Why? Because everything that is given as an object (thing, painting, text, body . . .) is a product, that is to say, a result of the metamorphosis of this energy from one form into other forms. Each object is energy at rest, quiescent, provisionally conserved, inscribed. The apparatus or figure is only a metaphoric operator. It is itself composed of stabilized and conserved energy.[8]

Written in 1913, Valentine de Saint-Point's "Futurist Manifesto of Lust" is one of the earliest statements by a European avant-gardist intent on explicitly linking eruptions of human psychosexual energy with the creative impulses of technological modernity: "Lust, when viewed without moral preconceptions and as an essential part of life's dynamism, is a force. . . . Lust is the expression of a being projected beyond itself. . . . LUST EXCITES

ENERGY AND RELEASES STRENGTH."⁹ On the other hand, probably the best known example of an early twentieth-century work of art which, like de Saint-Point's manifesto, directly draws its dynamic qualities and kinetic potential from a dual, psychosexual and machinic grounding, is Duchamp's *The Bride Stripped Bare by Her Bachelors, Even* (also known as the *Large Glass*, 1915–1922) (fig. 1.3). Particularly significant for our purposes is the fact that, according to Duchamp, his *desiring machine* was intended to give rise to a distinctly cinematic effect: a certain "cinematic blossoming" realized in the domain of the Bride (the upper portion of the work). Duchamp describes it as a machinic orgasm of sorts, triggered by the "desire-gears" at the point when all the elaborately interconnected component-parts of the apparatus are sufficiently fueled by the "love gasoline."¹⁰

Numerous other models of "techno-libidinal" art and literature, which flourished in Europe during the first two decades of the twentieth century, similarly claimed for themselves a cinematic character or orientation and profusely and imaginatively drew upon film—its various principles, dynamics, and effects—to fuel their conceptual engines. For instance, in his 1926 prose poem, *Ixion*, the Yugoslav writer Monny de Boully (whose engagement with the cinema I discuss at length in chapter 3) imagines and even draws a detailed diagram of a fantastic libidinal machine: a "chariot of desire" which, by assisting in the narrative formation of the romantic couple, propels "the poem toward its cinematic ending."¹¹

Figure 1.3 Marcel Duchamp, *The Bride Stripped Bare by Her Bachelors, Even* (*The Large Glass*, 1915–23) © 2011 Artists Rights Society (ARS), New York / ADAGP, Paris / Succession Marcel Duchamp; photo: The Philadelphia Museum of Art / Art Resource, NY

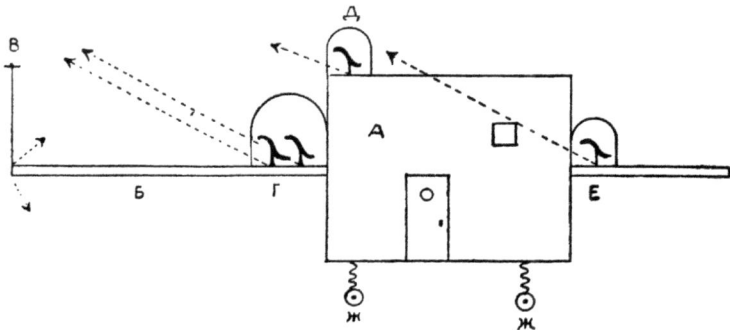

Figure 1.4 Monny de Boully, *Ixion* (1926): diagram of the air-carriage powered by the sexually starved eagles

The heroine of Boully's *Ixion* describes the operational logic of her "air-carriage" as follows: "It is flown by eagles, who are at first kept inside their cages. In the big front cage [Γ], are a male and a female eagle. In the middle cage [Δ], above the cabin, is a female. In the last cage [E], there is a male again. If I decide to fly, I step inside the cabin [A], open the cages, and here's what happens: the male and the female in the front cage are sexually satisfied, but they are hungry; they both fly toward the platform [B] to which some fresh meat is attached. However, they cannot reach the meat because they are chained to the cabin. Wanting to free themselves by force, they lift the entire apparatus off the ground with the power of their wings. Something similar happens with the other pair of eagles. They are well fed, yet they crave sex. When I open their cages, the female rushes out fleeing the male (as all animals instinctively do). The male cannot catch up with the female for his chain is too short. This is how the four eagles lift the carriage into the clouds."

Consider also, in a similarly techno-libidinal vein, the case of Zenithism, one of the more insistently East European avant-garde movements of the early 1920s. Based first in Zagreb and then in Belgrade, Yugoslavia, Zenithism was invested in "Balkanizing Europe"—its fundamental ambition was to revitalize the "old," "tired," "decadent," and "syphilistic" European West with steady injections of Eastern "vitality," "irrationality," and "barbarism." Ljubomir Micić, the leader of Zenithism and the founder and editor of the journal, *Zenit* (Zenith), devoted a number of his major programmatic texts to describing the sources and trajectories of the creative energies fueling his movement. In "Zenithosophy, or the Energetics of Creative Zenithism," Micić begins by positing the "Zenith-Man" as "the central transformer of our lively and noisy sparks, of our wild and barbaric energies."[12] He then describes the human being's creative activity as "the pulse of Zenithism," the movement's "energetic imperative."[13] In a manner that betrays a combined influence of Futurism and Constructivism, Micić further asserts that "Zenithism is the awakening of the elemental and vital forces of labor, . . . energy in permanent conflict with the stinking matter of cultural impotence, . . . free of all traces of symbolism, of all phraseological jewelry: the thought is like a machine—the work is a mechanism."[14]

Born the same year as the cinematograph (as he liked to point out), Micić envisions his "Zenith-Man" (also known as the "Barbarogenius") as an extremely powerful corporeal machine—a combination of a relay and a dynamo, which perpetually receives, orientates, amplifies, and emits streams of energy, thus maintaining a direct and uninterrupted (at times almost psychotically intoned "Schreberian") material exchange with its surroundings. This fantasy of unrestrained and all-encompassing corporeal interaction with the world bespeaks another important early influence upon Zenithism: Expressionism. One of the many definitions of the movement, presented in the first issue of *Zenith*, reads: "Zenithism is the abstract meta-cosmic Expressionism." The figure of the Barbarogenius partially echoes Micić's favorite film character, Cesare the Somnambulist (played by Conrad Veidt), from Robert Wiene's silent classic, *The Cabinet of Doctor Caligari* (1920). And not unlike the obsessed Caligari, who experiences a radical conflation of sound and image in the form of language assuming a menacing material presence in his immediate surroundings, Micić prophesized a superimposition of a variety of media and poetic impulses. For instance, he saw Zenithism as effortlessly conflating "WORDS IN SPACE" with "A TRUE CINEMATIC PROJECTION OF TIME." Written and spoken poetry could become one with film, Micić asserted, as long as the artist's creative labor remained firmly oriented toward "INFINITY."[15]

In section 15 of Micić's long serial poem "Words in Space," published across a number of issues of his journal, *Zenith*, the cinema is even granted the status of a new artistic religion:

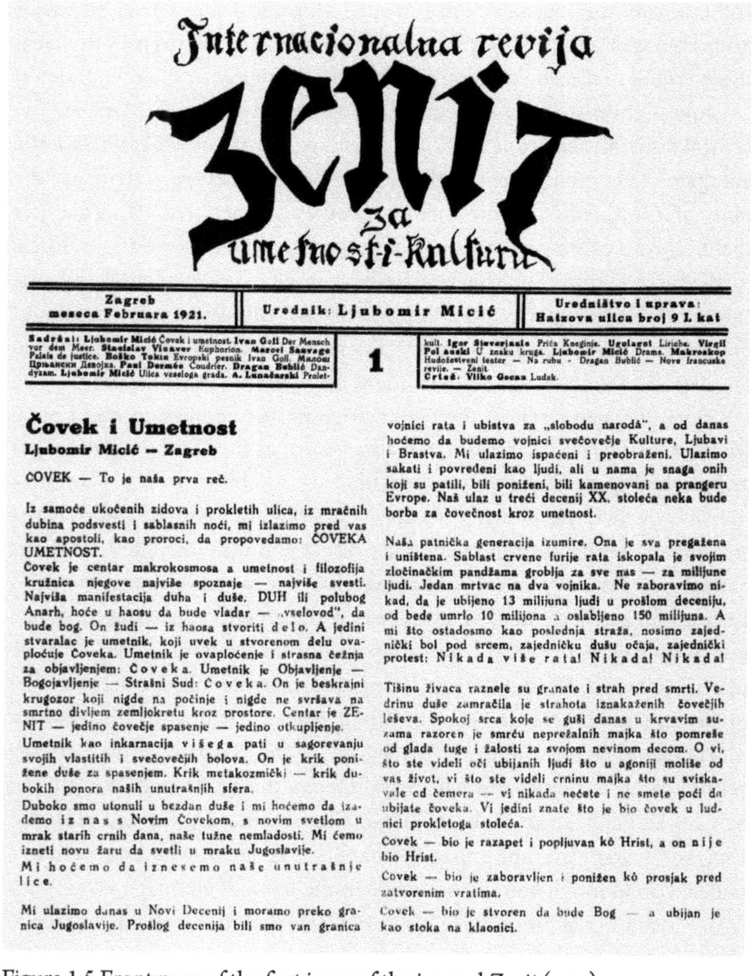

Internacionalna revija

ZENIT

za umetnosti i kulturu

Zagreb meseca Februara 1921. | Urednik: Ljubomir Micić | Uredništvo i uprava: Hatzova ulica broj 9 I. kat

Sadržaj: Ljubomir Micić Čovek i umetnost. Ivan Goll Der Mensch vor dem Meer. Stanislav Vinaver Euphorion. Marcel Sauvage Palais de justice. Boško Tokin Evropski pesnik Ivan Goll. Милош Црњански Девојка. Paul Dermée Coudrier. Dragan Bublić Dandyzam. Ljubomir Micić Ulica veseloga grada. A. Lunačarski Proletkult. Igor Sjeverjanin Priča Kneginje. Ugolagot Liriche. Virgil Pol auski U znaku kruga. Ljubomir Micić Drama. Makroskop Hudožestveni teater — Na rubu - Dragan Bublić — Nove francuske revije. — Zenit.
Crtež: Vilko Gecan Ludak.

1

Čovek i Umetnost

Ljubomir Micić — Zagreb

ČOVEK — To je naša prva reč.

Iz samoće ukočenih zidova i prokletih ulica, iz mračnih dubina podsvesti i sablasnih noći, mi izlazimo pred vas kao apostoli, kao proroci, da propovedamo: ČOVEKA UMETNOST.

Čovek je centar makrokosmosa a umetnost i filozofija kružnica njegove najviše spoznaje — najviše svesti. Najviša manifestacija duha i duše, DUH ili polubog Anarh, hoće u haosu da bude vladar — „vselovod", da bude bog. On žudi — iz haosa stvoriti delo. A jedini stvaralac je umetnik, koji uvek u stvorenom delu ovaploćuje Čoveka. Umetnik je ovaploćenje i strasna čežnja za objavljenjem: Čoveka. Umetnik je Objavljenje — Bogojavljenje — Strašni Sud: Čoveka. On je beskrajni krugozor koji nigde na počinje i nigde ne svršava na smrtno divljem zemljokretu kroz prostore. Centar je ZENIT — jedino čovečje spasenje — jedino otkupljenje.

Umetnik kao inkarnacija višega pati u sagorevanju svojih vlastitih i svečovečjih bolova. On je krik poniženе duše za spasenjem. Krik metakozmički — krik dubokih ponora naših unutrašnjih sfera.

Duboko smo utonuli u bezdan duše i mi hoćemo da izađemo iz nas s Novim Čovekom, s novim svetlom u mrak starih crnih dana, naše tužne nemladosti. Mi ćemo izneti novu žaru da svetli u mraku Jugoslavije.

Mi hoćemo da iznesemo naše unutrašnje lice.

Mi ulazimo danas u Novi Decenij i moramo preko granica Jugoslavije. Prošlog decenija bili smo van granica vojnici rata i ubistva za „slobodu narodâ", a od danas hoćemo da budemo vojnici svečovečje Kulture, Ljubavi i Brastva. Mi ulazimo ispaćeni i preobraženi. Ulazimo sakati i povredeni kao ljudi, ali u nama je snaga onih koji su patili, bili poniženi, bili kamenovani na prangeru Evrope. Naš ulaz u treći decenij XX. stoleća neka bude borba za čovečnost kroz umetnost.

Naša patnička generacija izumire. Ona je sva pregažena i uništena. Sablast crvene furije rata iskopala je svojim zločinačkim pandžama groblja za sve nas — za milijune ljudi. Jedan mrtvac na dva vojnika. Ne zaboravimo nikad, da je ubijeno 13 milijuna ljudi u prošlom deceniju, od bede umrlo 10 milijona a oslabljeno 150 milijuna. A mi što ostadosmo kao poslednja straža, nosimo zajednički bol pod srcem, zajedničku dušu očaja, zajednički protest: Nikada više rata! Nikada! Nikada!

Tišinu živaca raznele su granate i strah pred smrti. Vedrinu duše zamračila je strahota iznakaženih čovečjih leševa. Spokoj srca koje se guši danas u krvavim suzama razoren je smrću neprežalnih majka što pomreše od glada tuge i žalosti za svojom nevinom decom. O vi, što ste videli oči ubijanih ljudi što u agoniji mološe od vas život, vi što ste videli crninu majka što su sviskavale od čemera — vi nikada nećete i ne smete poći da ubijate čoveka. Vi jedini znate što je bio čovek u ludnici prokletoga stoleća.

Čovek — bio je razapet i popljuvan kô Hrist, a on nije bio Hrist.

Čovek — bio je zaboravljen i ponižen kô prosjak pred zatvorenim vratima.

Čovek — bio je stvoren da bude Bog — a ubijan je kao stoka na klaonici.

Figure 1.5 Front page of the first issue of the journal *Zenit* (1921)

Balconies of the darkened Esperanto-temples are collapsing.
Cinema
THE BALKANS
Cinema
the crowd moans in front of the white altar of the living pictures
. . .

Turn the churches into the cinematographs of the living iconostases!
The children are collapsing in front of the movie-doors
as they watch the work of the living pictures[16]

The film medium's unique, machinically grounded ability to perform an ongoing dynamization of matter was understood early on by the Zenithists as its privileged, integrative function among the arts. This is true of Micić and even more so of Boško Tokin, one of the three cosigners of the original "Manifesto of Zenithism" (1921) and a pioneer of film theory and criticism in pre-war Yugoslavia. Tokin, whose pseudonym was Filmus, believed that "cinematography is omnipotent!" He claimed: "The cinematograph is capable of uniting the elements of all other arts, it presents the STYLE of its epoch. As Canudo put it... the cinematograph has already given the world a new artist: the painter-sculptor-architect of light-musician-poet-choreographer of black and white, it has given it the metteur en scene."[17]

Tokin/Filmus designed some cinematically conceived photo-collages (see color plate 3) and cherished the genre of "cinematographic poetry." Writing in praise of the film apparatus, that foremost symptom of the modern times, he also sought to directly introduce a number of cinematic effects—movement, speed, rapid succession, and abrupt change—into the poetic structures of the written language. His cinematographic poems 3 and 4 are particularly representative in this respect:

> 3.
> The life of majority:
> Question answer, answer question.
> Eternity: question to an answer.
> The life of minority, our life?
> Airplane, climbing,
> Cinematograph, movement,
> Speed and art.
> Art.
> 4.
> Thousand lines in a drawing.

> Hundred possibilities in an airplane.
> Million movements in a film.
> To encompass. To be an artist.
> Eternally.[18]

Tokin's celebration of art in general and cinema in particular, as life's speedways into eternity, corresponds with Micić's infatuation with a limitless outpouring of creative energies and their channeling into "infinity." For Tokin, the line is the embodiment of countless possible techno-libidinal movements. Micić similarly declares a preference for "direction over the circle"—for the open, unending linearity of the former, over the self-enclosed formal completeness of the latter: "Zenithist energy turns all raw elements of life into works. Our life burns like the diameter of death. Death is a circle. It is impossible for people to function as directions and circles at the same time. Run out of the circle—become a direction, a direction!"[19]

In the early 1920s, the Surrealist practice of automatism—which similarly grounded itself in the principles of the free outpouring of energy and insubordination of desire to formal coherence—was brewing in Paris. Significance and functions of automatism—of automatic writing in particular—are elaborated at great length in André Breton's first surrealist manifesto, produced in 1924 (which also happens to be the year of Micić's "Zenitisophy"). In a well-known passage, Breton defines automatism as the essence of Surrealism: "Surrealism, *n*. Psychic automatism in its pure state, by which one proposes to express—verbally, by means of the written word, or in any other manner—the actual functioning of thought. Dictated by the thought, in the absence of any control exercised by reason, exempt from any aesthetic or moral concern."[20]

In the realm of visual arts, the foremost proponents of Surrealist automatism were André Masson and Max Ernst, the former with his drawings and paintings and the latter with his *frottages*. In Masson's drawings, for example, the line traced by the pen aspires to assert itself faster than the thought accompanying it. Only subsequently does the artist begin to take into consideration the contours and the shapes he has produced. Masson explains: "I begin without an image or plan in mind, but just draw or paint rapidly according to my impulses. Gradually, in the marks I make, I see suggestions of figures or objects. I encourage these to emerge, trying to bring out their implications even as I now consciously try to give order to the composition."[21]

But as it temporarily contains and fixates the pulsating libido, the emerging shape always also introduces the promise of a new energetic disequilibrium. The forming of an object thus simultaneously functions as the process whereby the object hints at the possibility of "undoing" itself. Bataille called this operation *informe* or "formless-ing."[22] In the final analysis, it is precisely its potential for formless-ing that makes an object, a structure, or a formation a proper libidinal *dispositif*.

The logic of *informe* distinguishes Masson's (Bataille's friend and collaborator) automatic drawings, but it is equally applicable to a variety of paintings, collages, and sculptures by Ernst, Salvador Dali, and Hans Belmeer as it is to a number of Man Ray's photographic works and to his film *Return to Reason*. What is more, the same logic exists outside the framework of the 1920s French avant-garde, in, say, the paintings of Egon Schiele (*Fighter,* 1913) or, more recently, those of Francis Bacon (notably, *Three Studies for Figures at the Base of a Crucifix*, 1944); and in the films of Jack Smith (*Flaming Creatures*, 1962–1963). Most frequently, it is the body—human, animal, or otherwise—that is the center of attention, confronting the viewer with the oscillations (quantitative as well as qualitative) of the primary force of life in the act of materializing itself, becoming visible. Such is the case, for example, with the morbidly "deformed" appearance of Schiele's characters (much appreciated by Ljubomir Micić); or the disturbingly impossible corporeal montages of Belmeer's dolls; or the homunculuses and the half-human half-animal figures repeatedly conceived by the Yugoslav Surrealist painter Radojica Živanović Noe.

In Noe's *Pulse* (1930, figure 1.6) or *Curtain at the Window* (color plate 4), for instance, the body does not strike one as a stable, pre-determined ground upon which the artist has chosen to intervene. Nor does the body in these drawings represent an autonomous, singular entity, clearly distinguishable from other living forms that populate its surroundings. Instead, Noe's morphing and vulnerable corporeal entities—at times tense, at other times relaxed and seemingly "leaking away"—are offered first and foremost as evidence of what lies underneath or within the body: libidinal

Figure 1.6 Radojica Živanović Noe, *The Pulse* (1930)

energy and desire; a concoction of lust for life and illness, splattered across the paper, substantialized in the line, the ink, and the very gesture of drawing.

On the level of (infra-)structural analysis, carnal "activation" and the "awakening" of matter may also be posited as the processes that underwrite the operational logic of *all* media *dispositifs*, of each and every channel and act of communication or artistic expression. That is, before it is used to transmit some content—auditory, visual, or audiovisual—the fundamental "message" conveyed by every medium is always, quite literally, the dynamization of its own pure materiality, a "pre-sublimatory" vibrancy of its body.[23] From this perspective, Man Ray's *Return to Reason* may be seen as a perceptive exercise in filmic reflexivity: by thoroughly focusing on the "libidinal-material" dimension of the projected moving image—by casting the forming and the formless-ing of its rapidly changing on-screen content as functions of cinematic flow and duration, it forges a direct connection between the cinema's "imaginary signifier" and the hard physical existence, the immediate and vital presence (beyond the screen) of the film apparatus itself. (I will discuss some additional physical features of *Return to Reason* in chapter 5.)

Among the experiments conducted by the historical avant-garde, active engagement with the bare corporeality of various media apparatuses was perhaps nowhere more obvious than in certain automatic uses of language, in instances of automatic writing and speech. Here, I am not primarily thinking of Breton's Surrealist model of automatist liberation of language (which remains poetic and idealized and takes place under the elevated credo of "words making love"), but of the slightly earlier phonetic and opto-phonetic poetry of the Dadaists or of their close "Barbarogenial" kin, the Zenithists. These works forcefully demonstrated ways in which language, that foremost guardian of reason and the socio-symbolic order, may itself be "savaged"—transformed into both an apparatus and the crude substance of pure and direct enjoyment. Among the most dedicated practitioners of sound and audiovisual poetry were Hugo Ball in Zurich, Kurt Schwitters in Hannover, Raoul Hausmann in Berlin, and Dragan Aleksić in Prague and Belgrade. Man Ray, too, produced some so-called "dumb poetry," which, notably, made its initial public appearance in the cinema in a brief shot from *Return to Reason* (in 1924, a different Dumb Poem by Man Ray would be published in Francis Picabia's magazine 391; see figures 1.7 and 1.8).

Consider, for instance, the following excerpt from TABA CIKLON II, a sound poem by Dragan Aleksić, the leader of the Yugoslav Dadaists, which appeared in 1922 in the avant-garde journal *Ma*:

>AbU TABUATA AUBATAUBA
>taba
>re re re RE RE
>Rn Rn Rn Rn
>Reb en en Rn
>Ren RN Ren ErNReN
>abu tabu abua u tabu abuaaa
>abu tabu abaata
>babaata tabu tabauuuta
>taba Rn

tabaren
tabararararan
tabaren ENEN tabarerenn/parlevufranse/

With the exception of the last phrase ("parlez-vous francais," spelled phonetically in the Serbo-Croatian language), each word and each sound functions as an entirely self-sufficient articulation not bound by meaning. For Aleksić, as for all Dadaists, language is, at its root, no more and no less than its own *phonetic body*, enjoyed by the body of the poet/performer in whose mouth it is being devoured. In his manifestoes of Dadaism, Aleksić accordingly claimed that art is a straightforward "expression of the nerves." "Nerves are primitivism . . . nerves are primordial," he asserts, and proceeds to assault art when "language [is] used to transmit impressions." "Have nerves, not brains. . . . A detailed understanding of art . . . is a plan concocted by madmen and professors. . . . A naked man in the year One is a Dadaist. Speech is an apparatus. I am narrowing it down to seconds. . . . A wave of abstraction can replace numerous comparisons (Schwitters Kurt, Kurt, Kurt!!) . . . . The mind cries after clarity, it drowns in the whining barber shops, museums, powder boxes, hair."[24]

Dadaist sound poetry may be said to employ the type of ahistorical and meaningless language that Jacques Lacan termed *lalangue*: its primary objective, like that of a child's babble, is not simply or merely communication with another, but a nonsensical, narcissistic enjoyment—the "satisfaction of blah-blah."[25]

The procedure of *writing* sound poetry explicates still another interesting feature of what may be termed the "materiality of blah-blah." As Friedrich Kittler authoritatively points out in his analysis of Christian Morgenstern's work "The Great Lalula," before this author's "1905 collection *Gallows Songs*, no poem had existed as a small discourse network. Literary historians have sought classical-romantic models for these poems and have found some nonsense verse here and there. But even the 'Wien ung quatsch, Ba nu, Ba nu n'am tsche fatsch' . . . is at least speakable. No voice, however, can speak the parentheses that enclose a semicolon (as specified in 'The Great Lalula') or even—to demonstrate once and for all what media are—brackets that surround an empty space."[26]

VIBRANCY OF MATTER

Figure 1.7 Man Ray, *Dumb Poem* (1924) © 2011 Man Ray Trust / Artists Rights Society (ARS), NY / ADAGP, Paris; image courtesy of the International Dada Archive, Special Collections, University of Iowa Libraries

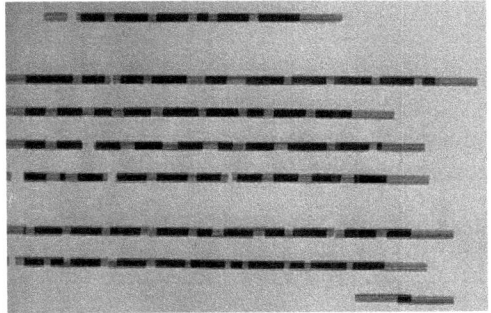

Figure 1.8 "Dumb poem" in Man Ray's *Return to Reason* (1923)

Opto-phonetic poetry, originating with Morgenstern and subsequently actively pursued by the Dadaists, is a type of inter-media practice in which meaning is "bracketed off" (as in Morgenstern's () or (;)), while the bracket itself (the desublimated physical substance of the media *dispositif*) is what is communicated in the process of infinite conversion of sounds into images and vice versa. Opto-phony is the master-dynamic of what Marcella Lista calls "the universal convertibility of the senses"; it bespeaks "an extended sensoriality in direct contact with the continuous movement of vibratory space."[27] But opto-phony may also be said to constitute the horizon of fantasy for a reality in which the image is, ultimately, no more than the *failure* of sound and, likewise, sound is nothing but the *failure* of the image. In the final analysis, it is the human body itself that operates as one of the most accomplished opto-phonetic apparatuses. This becomes apparent when the body entangles itself in the act of actually attempting to read/perform a work such as one of Man Ray's Dumb Poems.

"Dumb poetry" rests on the principle of circular feedback, characteristic of all opto-phonetic works: sounds *visualized* and/or images given to be *auralized*. More than that, the irreducible materiality of the signifier is explicitly captured in the performer's body's (predetermined) failure to articulate it, to "emit" it. For how else can one read "out loud" the blank, entirely content-less verse of Man Ray's poem, but as purely carnal manifestations of *mute sounds*? In other words, the body, the conductor, and the converter mediating between images and sounds can only perform a Dumb Poem by acting itself out (through movements and contortions originating in the area of the mouth), after having been caught in the situation of not being able to discharge. Deprived of the possibility of a properly sonorous energetic/libidinal release, the body dynamically materializes what forever remain the "not-yet sounds": sounds that *ought to be* articulated, but at the same time *cannot* be articulated for they remain unknown, unspecified by the poem. To perform Man Ray's "dumb poetry" is, more than anything, to trap the body in the interregnum caused by a double "imperfection": after the "failure" of both sound and image as containers of meaning, all that is left is the libidinally fueled corporeal hardware, the *informe* material support of audio-vision.

As exercises in opto-phonetics such as this one demonstrate, the Dadaist imaginarium went well beyond the transgressive combinatory of the already familiar, stable, and legible regimes of signs. It strove to establish elements of new, dynamic-materialist forms of art—art that would embody the signifying impermanence caused by the incessant conversions (rather than simple juxtapositions) and convergences (rather than mere differentiation) between all sorts of auditory and visual signifiers, static and kinetic forces, rational and irrational impulses. Searching for precisely such art, Dragan Aleksić declared: "Ask for your thoughts to be turned into iron: the spirit of matter. *Conversion of energies into abstract effects.* Synthesis of the spirit and the raw mass converted into abstraction: instinctual metamorphosis."[28] Like a number of his contemporaries, most notably perhaps Raoul Hausmann and Ljubomir Micić, Aleksić was inspired by Tatlin and Constructivism, but he also interpreted what he called "Tatlinism" somewhat liberally. He set out in search of "the measure of physical-intellectual energy," hoping to stimulate a complex Dadaist alignment of straightforward *acephalic* impulses ("Have nerves, not brains") with the processes whereby "the forces of the mind, learned by the muscles, [turn] into matter."[29]

Aleksić also enthusiastically endorsed the cinema, seeking in it a possible ally for his firm Dadaist refusal of signification as a stable and uninterrupted process, and for his corresponding commitment to turning or reducing different media apparatuses into vibrant clusters of basic matter. "Film is a moving body," Aleksić declared. "That is what Confucius would say, but Hako would also add: it is a modern barbarian wishing to conceive of a miracle. Parrots can recite by heart 30.000 hexameters from the *Odyssey* and the *Iliad*, but film spins around faster than the brain in a perfect divine Homunculus. No country is without it. The sin of the cinema has penetrated the bodies of all the planet's inhabitants. . . . Biological progress follows the same laws which led to the creation of the optical-chemical body of film."[30]

Aleksić's insistence that the cinema is a prime instrument of a kind of bio-political internationalism is not unlike Ljubomir Micić's own praise of the medium. But the Dadaist's engagement with film was both theoretically and practically more substantial than that of his Zenithist counterpart (in whose journal, *Zenith*, he had initially published a number of his texts). With Micić's brother, Branko Ve Poljanski, Aleksić co-edited *Kinofon* (1921–1922) (fig. 1.9), the first ever journal in Yugoslavia dedicated exclusively to film. He wrote inspired film criticism and even co-directed, with Boško Tokin, a short film, *Outlaws in Topčider, or God Be With Us* (1924). Partially inspired by the American burlesques and slapstick comedies, *Outlaws* is significant as the earliest instance of filmmaking undertaken by the members of the Yugoslav avant-garde. The film is now considered lost—it is said that in a moment of rage, its cinematographer set the negative on fire!

An important lesson of Dadaist experimentation with a wide array of media including film (which was frequently granted the status of the first among the equals) is that a correlation exists between the impulse toward

Figure 1.9 Front page of the second issue of the journal *Kinofon* (1922)

one media-dispositif's material debasement and the potential for its convergence with another. A superb demonstration of this is found in *Return to Reason*. As already noted, this cinematic conglomerate of all kinds of "stuff" contains, among other things, one of Man Ray's Dumb Poems (fig. 1.8). In a particularly shaky shot that shows this opto-phonetic work, the camera acts as if it has assumed upon itself, and then further amplified, the spasms of the (camera operator's) body attempting to utter the Dumb Poem. That which "is learned by the muscles," as Aleksić put it, is here successfully "turned into (filmic) matter"—the cinematograph and the human body have thoroughly "penetrated each other." In a way, this shot emblematizes the central ambition of Man Ray's entire film. This swiftly moving chain of often illegible images confines all signification to the rampant carnality of the cinematographic apparatus. As it foregrounds the material base of the motion pictures, *Return to Reason* puts forth a rather physiological, at times even excremental, vision of the film medium. Man Ray's short may be thought of as a projected (released? lost? detached?) piece of a larger cinematographic body, a small fragment of raw film matter overflowing with libidinal pulsations: simulated and actual flicker effects; appearance of empty black and white frames; segments of scratched filmstrip interpolated between shots; destabilized and at times even uncontrolled camera work; preponderance of rapid discontinuous editing.

Man Ray stimulates an incessant imagistic flow *without* encouraging meaningful and significant shot relations to emerge. Although a variety of representational images do appear throughout *Return to Reason*, only a few of these are denotatively meaningful—they include the already-mentioned negatives of tacks and nails, night shots of a merry-go-round, and an egg carton suspended in the air. Other images in the film have been rendered either entirely abstract (as is the case with the circles, lines, and spirals that periodically move across the screen), or unrecognizable (a good example is the brief appearance, in smoke, of *The Dancer*, another unusual, auto-referential Dadaist object invented by Man Ray). It is only in the very last image of the film that representational certainty (a return to reason?) is established, providing an antithesis to the preponderance of visual ambiguity and serial randomness that went on before it. Not unlike Aleksić's earlier quoted phonetic poem, *TABA CIKLON II*, which ends at the point when language becomes sense ("parlez-vous francais"), *Return to Reason*'s cinematic irrationality finally comes to a halt as it "stumbles upon" some familiar content, filmed in a steady and patient manner.

The film ends with a shot of a naked, rotating female torso. The shot is, in fact, shown twice, first as a positive then as a flipped negative image. Compositionally, the shot foregrounds the breast—the original "lost object" and the first object of desire, as psychoanalysis teaches us. It is as if the emergence of the breast announces the fact that the field of visual representation has been sufficiently formed, fixated, and coded. It has been properly aligned with the economy of spectatorial desire. For Man Ray, this is also the signal that his film ought to come to an end.

Chapter 2

On Re-materialization of the Cinematographic Apparatus

When is a film not a film? And when is a film a movie? And, as they say, 'What is cinema?'

—Annette Michelson

During the 1920s, Man Ray made four films—*Le Retour à la Raison, Emak Bakia, L'Étoile de mer,* and *Les Mystères du Château de Dé*. In the mid-1930s, however, he decided to abandon the cinematographic medium. He explained this decision—made in the wake of, but not directly prompted by, an aborted collaboration with Andre Breton and Paul Eluard on what the three conceived as an "Essay on the Simulation of the Cinematic Delirium"—as follows:

> A book, a painting, a sculpture, a drawing, a photograph, and any concrete object are always at one's disposition, to be appreciated or ignored, whereas a spectacle before an assemblage insists on the general attention, limited to the period of presentation. . . . I prefer the permanent immobility of a static work which allows me to make my deductions at my leisure, without being distracted by attending circumstances. And so, the last few years before the war, in between my professional photographic activities, I concentrated on painting, drawing, and the making of Surrealist objects—a substitute for sculpture—which figured in magazines and exhibitions sponsored by the group.[1]

Man Ray's claim, made in the midst of the age of Surrealism, suggests a set of aesthetic and ontological expectations different from, say, Louis Aragon's praise of cinema's power to "transport" the viewer and to "transform" the objects it depicts; or, from Breton's enthusiasm about the medium's potential for "deracination."[2] Beyond its material properties, the Surrealists seized upon the psychic delirium triggered by the cinematographic apparatus—its imaginary, oneiric, and hallucinatory effects. By contrast, Man Ray's renunciation of filmmaking seems symptomatic of an anxiety over the fact that his own engagement with the medium had increasingly gone in a direction different from that announced in 1923 by his first film, *Return to Reason*. As Stephen Kovács aptly put it: "Unlike the poets, who saw film as a perfect vehicle of Surrealism, Man Ray was rather interested in its plastic possibilities . . . . Characteristically, the abandonment of his last film project with Breton and Eluard meant more to them than it did to him. The ephemeral quality of film that had endeared it to them made Man Ray feel uncomfortable with it."[3]

When, in 1930, two Yugoslav artists, Aleksandar Vučo and Dušan Matić, produced one of their own Surrealist objects, *The Frenzied Marble* (fig. 2.1; also color plate 5), they gave body to a Man Ray-like fantasy of tactile, plastic cinema: a synthesis of material elements and relations characteristic of an assemblage into a structure that is, at the same time, unambiguously cinematic.

This "apparatus," as its authors called it (an apparatus that, like Man Ray's cinematic sensibility, seems more properly Dadaist than Surrealist),

Figure 2.1 Aleksandar Vučo and Dušan Matić, *The Frenzied Marble* (1930) © Museum of Contemporary Art, Belgrade

is an assemblage made of wood, metal, clay, hay, and paper, on a painted wooden background. The autonomy of its component-parts (one of which is a fishing reel, irresistibly reminiscent of a film spool) is foregrounded even as these are "framed"—organized into successive rectangular, screen-like formations, creating the overall impression of a filmstrip. *The Frenzied Marble* is thus a "permanently immobile," "concrete object . . . always at one's disposition" (as Man Ray would have it), while at the same time, it evokes the serial character of the "cinemage" (also Man Ray's term).[4]

Vučo and Matić's dynamic structure is a good example of what I wish to call "cinema by other means": the practice of positing cinema as a system of relations directly inspired by the workings of the film apparatus, but evoked through the material and technological properties of the originally nonfilmic media. Thus, in *The Frenzied Marble*, the notion of cinema as a temporal flow of moving images—but also, more literally, as a material succession of frames—finds its realization in the static objectness of an assemblage made of wood, metal, paper, and other material. Crucial here, of course, is the fact that a discrepancy clearly manifests itself between the medium as a concept (as a nexus of different elements, understood and/or imagined as capable of generating specific effects), and the medium as an actual apparatus (as concrete technology embodying this nexus of relations). Considered exclusively as a "working" artifact, *The Frenzied Marble* is a forever inappropriate version of the cinematograph: it just is not capable of offering its viewers an actual flow of moving images. On the other hand, by being thought through the framework of the cinema, the material form and structure of this assemblage are invested with a creative potential to generate an entire set of kinetic, film-like effects.

My primary concern here is *not* with the numerous instances of avant-garde art inspired by the cinema. Rather, what interests me is the *obverse* of this dynamic: not art made under the influence of or referring to the cinema, but conceptualization of the cinema as itself a type of practice that, *since the invention of the film apparatus*, has also (simultaneously) had a history of execution through other, often "older," artistic media. Among the works representative of this alternative cine-history one counts some of Man Ray and Francis Picabia's diagrammatic drawings from the late 1910s; a number of Raoul Hausmann's collages and optophonetic works from the late 1910s and the early 1920s; László Moholy-Nagy's Typophotos; Karel

Teige's "static films"; and El Lissitzky's "bioscopic books" and autobiographical "film sketches," all from the 1920s; "films without film" produced, also in the 1920s, in Lev Kuleshov's Workshop; "written" and "radio-films" created throughout the first three decades of the twentieth century by Guillaume Apollinaire, Ljubomir Micić, Philippe Soupault, Salvador Dali, Antonin Artaud, Boško Tokin, Monny de Boully, and others; Lettrist hyper-graphics, performative "syncinema," and "imaginary" films from the 1950s and the 1960s (Maurice Lamaitre, Isidore Isou, Roland Sabatier); "orthodialectical film-poems," written in the early 1970s by the Yugoslav Signalist artist, Ljubiša Jocić; Alain Resnais's *Repérages*, a 1974 photographic book of "future films"; and much more.

Jonathan Walley has recently developed an elegant theoretical framework within which he situates a variety of the so-called "paracinematic" practices:

> Paracinema identifies an array of phenomena that are considered "cinematic" but that are not embodied in the materials of film as traditionally defined. That is, the film works I am addressing recognize cinematic properties outside the standard film apparatus, and therefore reject the medium-specific premise of most essentialist theory and practice that the art of cinema is defined by the specific medium of film. Instead, paracinema is based on a different version of essentialism, which locates cinema's essence elsewhere.[5]

Espousing a broadly conceived separation of the idea of cinema from its normative technological apparatus—its liberation, as it were, from the material of film; its opening unto other artistic forms and techniques (performance, sculpture, still photography, and so forth)—Walley eventually identifies the cinematograph as a historical contingency. He argues (finding inspiration in, among others, Sergei Eisenstein and Andre Bazin) that the cultural dream, or the "myth," as Bazin would put it, of cinema preceded its technological realization in film: "The paracinematic works of this period [1960s and 1970s] are premised on the *historicized* conception of the medium of film we find in the writings of Eisenstein and Bazin—namely, that the film medium (. . . 'as we know it') is not a timeless absolute but a cluster of historically contingent materials that happens to be, for the time being at least, the best means for creating cinema."⁶ The conclusion Walley draws from all this is the following: "The idea of cinema, then, is not a function of the materials of film, but the other way around—the materials of film are a function of the idea of cinema."⁷

Walley's argument is rich in theoretical insight and stated with eloquence. However, despite the author's implicit claim for its general applicability, his model cannot sufficiently account for the peculiarities of some of the most complex instances of "paracinematic" practice—whether in the prewar era (Vučo and Matić, Man Ray, Raoul Hausmann), or in the postwar period (with which Walley is primarily concerned). It is true that in the late 1960s and the 1970s, during the post-minimalist epoch, cinema's conceptual expansion through film's "dematerialization" gained much momentum, motivated as it was by a desire on part of many artists and filmmakers to subvert and move beyond the reigning, essentializing legacy of medium-specificity. But it is also true that, just as during the prewar years, many of the most innovative 1960s and 1970s endeavors to differentiate the concept of cinema from the actual cinematographic apparatus were at least as strongly expressive of their practitioners' radicalized—even perverse—*fidelity* to the notion of medium-specificity. Two prime examples are found in the work of Paul Sharits in the United States and Slobodan Šijan in Yugoslavia.⁸ I discuss both filmmakers in chapter 5; in the present chapter, I will limit myself to a consideration of "cinema by other means" in the 1920s and the 1930s.

The theoretical writings of László Moholy-Nagy are especially telling where this question of the extent and the modality of one's "fidelity" to medium-specificity is concerned. In his visionary book, *Painting, Photography, Film* (1925–1927), the innovator of modern art forms and a champion of wide-ranging experimentation with the new technological media frequently espouses what Walley deems a "mediumless art practice."⁹ For instance, Moholy-Nagy claims that "in comparison with the inventive mental process of the genesis of the work, the question of its execution is important only in so far as it must be *mastered* to the limits. The manner, however—whether personal or by assignment of labour, whether manual or mechanical—is irrelevant."¹⁰ Similarly, he asserts:

Men discover new instruments, new methods of work, which revolutionize their familiar habits of work. Often, however, it is a long time before the innovation is purely utilized; it is hampered by the old; the new function is shrouded in the traditional form. The creative possibilities of the innovation are usually slowly disclosed by these old forms, old instruments and fields of creativity which burst into euphoric flower when the innovation which has been preparing finally emerges. Thus for example Futurist (static) painting stated the problem of simultaneity of movement, the representation of the time impulse—a clear-cut problem which later brought about its own destruction; and this was at the time when film was already known but far from being understood. Similarly, the painting of the Constructivists which paves the way for the development on the highest level of reflected light composition such as already exists in embryo.[11]

But throughout the same book, Moholy-Nagy also promotes autonomy and specificity of different artistic media and is particularly enthusiastic about the possibilities unique to the young technological medium of film. Thus, he praises the purely "FILMIC"—that which "proceeds from the potentialities of the camera and the dynamics of motion" and involves "optical effect proper to the film alone."[12] At one point, he even concludes that "[t]he practical prerequisites of an absolute filmic art are excellence of materials and a highly developed apparatus. . . . What seems to be needed is a camera which will shoot automatically or otherwise work continuously."[13]

A similar dynamic underlies Raoul Hausmann's longstanding investment, ever since the 1910s and the early 1920s, in the field of optophonetics. On the one hand, he devoted much attention to the questions and problems of the practical realization of the Optophone—a novel technological apparatus envisioned as more powerful than even the cinematograph; an instrument of media convergence, capable of a total conversion between sounds and images. On the other hand, at the same time, Hausmann also pursued the idea(l) of optophony—a continuous flow of energy and information grounded in a series of (more or less) unhindered sensorial slips and slidings—in the technologically nondetermined realm of audiovisual poetry. Hausmann even explicitly acknowledged that something of a prototype for the Optophone, this "ultimate" machine of the future, is to be found in the rather artisanal assemblage of the already existing technology—a telephone placed in the vicinity of a bulb: "If one places a telephone in the circuit of an arc lamp, the arc of light is transformed because of the sound waves that are transformed by the microphone in accordance with variations corresponding exactly to acoustic vibrations, that is to say, the rays of light change form in relation to sound waves. At the same time, the arc lamp clearly reflects all the different variations from the microphone, i.e. speech, singing, etc."[14]

For Hausmann, as for Moholy-Nagy, consideration of a medium's potential for various degrees and forms of "dematerialization" and the practical concern with advancing the state of its "proper" technological apparatus are, then, not mutually exclusive but complementary endeavors.

All the conceptual complexity of a work such as *The Frenzied Marble* would, similarly, be lost if its sole point of reference were sought in some general, materially "uprooted" idea(l) of cinema, rather than in a fairly exact set of structural relations inspired by the workings of the film apparatus itself. For, built into Vučo and Matić's assemblage, more than anything, is a desire to *sublate* the cinematograph: to oppose normativization and technological reification of the apparatus by inviting the process of its infinite *re*-materialization (rather than dematerialization)—an endless game of medium-specificity's dialectical denial and reassertion, disavowal and restitution, negation and . . . negation of the negation.

The separation of film technology from the more inclusive (and thereby less precise) idea of cinema needs to be acknowledged here in its historical dimension as a recurring *performative act*. Rather than being *a priori* given as an undisputable and unalterable fact, this separation must be claimed, insisted upon, and its terms negotiated, every time it is summoned into existence in the realm of art/media practice. It is here that the value of the 1920s and 1930s "cinema by other means" becomes most apparent in all its unorthodox devotion to medium-specificity. For if the Idea or the dream of cinema may, indeed, be said to have preceded and motivated the invention of the film medium, it seems equally necessary to recognize, in a true dialectical reversal (which the above practices enact), that this Idea acquired sufficient conceptual precision—that it gained its own, albeit immaterial, specificity—*only after the cinematographic apparatus had already been invented*. To paraphrase Edgar Morin, the French anthropologist and theorist of cinema (Bazin's contemporary who further explicated the complexity of the notion of "the myth of total cinema"): *the cinematograph is heir to the cinema and at the same time transforms it*. "[T]he ultimate myth of cinematography . . . is at the same time its original myth."[15]

It is in this light that one needs to approach the numerous cinematographically underwritten, yet from a utilitarian perspective often entirely impracticable, visual contraptions and "new media" apparatuses that were being invented and designed by the Dadaists, the Constructivists, and the Surrealists. Following the standardization of the intersection of optical, mechanical, and chemical technology in the form of the film machine, various alternative quests for novel modes of seeing symptomatically, and for the first time, began to reveal the whole of reality as having, in fact, all along been *proto-cinematic* (a form of "cinema degree zero," so to speak). "Life. The film studio," declared Dziga Vertov in the 1920s; around the same time, members of Lev Kuleshov's Workshop were responding to the severe shortage of raw film stock in the Soviet Union by staging and performing "films without film."

"Film is a form of life," Hausmann similarly wrote in 1930, "and, like all forms, it is to be understood only as an expression of the correspondences among the forces living in things."[16] The significance of this claim is in the subtlety of what it seems to be suggesting—in the peculiar way in which it dialecticizes the relationship between the film medium and the living reality. It is as if Hausmann is here recognizing the fact that in the aftermath of its technological realization, mankind's ancient "dream" of cinema retroactively established itself as an aspect of a larger "reality of total cinema," of a worldwide network of latent moving images: images not yet concretized, waiting to be materialized through inscription by and into a specific technological medium such as the cinematograph.

As early as the beginning of the 1920s, the Berlin avant-gardist proclaimed: "Our art is already today film! At once event, sculpture, and image."[17] Understanding perception and thought as machinic-like processes, the author of the *Mechanical Head* (1919) increasingly posited film—that foremost vision-machine—as the instrument of a generalized "cinematic thought." "Cinémademapensée," or "cinema of my mind," is what is written across the forehead of Hausmann's 1919 collage, *Gurk* (fig. 2.2). On the other hand, his *Self-Portrait of the Dadasoph* (1920, color plate 6) features a tiny film projector placed in the back of the Dadasoph's head. Hausmann engaged the cinema as the master signifier of his dynamic and physiological conception of reality which, in both its objective and subjective manifestations, represents a perpetual flow and conversion of matter and energy from one form to another, from one medium (human) to another (filmic/machinic). As Timothy O. Benson was among the first to point out, around the time he made *Gurk*, Hausmann retitled his "Das Neue Material in der Malerei" (The New Material in Painting) manifesto "Syntetisches Cino der Malerei" (Synthetic Cinema of Painting): "As was the case for Heartfield, Moholy-Nagy, and others, film was becoming a central metaphor in Hausmann's theory of consciousness."[18] And while Hausmann may have been more of a psycho-materialist than the already-mentioned film-anthropologist Morin, a work like *Gurk*, and especially the *Self-Portrait of the Dadasoph*, stages precisely the type of dynamic that Morin would subsequently describe thus: "Film is constructed in the likeness of our total psyche. To draw the whole truth from this proposition, we must turn it inside out, like a pocket; if the cinema is in the image of our psyche, our psyche is in the image of the cinema.... [*T*]*his little cinema that we have in our head*."[19]

Consider in this light also *The Mirror*, an optical toy invented by Vučo the same year he and Matić created *The Frenzied Marble*. All that is left of this apparatus today are the author's detailed instructions on how to construct it: "Take a broken mirror. Paste its pieces onto a cardboard in such a way that they do not touch, do not abut, always leaving a space of uncovered cardboard between them, like a river or a path. Cut out photographs of celebrities from newspapers, picture magazines, and specialized journals. Mirror these photos in the broken abysses. If you wish to have a permanent apparatus, make a cardboard cube with the changeable upper side. Punch a hole and stick a magnifying glass into it—you will get an interesting panorama, an illusion of ungraspable reality."[20]

Above all else, Vučo is here interested in giving material immediacy to the ruptures and the limits of visual signification. By casting both the human subject and the world around him/her as irreparably fragmented, Vučo's "para-cinematograph" provokes a failure of conscious-perceptual totalization and evokes the threat of corporeal dispersal. In *The Mirror*, the

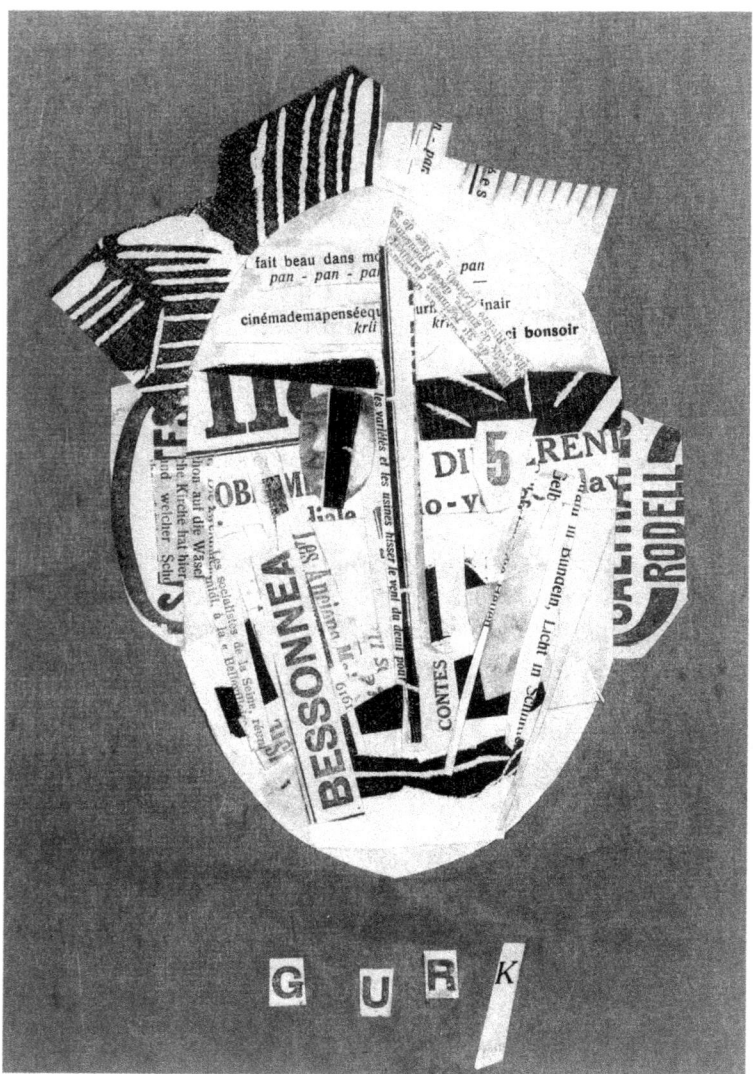

Figure 2.2 Raoul Hausmann, *Gurk* (1919) © 2011 Artists Rights Society (ARS), New York / ADAGP, Paris

author-as-spectator is subjected to a violent operation of (de-)montage modeled after the elementary film procedure of "in-camera" editing. With its partial and discontinuous reflections, the apparatus effectively opens up fissures within one's perception of reality. In this precise sense, it may be said to both produce and manifest a cinematic unconscious: it evinces spaces irreducible to meaning, an unaccountable surplus in the visible world—the "between" that separates, but at the same time also holds together, all the pieces of an image, all the fragments of reality as itself a serialized image, a "movie." In short, *The Mirror* bespeaks the fact that with the advent of film technology, reality revealed itself as cinema's "Uhr-state" (to use a phrase dear to Hausmann[21]); as film theorist Stephen Heath would later put it, it asserted itself as "a primal scene of cinema (a history that is always there before the meanings of its films and as their ultimate return)."[22]

Two examples will further illustrate exactly this connection between reality and camera-based, film and photographic technology. The first is Max Ernst's collage, "The Failed Immaculate Conception" (fig. 2.3), from his "picture book," *100 Headless Woman* (1929). The mise-en-scène, the composition, the emotional tone (and, of course, the title) of the image suggest the ambivalence of the primal scene: the child witnesses an enigmatic affective act, and is unable to understand its exact nature; the child interprets parental intercourse as an act of violence.

But *The Failed Immaculate Conception* is, in fact, Ernst's "revision" of an appropriated nineteenth-century newspaper illustration (fig. 2.4), which depicts the act of framing, of setting up a shot—translating "raw life" into a staged scene. Visible in the newspaper original, the camera turns out to function here as a trigger of sorts: as an unacknowledged, repressed initiator of that primal fantasy that fundamentally frames our perception and understanding of reality. What is more, with Ernst's intervention, the camera-apparatus is, in fact, retroactively explicated as itself also contained within the mise-en-scène of the very phantasm that it generates.

The second illustration of the entanglement between reality and cinematographic technology comes from Ljubomir Micić's montage-driven typographic poem, "In the Name of Hundred Gods!" (1922) (fig. 2.5). In this Zenithist text, declarations, announcements, news-briefs, truncated ads, calls to revolutionary artistic and political action succeed each other in telegraphic fashion—rapidly, and by arriving from all sides and from all

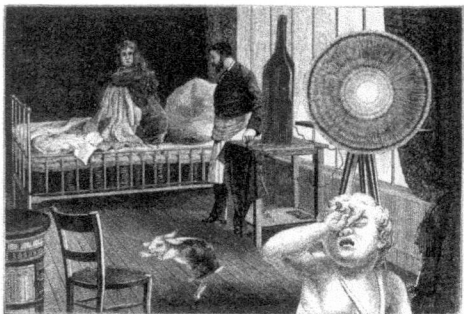

Figure 2.3 Max Ernst, *The Failed Immaculate Conception* (plate 2 from *100 Headless Woman*, 1929) © 2011 Artists Rights Society (ARS), New York / ADAGP, Paris; photo: CNAC/MNAM/Dist. Réunion des Musées Nationaux / Art Resource, NY

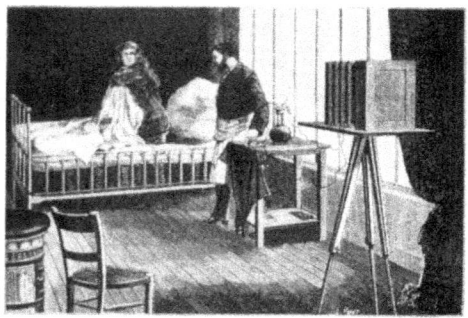

Figure 2.4 Nineteenth-century newspaper image appropriated by Ernst (discovered and first published by Dr. Werner Spies, in his book *Max Ernst Collages: The Invention of the Surrealist Universe*)

corners of the page. Every once in a while, there also pop up on the page—as if they have pierced through the textual stitches—what are best described as various reminders of cinema's ubiquity: descriptions of streets, hospital walls, and funerary cars decorated with posters for the film *The Cabinet of Doctor Caligari* (1920); theoretical quips about "film as Esperanto" and the science of "kinoism"; didactic calls to "turn churches into cinematographs"; and even images, such as the one seen here, of the film apparatus itself.

Figure 2.5 Ljubomir Micić, *In the Name of Hundred Gods!* (1922)

Reality, the Uhr-state of cinema! In Micić's typographic poetry, "cinema degree zero" is nothing other than reality understood as somehow always already "penetrated by technology," impure and "equipment-based."[23]

From *Gurk* and *The Self-Portrait of the Dadasoph*, to *The Frenzied Marble* and *The Mirror*—diverse as they are, these works are all motivated by their authors' desire to posit cinema-as-design. They locate this cinematic design in the space—or, more precisely, in the difference—between the concept of the film medium and its unconventional technological realization.[24] (In this sense, *Gurk* and *The Self-Portrait of the Dadasoph* may even be thought of as a dynamic couple.) In each case, artistic practice thus asserts itself as a sort of "philosophy of technology." It belongs to the realm of conceptual-materialist *praxis*, in which the *techne* and the *logos* coexist in each other as *technologie* (to use Alexandre Koyré's formulation), and precisely because they are, in fact, prevented from ever entirely coinciding.

As the Futurist leader Filippo Tommaso Marinetti understood very well: once it is practically perfected and made common, every medium in a sense becomes obsolete. Design, therefore, in a manner of "eternal critique"—or, perhaps, of Hegelian "infinite judgment"—fulfills the need for strict formalization: it treats the given medium as an absolute, as a pure form or structure, realizable even through the "inadequacies" of the media technologies that are, properly speaking, not its own. In this sense, all the technological "imperfections" of an apparatus such as *The Frenzied Marble*, *The Mirror* or, for that matter, Hausmann's *Synthetic Cinema of Painting* are only secondary in importance. What matters is that an artifact can be proposed that will ground a dynamic and largely imaginary film-system; that it will give body to a *diagram* fueled by what is, at its origin, a pure flow of thought. The more apparent the difference between the concept of a medium and its practical realization, the more pronounced the "primordial" status of the medium as a *set of structural relations*.

Let us now return to Man Ray. In 1919, almost five years before *Return to Reason*, he himself produced what is, arguably, an example of a "rematerialized" film apparatus. *Admiration of the Orchestrelle for the Cinematograph* (fig. 2.6) is an airbrush painting that presents an audiovisual machine of dubious operability, a strange relative, one might say, of Sound Film. The apparatus at stake is here "suggested" as the outcome of a simple, linearly traced montage (sexual in implications) of the depicted technologies of sound and image reproduction (top and bottom of the drawing, respectively).

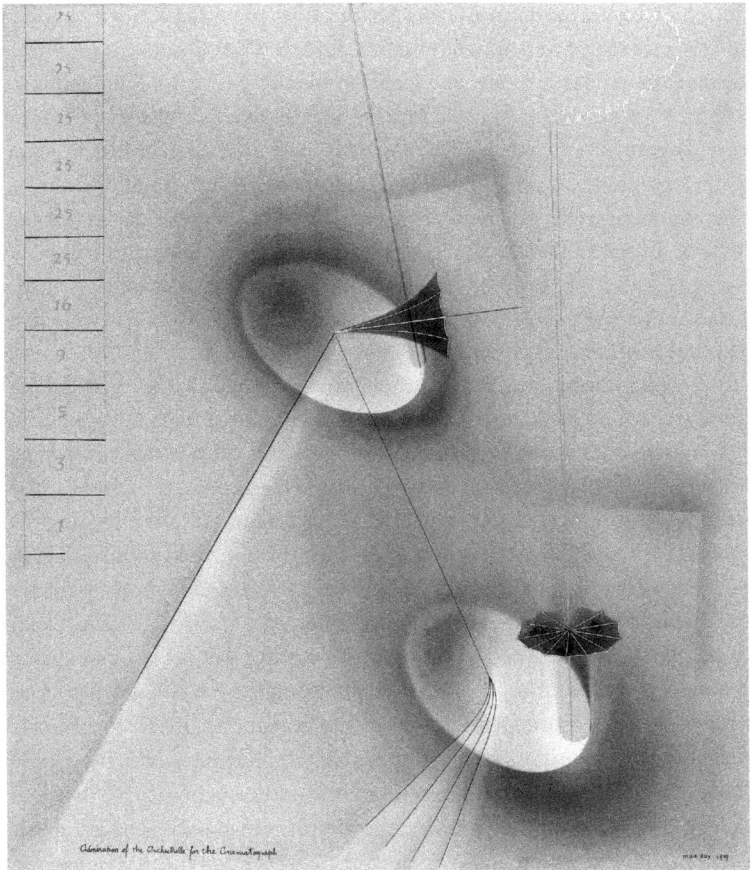

Figure 2.6 Man Ray, *Admiration of the Orchestrelle for the Cinematograph* (1919) © 2011 Man Ray Trust / Artists Rights Society (ARS), NY / ADAGP, Paris. Digital Image © The Museum of Modern Art/Licensed by SCALA / Art Resource, NY

The kinetic nature of the "medium" posited in the painting is registered, in Barbara Rose's words, through the "rectangular grid on the left margin reminiscent of a film strip, marked with numbers indicating a progression in time."[25] Significantly, the active component of the "medium" depends on an interpretative projection being mapped over its material design: it is equal to inscription of desire within the diagram for a possible re-conceptualized film apparatus of the future. What Deleuze said of diagrams in general is certainly applicable to Man Ray's *Admiration* (as it is to *The Frenzied Marble*, or to *Gurk* and *The Self-Portrait of the Dadasoph*): "(E)very diagram is intersocial and constantly evolving. It never functions in order to represent a persisting world but produces a new kind of reality, a new model of truth. It is neither the subject of history, nor does it survey history. It makes history by unmaking preceding realities and significations, constituting hundreds of points of emergence or creativity, unexpected conjunctions, of improbable continuums. It doubles history with a sense of continual evolution."[26]

As "philosophy of technology," conceptual-materialist art is, then, the art of presenting media that are in a permanent state of "becoming": media that are simultaneously objectively executed and subjectively motivated, universal in their abstractness and particular in their concrete existence. The material (or re-materialized) aspect of the medium—its specific, tangible "hardware" (painted by Man Ray; Hausmann's corporealized photo-collages; or, pieces of wood, metal, clay, etc., assembled by Vučo and Matić)—provides the stable and objective, formal coordinates of an "absolute" film apparatus. At the same time, its conceptual component—the subjectively grounded process of *thinking* and (thus) *mapping the relations* between these material coordinates—serves as the "cinematic dynamo" that sets the apparatus in motion, so to speak, by determining its specificity. That is to say, it is only because the diagrammatically outlined connection between different elements of the "working" apparatus remains subjectively motivated that the outcome of this "work," the effects it is expected/imagined to bring about can come across as having universal validity. The objective/material and the subjective/conceptual components of the "medium" supplement each other in such a way that it functions as a total, perfect version of itself, while at the same time it directly depends on (and is, moreover, repeatedly re-defined by) whatever subjectivity it engages at any given point in time.[27]

During his prolific "mechanical period," Francis Picabia produced numerous diagrammatic drawings and paintings such as *Voila Haviland!* and *Here, This is Stieglitz* (both 1915); *Balance* (1919); *Ezra Pound* (1922); and

Tickets (1922). Made by a restless bon vivant infatuated with the new and emerging technologies and with the speed and frenzy of the modern era, these works all explicate the general orientation of Picabia's art at the time: an orientation, in George Baker's words, toward "a hybrid form of artistic practice with new conditions of possibility, . . . a work between mediums, an interrelationship of forms, a hybridization of the image."[28] In some of these works, such as the rarely evoked *Portrait of Max Jacob*, a lamp drawing from 1915, the modality of this "hybridization" seems to be, in particular, that of the static image-turned-cinematic. The suggested circular dynamization of the depicted flashlight here comes across as a kind of structural simulacrum of what the film medium, at its most elementary, is: an instrument of kinesis of light—technology in the service of light moving through space, in time.[29] Furthermore, the anthropomorphic qualification—the act of assigning a proper name (Max Jacob) to the portrayed apparatus—hints at spectatorship as, literally, a hybrid of technology and human subjectivity.

The best known and the most commonly evoked example of Picabia's involvement with the cinema is found in his collaboration with Rene Clair on the production of the classic avant-garde film, *Entr'acte*.[30] Made in 1924, almost a decade after his diagrammatic drawings, the film—Picabia's brain-child—was situated in the intermission of his ballet *Relâche*. But the artist's immersion in the cinema (brief as it was) also had another, less conventional, post-*Entr'acte* phase. It is a phase distinguished, essentially, by a return to his pre-normative engagement with the medium and a further pursuit of the explorations he had already undertaken in some of the diagrammatic drawings. Specifically, following his excursion into the realm of filmmaking proper, Picabia revisited the domain to which he had already contributed his "film machine-that-is-not-the-cinematograph" (*Portrait of Max Jacob*) by creating further instances of "hybridized cinema": cinema indebted to, but not exactly realized by, the means of film. Thus, in 1924, after *Relache*, the artist worked (once again with Clair) on another theatrical performance, this time in its entirety conceived as, and given the title of, a "CineSketch." This short piece of "performed" cinema (staged only once, on New Year's Eve) sought to appropriate, to re-materialize within the practical limits of the theatrical apparatus, a number of rigorously filmic techniques and devices, such as parallel editing, slow motion, and the stroboscopically achieved flicker-effect. (Interestingly, around the same time the latter technique was also being explored in the Soviet Union: the Blue Blouse theatrical collectives used stroboscopic flicker effects in some of their agit-performances known as "kino reviews" or "living films.")[31] A few years later, in 1928, Picabia also tried himself out in the then fairly widespread genre of "written cinema": he created a written film "in three parts" called *La Loi d'accomodation chez les borgnes* (The Law of Accommodation among the One-Eyed). The preface to this film-text invited the viewer to "[d]o the filming yourself as you read...."[32] Importantly, the extraordinary conception of film practice and cinematic imagination underlying both of these projects was not for a moment lost on Picabia. As George Baker points out, at the time he was developing the *CineSketch*, the artist argued: "[U]p to now the cinema has been based on the theatre; I tried to do the opposite, bringing to the stage the techniques and lively rhythms of cinema."[33]

In general terms, the logic of Picabia's, Hausmann's, Man Ray's, or Vučo and Matić's "cinema by other means" rests on the point subsequently (in the 1960s) made famous by Marshall McLuhan: that "the content of one medium is always another medium." More precisely, these works may be situated within the parameters of Jay Bolter and Richard Grusin's category of "remediation." Beyond the foundation laid down by McLuhan, the two authors emphasized instances of different media *explicitly* following, reshaping, and reactivating each other's logic and forms.

Most commonly, "remediation" involves newer forms of media appropriating—surpassing but also on some level preserving—the older ones. Television, for example, presented an advanced form of radio, while virtual reality offered itself as a better, improved form of the cinema.[34] However, what interests me here is a peculiar version of this process—what may be termed "retrograde remediation": instances of remediation distinguished by some inherent discrepancy, by a pronounced practical/technological *inadequacy* of one ("older") medium to fully assimilate certain aspects of another.[35] Thus, *The Frenzied Marble* is to be understood as a modality of cinema even though—or precisely because—it represents a static object that is simply unable to generate an actual series of moving images. Although "petrified," it *is* real cinema, as it were, only realized through the technology of another medium: the imaginary signifier (Christian Metz's famous definition of the film image) made entirely material; movement or "change" literally "mummified" (as Andre Bazin would say). Similarly, although *The Self-Portrait of the Dadasoph* is strictly speaking a static collage, it is in fact thoroughly overcome by the flow of the cinematic imaginary–by its unique interweaving of mental and technological labor.

"Retrograde remediation" complicates the logic of unidirectional causality, frequently applied to the rapport between the idea of a medium and its technological implementation. Consider the case of Walter Benjamin who, in his well-known 1930s essay "The Work of Art in the Age of Technological Reproducibility," suggests a causal link between certain Dadaist practices and the advancement of film technology. Interested in the relationship between the general disappearance of artistic "aura" and the development of technologies of mechanical image production and reproduction, Benjamin lays emphasis on the fact that, before it is practically realized, every technological innovation is first articulated as a desire for a novel form:

> It has always been one of the primary tasks of art to create a demand whose hour of full satisfaction has not yet come. The history of every art form has critical periods in which the particular form strains after effects which can be easily achieved only with a changed technical standard—that is to say, in a new art form. The excesses and crudities of art which thus result, particularly in periods of so-called decadence, actually emerge from the core of its richest historical energies. In recent years, Dadaism has amused itself with such barbarisms. Only now is its impulse recognizable: *Dadaism attempted to produce with the means of painting (or literature) the effect which the public today seeks in film.*[36]

The "demand" made by an art form precedes, then, the means of its technological realization. Eventually, technology "catches up" with this demand, with the idea it seeks to realize: "First, technology is working toward a particular form of art. Before film appeared, there were little books of photos that could be made to flit past the viewer under the pressure of the thumb, presenting a boxing match or a tennis match; then there were coin-operated peepboxes in bazaars, with image sequences kept in motion by the turning of a handle. Second, traditional art forms, at certain stages in their development, strain laboriously for effects which later are effortlessly achieved by new art forms. Before film became established, Dadaist performances sought to stir in their audiences reactions which Chaplin then elicited more naturally."[37] Cinema thus realized the demand the Dadaists had already made "by other means"—through their performances, objects, collages, assemblages, optophonetic poetry. One could say that, according to this account, the cinematographic apparatus stands for technology having been advanced to the point where an authentic Dada machine can be created.

Significantly, however, Benjamin's argument rests upon what is in fact a chronological error. Dadaist practice *was not* simply anterior to the epoch of early film—rather, it *coincided* with it. The age of Dada and the age of cinema are not two successive eras, but one and the same. The question, therefore, inevitably arises: why did Hausmann, Man Ray, Picabia, and many more of their contemporaries repeatedly articulate a demand for the cinema by employing the techniques and forms of other, "older" means of expression? Why did these lovers of the machine continually insist on the cinematic character of their literary, visual, and performative practice, at the time when the actual film apparatus had not only already seen the light of day, but had even begun to assert itself as *the* medium of the twentieth century?

I would argue that it is here, actually, that the dialectic of "demand and its realization," at the root of all media, is truly put to work: the work of fundamentally opposing the teleological historical movement of technological essentialism.[38] It is in this light that one should read Thomas Elsaessser's perceptive assertion that "the Dadaists' attitude to the new technologies of visual reproduction and imaging was retrograde, but necessarily so, given their radical aspirations."[39] For the radical aspiration that is at stake here is precisely that of foregrounding and preserving the dual nature of all media. Every medium is, from the moment of its inception, a dynamic conceptual design: an imagined cluster of (desired, projected, assumed) functions—a "theoretical object," in Rosalind Krauss's sense of the term.[40] But this conceptual circuit also requires—it is perpetually in search of (this search being its history)—concrete material-technological support that will give the medium its operational body. Eventually, operational technology is declared normative. At that point, however, the Idea of the medium is also substantially transformed: its immaterial conceptual design acquires a thus far unprecedented degree of specificity by being forever related to the structural-material dynamics of the standardized apparatus. What is more, at the point when the concept and the technology fully coincide, when the new medium has successfully been turned into a working artifact—*the medium would, in some sense, also have already been excessively reified (and commodified)*. It is, therefore, only by repeatedly evoking, by enacting, the discrepancy between the idea and its technological implementation that the essential qualities and the radical, noninstrumentalist creative potential contained in any new medium are maintained. (Thus, for instance, it is in the failure of *The Frenzied Marble* as film technology proper that the conceptual purity of the cinematic idea(l) was preserved; against the historical background of the cinematographic machine simultaneously asserting its hegemony.)

The main current within the historical trajectory of any established medium will inevitably lead to a higher or lesser degree of technological alienation and fetishization. On the other hand, as design embodied in technology that is effective/productive only insofar as it is still, at least partially, motivated by the human/mental projection of its desired effects, the medium maintains the non-reified form of an apparatus set in motion by thought-relations (what Marinetti referred to as "anonymous gears"). Realized "by other means," it functions as a sort of Tauskian "influencing machine" in reverse: a "suggestion apparatus" firmly controlled by, rather than controlling, the psycho-perceptual activity of the human subject.[41] Seized upon by the avant-garde artists in the early decades of the twentieth century, the significance of this mentally and conceptually driven reversal of influence with respect to technology continued, with some key adjustments, in the postwar era. During the 1950s, it manifested itself in a variety of attempts—first made programmatic by the Lettrists—to redefine the existing media by re-materializing them ("chiseling" was the term put forth by the movement's leader, Isidore Isou) as so many corresponding *situations*.

Chapter 3

Written Films

Hypnison swallows the moon, puts clouds in his pocket, raises his arm, and transforms the arbitrary landscape into some other illusory setpieces: an endless purple desert surrounding a hill. There is a black tent at the bottom of the hill; ex oriente, a purple and square sun is rising. Ventilators (in the theater) blow a hot Saharan wind. Water and dates in front of the film viewers. The band plays oriental melodies. Hypnison finds the square sun quite tasteless. He changes it for another: a flaming ellipsoid. But he could not care for this sun either, and angry, with the speed of lightning, he kicks it like a rugby ball. The sun flies over the Milky Way, and somewhere, far away in the Cosmos, it breaks into pieces. African drums sound with all their force. Suddenly, things lose the aspect of perspective. Hyperbolas, spirals, ellipses, and coordinates, dance in front, behind, and on the screen: everyone senses that the explosion of the Sun has something to do with the hyper-space, the fourth or the fifth dimension.

In 1923, in Belgrade, Yugoslavia, a young poet named Monny de Boully wrote the above lines for the short text he entitled "Doctor Hypnison, or the Technique of Living."[1] The author conceived and designated the text as a "film scenario," yet it was never intended to be made into an actual film. "Doctor Hypnison" was, and forever remained, a "paper movie."[2] The space it occupies is to be located somewhere between literature and cinematography: a generic hybrid, Boully's text is neither a "rounded," self-enclosed literary work nor a film scenario proper (in the sense of representing a stage in the process of filmmaking). As such, it belongs to an unusual yet fairly extensive corpus of films that were all "written never to be filmed," the "unfilmable film scenarios" as Benjamin Fondane liked to call them.[3] In this corpus of "written cinema"—a genre that offers a prime historical example of the avant-garde practice of "retrograde remediation"—one finds works by numerous early twentieth century artists and poets, including Guillaume Apollinaire, Louis Delluc, Philippe Soupault, Antonin Artaud, Robert Desnos, Francis Picabia, Aleksandar Vučo, and others.[4]

Boully's immediate reasons for writing "Doctor Hypnison" clearly reveal that his "film" was from the outset predestined forever to remain in the written form. The poet's primary concern was with entering the circle of Belgrade avant-garde writers who frequented the "Moskva" cafe, and with publishing his work in *Hypnos,* a monthly review of "intuitive art" edited by Rade Drainac, the leader of the short-lived movement called Hypnism. The scenario did, indeed, appear in the second issue of *Hypnos* (fig. 3.1), and Boully joined the ranks of those whose manifesto proclaimed: "Death to Gods! Long live the Hypnist Zone, declared in the third section of the 'Moskva' cafe.... Feel free to enter the New Universe created by Rade Drainac." (fig. 3.2)

Hypnism was but one among the variety of avant-garde tendencies that developed in Yugoslavia in the early 1920s. As I pointed out in chapter one, Yugoslav modernists were overwhelmed by the recent blossoming of European literature and art. Drawing upon the ideas and aesthetic principles of Dadaism, German Expressionism, and Russian and Italian Futurism, they introduced a number of local versions of the rebellion against traditional values and the bourgeois society governed by nationalist myths and conservative morals. Disgusted by the Great War and the ethical hypocrisy that permitted such a human tragedy, seeking to cut off all links with the past and to produce art that would pave the path toward a new society grounded in internationalism, Ljubomir Micić founded Zenithism, while Dragan Aleksić organized and led the band of regional Dadaists. Other smaller and shorter-lived movements also emerged—Božidar Kovačević, Rade Drainac, and Miloš Crnjanski founded, respectively, Cosmism, Hypnism, and Sumatraism.

It is within this field of flourishing modernist literary activity that one locates the earliest attempts by the Yugoslav authors to engage the practice of "writing films." Boško Tokin, as we saw earlier, pioneered the writing of "cinematographic poetry." A few years before Boully's "Hypnison," Tokin was also developing *The Kingdom of Ghosts,* a novel envisioned

Figure 3.1 *Hipnos* no. 2 (1923), front page

as a film-story. As literary historian Gojko Tešić noted, Tokin is probably the author most responsible for introducing film as a narrative theme into Serbian literature.[5] Soon afterward, inspired by the techniques of film montage, other more radical authors also began experimenting with the

Figure 3.2 "Death to Gods. Long live the Hypnist Zone . . ."

possibilities of formal fragmentation and narrative discontinuity in their writing. Ljubomir Micić, for example, structured one of his most important prose texts, "Shimmy at the Graveyard in the Latin Quarter" (1922), as a constructivist collage, building "photo-montages from the newspaper clips depicting manifestations of the 'new spirit' around the world."[6] "Shimmy" is today recognized as a prime example of the narrative structure Micić referred to as "radio-film." "In Zenithist poetry," the author asserted programmatically, "we demand film realism and the totality of modern life, a quick exchange between the internal and the external worlds, strong and sharp contrasts of black and white by way of illogical associations and simultaneity. . . ."[7]

> Wanted: zenith-man-philosophy: zenitosophy
>   Wanted: cine-zenithistic new art: zenithism
>   Wanted: radio-film-zenithistic vertical: of spirit
>
> —Ljubomir Micić

> Traži se: zenit-čovek-filozofija: zenitozofija
> Traži se: filmo-zenitistička nova umetnost: zenitizam
> Traži se: radio-film-zenitistička okomica: duha«
> (LjM)

Figure 3.3

Micić's praise of radio as a foremost technological and artistic expression of the spirit of modernity coincided with the appearance of Velimir Khlebnikov's celebrated manifesto, "The Radio of the Future" (1921).[8] Overall, the influence of Russian Futurism and Constructivism on Zenithism was paramount. Starting with the tenth issue of his journal *Zenit*, Micić would regularly publish the works of Vladimir Mayakovsky, Aleksandr Rodchenko, Sergei Esenin, Illya Ehrenburg, and El Lissitzky. Correspondence and creative exchanges with the latter two (at the time, editors of the Berlin-based Constructivist journal, *Vešč'*) were particularly productive. Lisstizky even designed the cover for a double issue of *Zenit* (n.17–18, 1922) (fig. 3.4), entirely devoted to "the new art in Russia."[9]

But it was Vladimir Tatlin, more than any other Soviet avant-gardist, who reigned supreme in Micić's eyes. As Aleksandar Flaker points out, for the Zenithist leader, "the imperative of poetic creation" was, in his own words: "To persistently *think* of Tatlin's monument, and to stomp with one's foot the Morgan Bank in New York."[10] Images of "Tatlin's monument" (*Monument to the Third International*) were published in *Zenit* on a number of occasions. This seminal work of Constructivist architecture is also at the thematic center of Micić's seventeen-part radio-film, "Shimmy at the Graveyard in the Latin Quarter." In it, Micić employs the collage structure of the written text to convey the dynamic nature and the switchboard-like function of the *Monument*, envisioned (already by Tatlin himself) as a radio tower that disseminates the spirit of the Revolutionary internationalism around the globe: from Moscow and St. Petersburg, to Paris and Prague; from Tokyo to Zagreb, to Berlin, Belgrade, and New York. In Micić's rendition of Tatlin's *Monument*, avant-gardists of the world—Mayakovsky, Ehrenburg, Hausmann, Ivan Goll, Karel Teige, Charlie Chaplin, F. T. Marinetti (criticized for his fascist leanings), and

Figure 3.4 *Zenit* 17–18 (1922), front page

many others—have all become radio reporters, members of a "network" held together by the signals that incessantly pass through "Tatlin-central." "Shimmy" ends with a call for an all-Zenithist gathering, scheduled for "tomorrow." Location: Rodchenko's *Kiosk*![11]

Although Boully was never particularly impressed by Zenithism—which he somewhat simplistically tended to view as an inferior Balkanist version of Dadaism—he also employed the format of radio-film in parts of "Doctor Hypnison." A section of his film-text is entitled "Radio-Cinematographic Poem: Shadows of the Heart" (fig. 3.5). In it an image of a black rectangle framed by another rectangle—an abstract geometric shape, resistant to

РАДИОКИНЕМАТОГРАФСКА ПЕСМА
„СЕНКЕ СРЦА"

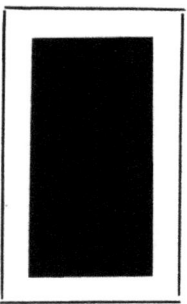

...И одједном, деконцентрацијом мисли, Доктор Хипнисон се нађе на улици. Он иде једним стрмим, балканским ћорсокаком где куће нису више од људи. Музиканти свирају *примитивне* мелодије у народне инструменте. Калдрма је од неотесаног камена а те турске стражаре од непровидног су стакла. Тада Васељенски Мудраци стадоше *млазевима светлости* да бомбардују *Стаклени Град*.

Figure 3.5 Monny de Boully, "Radio-Cinematographic Poem *Shadows of the Heart*"

immediate linguistic rationalizations and attributions of meaning—is freely incorporated into the text, juxtaposed ("illogically associated," as Micić would say) with a dramatic, Méliès-like narrative passage depicting Hypnison's fantasmatic adventures. To the accompaniment of some "primitive folk melodies," Hypnison, we are told, "walks down a steep Balkan alley where houses are not taller than people . . . [and] made of non-transparent glass," while "the Cosmic Sages begin to bombard this Glass City with rays of light." Only after this narrative episode has ended does Boully turn to elaborating the earlier mysterious appearance in the text of the black, upright (Malevich-like) rectangle. In the section of the scenario indicatively called "A Foretelling," he gives a brief description of "an open door, a rectangle full of darkness, akin to the secret entrances to the caves in which blind creatures reside in an eternal night." The image of the black rectangle is thus unveiled as a kind of proleptic visual echo of its own content—a perceptual advance amid linguistic signifiers, an image offered to the "film's" reader-spectator even as its meaning is yet to be fixated.

Such playfulness with the hallucinatory possibilities of the written text—stemming from an understanding of writing itself as a type of cinematic practice—permeates "Doctor Hypnison," making it one of the earliest forerunners of Surrealism in Yugoslavia. Driven by the paradoxes of irrational causality and soaked in a hypnagogic atmosphere, Boully's scenario saw the light of day at the time when the Parisian Surrealist movement was in its formative years, and the Belgrade poet's involvement with the "intuitive art" of Hypnism temporally coincided with the experiments by Breton, Aragon, Éluard, Soupault, and others in automatism, dream recollection, and hypnotic trances. During this period of transition from Dada to Surrealism, known as *le mouvement flou* (1922–1923), Marko Ristić—the future leader of the Belgrade Surrealists (and one of the co-signers of the "Second Manifesto of Surrealism")—had established correspondence with Breton and, keeping track of the activities of the Paris group, was regularly informing the Yugoslav public about this "vague and strange time when the mediums enter the stage . . ., when the sources of psychic automatism are sought and found yet another step lower, in the still lower galleries of the underground catacombs, in the lower world of labyrinths, in the forbidden zone."[12] Around the same time, the poet

Dušan Matić—one of the authors of the "petrified film," *The Frenzied Marble* (analyzed in the previous chapter)—was writing and lecturing on Freud, the unconscious, and the impact psychoanalysis was making on art and literature in the Western Europe.

Keeping in mind this context of the passionate interest in Parisian activities, it is not surprising that certain portions of Boully's scenario read as if the poet was himself directly experimenting in automatic writing, as if he had already aligned himself with the Bretonian struggle to "structure the spirit anew" by contaminating the everyday reality with the unconscious life of things. Consider, for instance, the following verse, attributed to Doctor Hypnison and inscribed in the sky of his fictional world "by the tail of a passing comet": "My eye/telescopic/only briefly/noticed tonight/a double star/thus for me/brought/from the Universe/were new themes/ and poems/my soul rides/on the double star. . . ." Little did Boully know at the time he produced these lines that two years later he would be sitting in a Paris cafe, writing his first "properly" automatic text under the close scrutiny of Benjamin Péret. During a visit to France in 1925, he established contact with Breton and his group (Aragon, then at work on *Le Paysan de Paris*,[13] took the newcomer on never-ending trips around the city), and "the bohemian table at the 'Moskva' thus gave way to the surrealist table at the café 'Cyrano.'"[14] Boully's automatic text, "Exercice surréaliste," as well as his adaptation of "Vampyr"—a short "illustrated novel" about mental disturbances, written by a Zagreb author, Miroslav Feler—subsequently appeared in the fifth issue of the journal, *La Révolution Surréaliste*.

Breton, we know, was weary (especially in the earliest days of Surrealism) of "the incursions of conscious elements" in the domain of "unconscious dictation." In "The Mediums Enter," a major statement on early Surrealist practices, he wrote: "[B]y heeding voices other than that of our own unconscious,. . . we risk compromising this self-sufficient murmur in its essence.[15] However, from the outset, Boully considered the possibility of an absolute elimination of the conscious intrusions as illusory, but even so, he praised automatism as a skill, an "acrobatic technique" capable, at its best, of striking a delicate balance and productive tension between the conscious and the unconscious. In a language unequivocally evocative of that in which "Doctor Hypnison" was written, Boully once asked: "Is there a surrealist, automatic technique of living? As far as I am concerned, the answer is yes." It consists in producing "instinctive lyrical syntheses" from "everything that the waters of the unconscious cast upon the shores of a specific consciousness," in a manner "akin to a sleepwalker balancing on the edge of an abyss.... A stubborn development of such a consciousness,... its strengthening to the point of monstrosity, might be the sole secret of the surrealist technique of living."[16] Like his Surrealist comrades, Boully was full of contempt for conventional logic and instrumental reason, yet he was also skeptical about treating the unconscious as an entirely self-contained realm, as a depository of the repressed content separable from consciousness. For him, what distinguishes an automatic text from any other piece of writing is the extent to which it creatively emphasizes and heightens the tension characterizing the state of intertwining between the primary libidinal processes generating the text and the inevitable, but de-normativized, efforts of the conscious mind to give these processes a form. It is out of this tension, this interaction, that the unconscious life of the text emerges, inscribing itself in the very form of the text's manifest appearance, as the surplus of its consciously "digested" ingredients.

Considered in this light, "written film" seems like a format particularly suited for turning psychic automatism into a cinematic practice. Image production becomes thus a major function of the spectatorial activity which, oscillating between the private screen of one's fantasy and the objectively given "*ekphrastic* coordinates" of the scenaristic blueprint, embodies the tension between the free libidinal flow and the form of its control, its censorship. "I've heard it said," claimed Francis Picabia, "that the scenario is nothing.... That's why I ask each of my readers to direct, to project it for himself on the screen of his imagination, a truly magical screen...."[17] Projecting the film beyond its material-written basis, onto the "screen of one's imagination," accords with Breton's conception of the surrealist image as "neither a descriptive mirror nor a narrative window, but a fantasmatic window"—a grid inscribed with "letters of desire," as Hal Foster puts it.[18] Obviously familiar with the mechanisms with which to stimulate his audience's desire, Boully gives only a schematic, intentionally incomplete description of Hypnison: he has "the characteristics of an Everyman," and he looks like "a mold for a man." Similarly, a woman whom

Hypnison encounters at one point "has no concrete physical properties": she is a "contour of a woman," produced by photographing "all the women of the world" in the "exact same position on the exact same photographic plate." Anticipating the literal framing of desire in the scopic field in what would become one of the most celebrated works of Yugoslav Surrealist photography—Nikola Vučo's "Untitled" (1930) (fig. 3.6)—Boully's Woman invites the reader-viewer to "project onto her the mask of an ideal from the heart."

In an inspired review of René Clair's film *Entr'acte*—published in 1926 in the short-lived, Surrealist-leaning journal *Večnost* (Eternity)—Boully praised cinema's "metaphysical" quality, its ability to move beyond

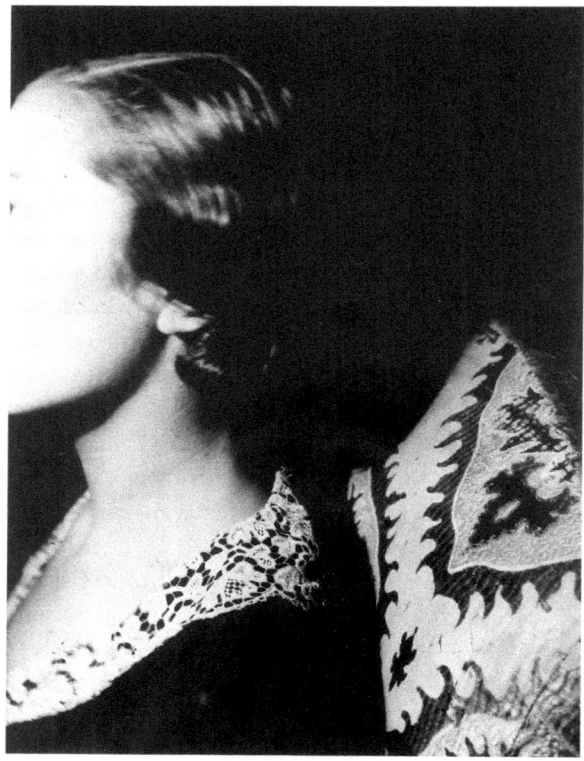

Figure 3.6 Nikola Vučo, *Untitled* (1930) © Museum of Fine Arts, Belgrade

the photographic reproduction of the physical world, into the realm of "transcendental irrationality."[19] This type of infatuation with "cinematic transcendence" was, at the time, also common among other Yugoslav avant-gardists. Marko Ristić, for instance, partially inspired by Jean Epstein, argued that the "metaphysics of the cinematograph leaves behind its aesthetics," for one "faces a film" not equipped "with one's own criteria, but with one's desires, hopes, and tears...."[20] Likewise, in Ristić's "An Example" (1924)—the first official, programmatically intended piece of "automatic writing" in Yugoslavia—cinema asserts its pivotal role in inducing an "unaltered flow of thought":

> The ship is emptied, and dry, it rises slowly and graciously in the air, while the Sea Snake lets it go with an unbearable, yet inaudible, life-endangering whistle from the locomotives in American films. The cinema was half-empty, but the rising of the ship on the screen filled hearts with such joy for the Eternal New Life that those few film viewers stood up on their seats and roared, asking that, in the purple blasts of celestial blood, the ship negligently takes them from reality to reality, with only its image, from dream to dream.[21]

Cinema is here invested with the power to perform the transition from one reality to another, from one dream to another (what, decades later, Breton would describe as its "power of displacement"[22]), and Ristić presents this transition as almost inevitable, as something his entranced, imaginary film-viewers yearn for. He thus shares the same sense of urgency as Boully, who, seeking to emphasize the awe-evoking power of Doctor Hypnison's hallucinatory world, incorporated within his scenario its desired effects upon the audience: "suddenly, all the viewers raise their hands"; "everyone senses that the explosion of the sun has something to do with the hyper-space, the fourth or the fifth dimension"; "silence and complete darkness in the theater. Only the ticking of watches in the waistcoats, and of hearts in the bosoms can be heard." So carried was Boully by the wish to ensure not only the exact emotional, but also the proper physiological impact of his film, that he imagined for his audience a theater "constructed as an elevator" so that when required, it can "suddenly descend into the depths of the underground." In this futuristic theater, "ventilators blow a hot Saharan wind" while water, dates, pineapple, bananas, and coconuts are placed in front of the viewers. Even the olfactory effects of his imagined cinema are taken into account by the young poet: "The scent of flowers is in the air, that thick, tropical scent of blooming."

As Branko Vučićević points out, Boully's concern with the power of art to affect the sense of smell is probably most accurately understood as a continuation of the Yugoslav Dadaists' almost obsessive attention to scents.[23] Suffice it to evoke here the most notorious Dadaist matinee, held in the town of Subotica only a couple of months before "Doctor Hypnison, or the Technique of Living" would be published. There, one of the participants, Endre Arato, questioned why

> all arts address primarily the eye and the ear, while neglecting other senses.... Since there already was Tactilism, Arato decided that a nose-art must also exist. Thus he arranged for a concert of scents in Subotica.... Arato had some trumpet-like instrument to blow, emitting scents together with the sounds. He wanted to make sure that the perfumes will reach the other end of the hall, so he blew very hard. Waves of scents flooded the audience, who enriched the concert with coughing.[24]

While it may have been partially inspired by the peculiarities of Yugoslav Dada, Boully's "cinema of scents" is, nonetheless, conceived more functionally, as part of an effort toward a rather systematic "synchronization of the senses." Reflecting on the artistic ideals underlying his work, Boully explained: "[E]schewing all clichés of stylization, no longer paying attention to the rational and the irrational, I gave rise to a personal intuition: to take what is known as word-play beyond its outer limits, into an entirely crystallized, new, coherent, marvelous universe."[25] One imagines that it is precisely this propensity for poetic sublimation—outstepping the boundaries of Dada in a manner typical of *le mouvement flou*—that attracted Breton to Boully's work. And yet, as we shall see, the "founding procedure" of Boully's surrealism—as it is narrativized in "Doctor Hypnison"—seems to correspond most directly to that sense of *convulsive beauty* described by Salvador Dali: "Beauty will be edible or it will not be."

The passage from the text in the opening of this chapter clearly illustrates that Boully's protagonist inhabits a space lacking all sense of perspective. He is capable of kicking the moon and of assigning different shapes to the sun. Later on, he also demonstrates a power to transpose himself from one place to another "by the sole power of his imagination"—and when he does so, "his head grows bigger, his hands, legs, and body diminish in size. His body becomes too weak to carry such a huge head, which soon falls down on the ground, immobile and with eyes closed." Such overlappings of realistic and fantastic/oneiric elements are so frequent and intense in the "film," that no point of reference can be established to distinguish between the two. When, two-thirds into the text, Boully introduces an intertitle that reads "dream," it seems to have an ironic rather than a practical narrative function. The intertitle, meant to announce a change in diegetic registers—from reality one moves into the realm of dreams—seems to signal only a change that never actually takes place. The "dream"—in which, according to Hypnison, "thus I travel/with the speed of thought/towards the distant star/blinking at me/my eyelashes caressing/the beloved sphere"—is as realistic (or nonrealistic) as the "reality" that precedes it, and this reality is just as oneiric as the dream itself. One wonders, indeed, whether Hypnison's reality is not, in fact, a dream of reality and whether the "dream" following it is not the actual reality into which Hypnison awakens. In Boully's Hypnos-world, as in Lewis Carroll's Wonderland, reality and dream/fantasy come together comprising one singular realm, a "living spatial magma," as the film critic Ranko Munitić put it, a "global elastic sphere—accessible at every moment and in every direction to the main character. A decision or a gesture by dramatis personae brings about an immediate reaction of this meta-space."[26]

What is most interesting about this conflation of reality and dream/fantasy, about their fusion into a single plane of surreality, is that Boully provides insight into the very means by which this fusion is accomplished. Hypnison is a character with an oral fixation. He demonstrates a tendency to lick and devour anything he does or does not like. At one time, for instance, he insatiably drinks the "moon honey" ("seeking to quench/the thirst of my gluttonous soul/I raise my tongue towards the sky/and I lick passionately/the Honey Moon"), while at another time he impatiently swallows the moon itself. It is not surprising, therefore, that the generative point of his surreal habitat marks its appearance during yet another one of his oral festivities:

> Endlessly joyous, Hypnison opened his mouth.... His mouth grew bigger and bigger, the huge throat was laughing.... What a terrible laughter, what dark, deep, huge and abysmal jaws. There! There! The teeth are turning into the stars of the Great Elephant: alpha, beta, gamma... and the monstrous gape becomes the entire sky. A comet etches in it Hypnison's verses....

As Hypnison opens his infinitely big mouth, Boully effectively initiates the unfolding of the process through which the external reality is internalized, Hypnison's interiority is externalized, and the standard, clear-cut distinction between the objective ("outer" reality) and the subjective ("internal states") is forever blurred. In the depths of Hypnison's throat, the darkness and monstrosity *instantaneously* turn into the sky filled with stars and comets. What is thus implied is that the *movement* along the path which connects the external reality with Hypnison's interior life—the movement along the path leading through his oral cavity—must have taken place *in both directions simultaneously*. The moment of reaching the deepest spheres of Hypnison's interiority is the same as the moment of their externalization. The consequence of Boully's use of this paradoxical simultaneity—which, not unlike *convulsive beauty*, conflates spatial movements and/or fixates time—is that the *cogito*, the subject's (Hypnison's) consciousness, is bypassed, short-circuited. Hence, the new reality established around Hypnison is not simply his subjective vision or his daydream of reality, but rather something more radical: it is Hypnison's own externalized fantasy, given an uncannily de-subjectivized, autonomous existence. In other words, by structuring the existence of the "abyss" of Hypnison's subjectivity around the paradoxical double movement negating the clear-cut distinction between the objective and the subjective, Boully establishes this abyss as an equivalent of the Freudian unconscious. And it is precisely on this account that the poet comes closest to sharing the concerns of the early Surrealists. The operation he performs inside Hypnison's mouth revolves around a key Surrealist paradox demanding, as Allen S. Weiss explains, that the "phantasm is not distinguished from perception: thus it becomes the scene which contains the very personages [producing it]. Such a visionary mise-en-scène is emblematic of the idealizing and the sublimatory position of Surrealist creativity: origins are metaleptically dissimulated in their effects...."[27]

This paradox is also the key to understanding why "Doctor Hypnison, or the Technique of Living" is conceivable only as an "unfilmable" film. Underlying Boully's written text is the meta-cinematic fantasy of a perfect, futuristic film apparatus—the one that would no longer have to dissimulate representation (projected images) in perception (viewer's activity), "origins in their effects," but could, rather, make this conflation *literal*. It is the fantasy of the imagistic yield of the psyche directly materialized in the space of its exteriority. It is, finally, the fantasy of a pure de-subjectivized spectatorship—of cinema as truly a "mental institution."

This extraordinary psychophysical cinematic fantasy is given further conceptual explication, as well as visual representation, in another Yugoslav surrealist "written film," *Crustaceans on the Chest* (1930). Written by Aleksandar Vučo (during the same year he worked on other cinematic objects and apparatuses, including the earlier discussed *Frenzied Marble* and *The Mirror*) and illustrated by Marko Ristić, *Crustaceans* was produced over half a decade after "Doctor Hypnison." It is also much more directly inspired by the film-related activities of the French Surrealists than Boully's text is, in particular by the publication of Buñuel and Dali's scenario for *Un chien andalou* in the journal *Revolution surrealiste*. Vučo's film uses a typically surrealist narrative structure: the logical progression of the story is repeatedly "frustrated" by unmotivated discontinuities and sudden interpolation of highly coded images: galloping giraffes, women's shoes, cut-off legs, gloves, scorpions, and glass jars in which fish and other aquatic creatures are kept. At the time of the film's writing, crustaceans, too, had already begun to populate Surrealist imagination, to some extent due to the work done by the scientist and nature documentarian, Jean Painleve. Man Ray used Painleve's footage of starfish for his own film, *L'Etoile de mer* (1928), while Georges Bataille's *Encyclopaedia Acephalica* included an entry on the "Crustaceans," illustrated by Painleve's images. Written by Jacques Baron (his sole contribution to the *Encyclopaedia*), this short reflection on lobsters, shrimp, crayfish, and crabs praised their often-overlooked heterological beauty and emphasized their symbolic ties to female sexuality.[28]

Ristić enriched Vučo's scenario with twelve collages (fig.3.7) which, far from directly translating words into images, suggest fluctuations of creative energy between the formats of "written cinema" and "visual literature."[29] Somewhat reminiscent of Man Ray filming his *L'Etoile de mer* as an "adaptation" of a poem by Robert Desnos, the Vučo-Ristić collaboration is an example of the intersubjective variant of the Surrealist practice of automatism: the two interlocutors complement each other by communicating a message unburdened by the fixity and the singularity of meaning.

Beyond the parallel that may be drawn between the mechanisms of collaborative visualization in *Crustaceans* and *L'Etoile de mer*, the inspiring shadow of Man Ray looms fairly large over Ristić's cinematic imagination in general. Well informed about the activities of the "Paris central," the leader of the Belgrade Surrealists knew early on about Man Ray's rayographic practice, and since 1928 was himself also experimenting with this medium. In the late 1920s, he produced a sequence of fifteen photo-collages which, in a rarely seen gesture, combined camera-less and camera-based photography, photogrames, and photographed content (figs. 3.8, 3.9, 3.10). As art historian Milanka Todić points out, Ristić's images are distinguished by the fact that, unlike the majority of the camera-less works produced at the time, they show not only objects but also soft-edged photographic silhouettes and portraits of human subjects.[30]

Ristić's series of fifteen collage-photograms is organized in a manner suggestive of a cinematic progression. By itself, each image presents a particular case of subject-object or subject-subject relations. And, as is only fitting for a Surrealist work, these relations rest upon an economy of desire (connecting representations of man, woman, lace, necklace, and so forth). When considered together, as a sequence, the fifteen images create a strong sense of kinesis: of spatiotemporal changes occurring as the depicted people and objects move, position, and reposition themselves. It is as if by combining and orchestrating the camera-less and the camera-based images, Ristić managed to excavate the ethereal "motion pictures" buried beneath the frozen surface of still photography.[31] "Digging" underneath the naturalized stability of the physical world, the Yugoslav Surrealist stumbled upon an elaborate but hidden system of kinetic fluctuations,

ЉУСКАРИ НА ПРСИМА
ФИЛМ

ПРЕДИГРА КОЈА СЕ НЕ ИГРА

Нека позадина буде сенка или црни талас. Најбоље би још одговарала мукла ноћ, тај мрки појас вечитог зида који не одаје тајне. Мокра, тамно-мрка боја има добру особину да крије трагове злочина: она упија као сунђер пруге од крвавих прстију. Нико према томе неће приметити да се на печатима ољуштеног малтера, на том сифилису зидова, могу под лупом открити отисци и сумњиви, проблематични трагови. Задржавамо се дакле на тој боји.

Са десне стране, где се под једном бледом руком угасила свећа долази стрела. Она је путоказ и смрт, али није још ослобођена од полазне тачке, за коју је везује сребрни конац, који сумњамо, да не ма ко видети. Конац полази из срца невине девојке, чије се груди као скривалиште појављују на свакој слици: у испупченом облику камена, у шарама рибљих крљушти, у воденим борама, а још најчешће у димовима јутра, то јест у планинама које се сваког јутра на хоризонту скупљају. Зато је неопходно да се догађаји посматрају са свих страна, из сваког положаја, врло радознало и са највећом пажњом.

Девојка ће продужити да живи и после Великог Свршетка. То је врло важно. То право само њој припада. Хоћемо да објаснимо да није тачно да све престаје кад срце прекине свој рад.

Да би се то потпуно осетило, потребно је лежати мирно и са притиснутим очима. Још је боље ако неко има љубавницу, вереницу или неку другу залубљену жену. Те дрхтаве, нежне, унемирене руке, у стању су, кад додирну очи, много да објасне.

I

Киша бије право у прозор. Окна се топе. Цела се соба покрива косим пругама кише. На средини собе, у којој још никога нема, додирују се три стола једнаке величине. На сваком се столу налази по једно стаклено звоно. Под првим звоном лежи једна бела, гумена рукавица. Под другим звоном једно запечаћено писмо и две коврџе плаве косе. Под трећим звоном кључ и једна мала, свилена, женска кошуља. Све су те ствари јако осветљене и необично чисте.

Истовремено, кроз јасне пропланке једне огромне шуме галопирају жедне жирафе. Пејзажи се врло брзо мењају. Река се налази иза пошумљеног брега, иза густе

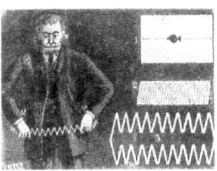

траве где су као муње пројуриле зебре. Сад у висини поред лишћа као облаци плове главе жирафа. Кроз густу траву пузе пругасте змије. Све је то врло пријатно и врло утешно. Моаре.

Преко кровова где се пуше димњаци, јури један човек у дугачкој пелерини. Он крије лице. Црна пелерина се вије иза њега као злослутна застава. На месту где престају редови кровова појављује се гвоздена конструкција једног великог моста. Човек скаче на тај мост и спушта се до његовог каменог свода. Под тим самим сводом, над водом која је црна, нагло се отварају једна мала врата. Иза њих стрме степенице. На прагу непознате собе, на

месту где се обично остављају ципеле, стоје две женске ноге, одсечене до колена. Ноге су обучене у танке чарапе и сјајне, лаковане ципеле. Човек им прилази са огромним задовољством и додирује их благо. Затим свлачи своје ципеле и чарапе, које оставља на истом том прагу, узима ноге у наручја, и бос, још увек врло радостан улази у један пространи хемиски лабораторијум. Из њега, на затвореним вратима остаје јако увеличано његово лице, окружено црном брадом и озареио дивним осмехом. У лабораторијум човек постаје узнемирен. Нервозно баца женске ноге на један отоман, покривен белим чаршавом, и журно прилази вели-

Figure 3.7 Aleksandar Vučo, Marko Ristić, *Crustaceans on the Chest* (1930), first page

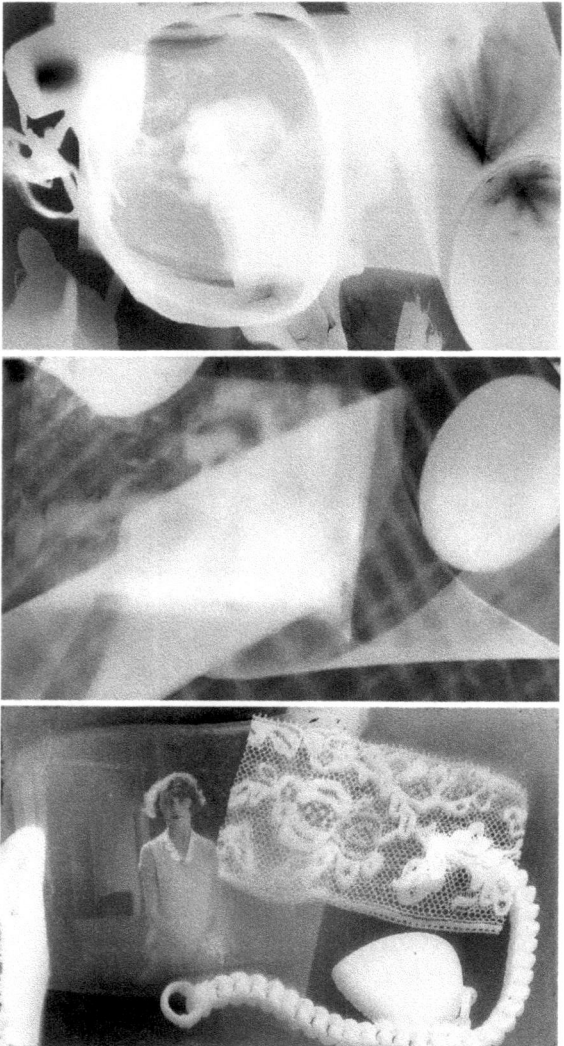

Figures 3.8, 3.9, 3.10 Marko Ristić, photograms (1928) © Museum of Fine Arts, Belgrade, and Museum of Contemporary Art, Belgrade

differences, and uncertainties. Fleeting, like reality itself, and anterior to visual representation, it is a system accessible only through a series of incomplete indexical traces that it leaves behind. One might say that through an insistent "mixing and matching" of camera-based and camera-less imagery, Ristić, like an alchemist, summoned into existence a meta-reality of the Cinema.

In his own conception of the "cinemage," Man Ray similarly strove for an all-encompassing superimposition of cinema and reality. Around the time his second film, *Emak Bakia*, was released, he described an ideal cinema capable of decisively affecting its audiences. Man Ray wished for the viewer "to rush out [of the movie theater] and breathe the pure air of the outside, be a leading actor and solve his own dramatic problems.... For that way, he would realize a long cherished dream of becoming a poet, an artist himself, instead of being merely a spectator."[32]

The spectator-turned-filmmaker, living the Film of his/her own life! This is what "cinema beyond film"—cinema beyond the production, distribution, exhibition, and consumption of individual film-texts—ultimately meant to Man Ray. This is the same logic that in 1930 motivated Ristić and other members of the Belgrade Surrealist Group to put forth a diagrammatic drawing entitled *Can You Recognize Her?* (fig. 3.11). The drawing presented to its viewer the most elementary, minimal apparatus required if the meta-reality of the Cinema were to be practically engaged. *Can You Recognize Her?* was no more, and no less, than an empty frame.

With this simple gesture, the Belgrade Surrealists effectively collapsed all established differences between image production and image consumption, between the objectively given and the subjectively generated (motion) pictures. The frame is here identified as the source of all desires and aesthetic sensations. It is the sole function mediating our perceptual experiences. Where its cinematic qualities are concerned, the empty frame represents simultaneously the viewfinder of the camera, the aperture of the projector, and the screen onto which images are to be cast.

Ristić was fond of nurturing an "ethereal cinema," a realm of ontologically imprecise images that are half-objective and half-subjective (we

ДА ЛИ ЈЕ МОЖЕТЕ ПОЗНАТИ ?

Figure 3.11 The Belgrade Surrealist Group, *Can You Recognize Her?* (1930)

recall from chapter 2 that Raoul Hausmann referred to precisely this type of image as "primordial"). This is also apparent from his creative contribution to *Crustaceans on the Chest*: the series of free visual associations he developed vis-à-vis Vučo's written text. Among the twelve collages he made, particularly relevant is the one that depicts a human head projecting a beam of light through its wide-open mouth onto the reflecting surface of a spoon (positioned as if it were a screen) (fig. 3.12). Or, perhaps, it is the beam of (candle)light, reflected off of the spoon that is somehow being projected through the mouth and inside the head, as in a camera obscura?[33]

Ristić's image of an anthropomorphically "re-materialized" film apparatus enacts the type of structural dynamic Vučo also assumes as the mandatory point of departure for the enterprise of cinematic writing. He makes this clear in the prologue to *Crustaceans*, "The Foreplay,"

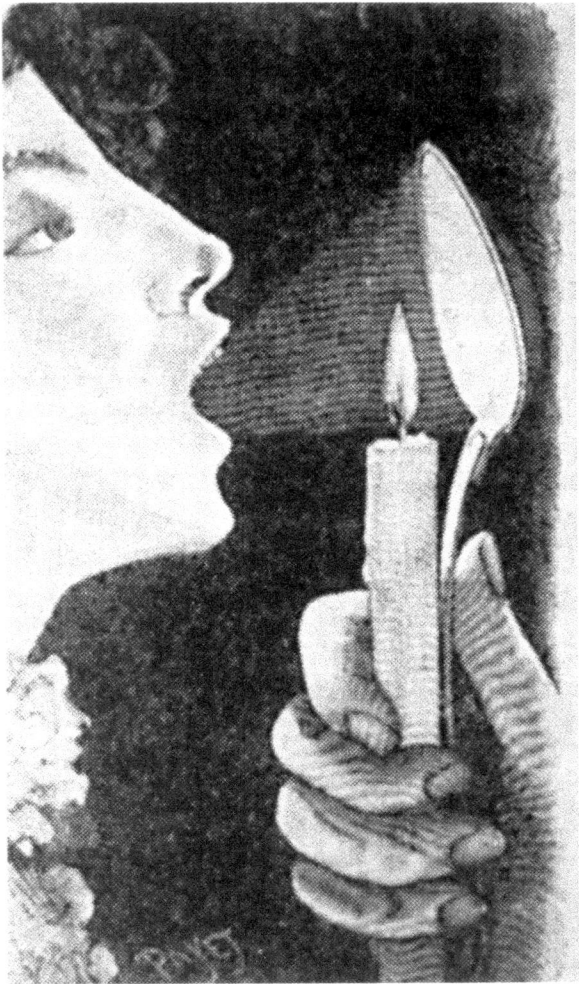

Figure 3.12 Marko Ristić, *Crustaceans on the Chest* (1930), detail

which, the author claims, "Is Not to Be Played." As is the case with most of Vučo's text, this prologue is largely an exercise in pure automatism. However, it also contains a precise, entirely coherent description of the material armature and the spatial arrangement within which the film proper (the "play itself") is to take place. That is, "The Foreplay

That Is Not to Be Played" is a written description of an improvised, minimal cinematic apparatus, the explanation of which the author deemed necessary if the oneiric and mental images of his film were to unfold, if they were to be successfully "projected." "Let the background be a shadow or a black wave," writes Vučo in the opening sentence of the "Foreplay": "Most suitable would, in fact, be the dead of night, that dark band of an eternal wall revealing no secrets. The wet, dark brown color has the good property of concealing all traces of a crime: like a sponge, it soaks the marks left there by the bloody fingers."[34] The screen and the darkened space of the projection room—two fundamental components of the film-viewing experience—are unmistakably evoked in an act of creative imaginary conflation. In the "dead of night," the screen is hallucinatorily expanded into its surroundings, presenting the reader with an extreme version of the cinematic apparatus, the "ultimate fantasy" of total cinema, as Edgar Morin would call it.[35] Drawing inspiration from the cinema's technologically normativized infrastructure—from the standard(ized) material elements and conditions of film projection and spectatorship—Vučo sublimates this technological-material foundation into a *conceptual crust*. He turns the film apparatus into a de-materialized relational structure, the contours of which become recognizable within the natural world itself. But while de-materialized, the medium is here by no means deprived of its specificity. To the contrary, Vučo's point is that even the purely imaginary activity of viewing a written film still directly depends on the operational logic of the basic cinematographic apparatus, although the apparatus may in this case be permitted to assume an immaterial(ized) state of existence.

"Doctor Hypnison" and *Crustaceans*, Boully and Ristić, both privilege the mouth—not the eye—as the site of the "cinematic," of an imagistic exchange between the subjective and the objective, the internal and the external. The two authors' choices bespeak a desire, common among the surrealists, to violate the faculty of sight insofar as it partakes of human consciousness. The mouth may be seen as a displaced incarnation of an *emptied* eye socket—deprived of its organ, yet still assigned the function of constituting the visible, the image.

The cinematic fantasy of violating the eye, of assaulting the apparatus of vision, was, of course, literalized in 1928 in the famous opening of Buñuel and Dali's *Un Chien andalou*. A man, the filmmaker, Buñuel himself, is shown sharpening the blade of a razor. Then, in an extreme close-up, he slices the eye of a woman. The stage is set for the film to begin. But Surrealist strategies of violating and displacing the eye as the organ of sight also frequently involved mapping and retailoring the lower regions of the body, and thus effecting various forms of sexual debasement.[36] Examples include:

—The Yugoslav Surrealist Koča Popović's automatic text, "Destiny Sold," in which the eye appears as the "navel-eye." Popović writes about the eye situated "to the side of the woman's navel. Wedged there, in the fat, powerless to transgress the basis of its own desire, the eye is deprived of its, by now superfluous, perseverance and reduced to a mere decoration, a stiff."[37] In a manner reminiscent of Salvador Dali's paranoiac-critical method, this navel-eye is identified as the point from which it is possible to witness one's own conception.[38] In other words, in Popović's text, the primal fantasy of origin is constructed from the "abdominal perspective" of the female actant in the parental intercourse.[39] The navel is presented as the marker of this paradoxical, not yet properly subjectivized, reflexive though "formless" (Bataille), instance of carnal looking/ knowledge.

–In the Surrealist imaginarium, the eye is at times pushed even further down, below the navel, and subordinated to the female genitalia. Such is the case with Max Ernst's plate 36 from *La femme 100 tetes* (fig. 3.13), the caption for which reads: "Without uttering a word and in all kinds of weather, magic light." The plate shows the image of a moustached man projected onto a canvas by a beam of light emanating from the vagina of a woman who floats suspended in the air.

In the original newspaper illustration, which Ernst appropriated for this plate (fig.3.14), the beam of light was cast by an optical device built on the principle of the camera obscura. The artist, however, chose the female sex as the apparatus for (re-)production and distribution of images. He thereby presented the woman as real and the man as only her ethereal projection (a symptom). In Ernst's proto-cinematic collage, the man does not exist except as an imaginary signifier. The man is born of the woman in a camera obscura.

Figure 3.13 Max Ernst, plate 36 from *Hundred Headless Woman* (1929) © 2011 Artists Rights Society (ARS), New York / ADAGP, Paris; photo: National Library of the Netherlands

Figure 3.14 Nineteenth-century newspaper image appropriated by the artist (discovered and first published by Dr. Werner Spies, in his book *Max Ernst Collages: the Invention of the Surrealist Universe*)

—Finally, in *The Landscape* (fig. 3.15), a 1930 collage by yet another Yugoslav Surrealist, Vane Živadinović Bor, the womb itself is envisioned by analogy with the camera obscura. Inspired, it would seem, by anatomy lessons and theatrical protocols alike, Bor drew the skin of the female body as if it were a curtain, exposing its interior to the viewer's gaze. But the exposed womb functions as the setting for what is, in fact, an exterior scene: a natural landscape, an outside image (and an image of the outside) is reflected inside the body, which is a hollow

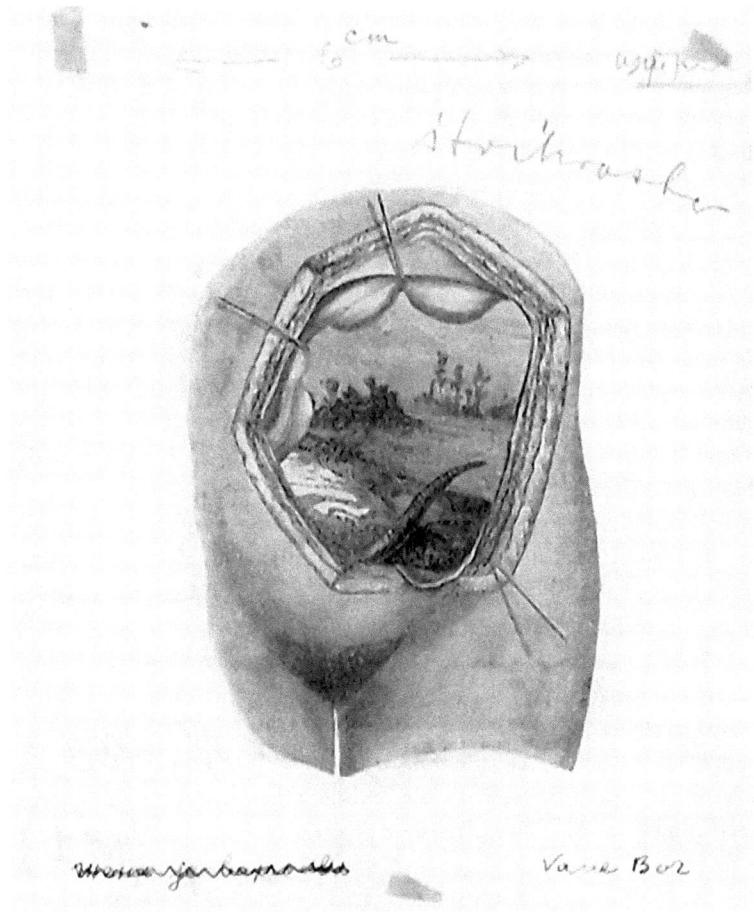

Figure 3.15 Vane Živadinović Bor, *The Landscape* (1930) © Museum of Contemporary Art, Belgrade

picture-chamber without the organs. As in Boully's rendition of Hypnison's mouth, so too in Bor's vision of the womb—spaces of exteriority and interiority are thoroughly conflated. All differences between the two are collapsed. The womb is presented as a fantasmatic apparatus that, not unlike the cinematograph, generates images that are "extimate."[40]

The beginnings of the written-cinematic fantasy (shared by "Doctor Hypnison" and *Crustaceans*) in which image-production becomes indistinguishable from spectatorship can be traced to a short text produced in 1910 by the "spiritual father" of the future Surrealists, Guillaume Apollinaire. In "The False Messiah, Amphion or The Stories and Adventures of the Baron of Ormesan," Apollinaire describes the activities of an imagined "cinematographic company" whose members kidnap people and force them to perform—to literally murder each other—in front of the camera.[41] Significantly, the content of Apollinaire's "great film" (as the poet labeled his text) is not limited to these violent events staged in front of the camera. "The False Messiah" is actually an account of the *watching of a film in the making*: an account of a film being simultaneously directed by the diegetic personages (members of the "company") and spectatorially engaged (and enjoyed) on the set by the same personages. A great champion of the film medium as a foremost manifestation of 'l'esprit nouveau,"[42] Apollinaire thus set the scene for exploring the possibilities of a writerly conflation of cinematic authorship and spectatorship, by narratively situating image consumption (the film viewer's activity) within the realm of image production (the camera's activity).

As Richard Abel points out, at the time when Apollinaire was endorsing cinema as the poetry of the future, film producers in France were themselves eager to engage "writers both inside and outside the industry to supply story ideas and scenarios for [their] films."[43] But things would change over the course of the next decade, and the film industry would become increasingly "unconducive to the kind of work Apollinaire had in mind":

> The production and distribution sectors of the industry were in a state of retreat before the "invasion" of American films; technical facilities were woefully outdated; industry leaders such as Charles Pathé were calling for scenarios appropriate for American audiences; fewer and fewer original scenarios were being filmed. The writers accepted into the industry, consequently, were not drawn from the avant-garde, especially those who were seeking to annex a popular art form such as the cinema to an aesthetic project intent on breaking radically with past literary conventions and with renewing or even revolutionizing textual forms.[44]

The widening of the gap between the literary avant-garde and the French film industry initially led to an intensification of the practice of publishing film scenarios, for it offered writers an alternative to or a substitute for seeing their work actually filmed.[45] However, by the end of the 1920s, this state of affairs (exemplified in Artaud's lack of success in having any one of his scenarios written after "The Seashell and the Clergyman" realized as a film) had led to a complete disappointment for a number of avant-garde authors with respect to the idea of filmmaking as such, and this disappointment, in turn, made possible a truly peculiar development in the theorization of cinema: the positing of the unfilmed scenario as no less than the cinematic form par excellence. Among the proponents of this eccentric theoretical position, Benjamin Fondane is probably the best known.[46] "Let us therefore inaugurate the era of unfilmable scenarios," he wrote in the late 1920s. "A little of the amazing beauty of a foetus can be found there."[47] And as Fondane wrote his unfilmable scenarios seeking to create "a provisional state of mind that is consumed by memory in the act of reading,"[48] around the same time, Monny de Boully offered one of the most explicit attempts at theoretically grounding "written cinema" in a severe ontological critique of the photographic image itself.

By 1928, Boully's love affair with the French Surrealist group was over. That year, he and his close friend Jean Carrive (one of the youngest Surrealists) entered the ranks of those who would be "expelled" from Breton's circle (Artaud, Desnos, Georges Riebmont-Dessaignes). As Surrealist dissidents, they joined forces with Arthur Adamov and Claude Sernet and published the only issue of the journal indicatively called *Discontinuité* (to which Fondane also contributed). Subsequently, Boully and Carrive joined the group Le Grand Jeu. Active between 1927 and 1932 and led by Roger Gilbert-Lecomte and René Daumal, Le Grand Jeu was a group of writers and artists who, in the spirit of avant-garde movements of their time, adopted a "systematically destructive" attitude of radical renunciation with respect to the ideas and values of Western culture. Enamored by the mystical and the esoteric and inspired by some Eastern philosophical and spiritual traditions (such as Hinduism), members of the group committed themselves to conducting research in what they called "experimental metaphysics." One of Grand Jeu's guiding principles was the search for the Absolute—for the essential, Universal truth of being and knowledge. The group's relationship with the Surrealist movement (in whose shadow it developed) was an uneasy one, not the least because Gilbert-Lecomte and Daumal were willing to associate with Surrealist dissidents, while declining Breton's offers to join his circle.

One of the last manifestation of the activities of the short-lived Grand Jeu was their contribution to the fourth issue of the journal *Les Cahiers jaunes*, devoted to the cinema. Under the title "Cinéma 33," the issue included polemics and essays by Fondane, Artaud, Gilbert-Lecomte, and Boully, as well as five "unrealizable" film scenarios by Desnos, Sernet, Maurice Henry, Hendrik Cramer, and Riebmont-Dessaignes.[49] As Alain and Odette Virmaux point out, what brought together members of Le Grand Jeu, associates of *Discontinuité*, and former Surrealists, was their shared disappointment with the state of contemporary cinema and their pronouncedly pessimistic, even hopeless, perspective on the future of the medium.[50]

In his contribution to the issue, "The Alchemy of the Eye: Cinema as a Form of Mind," Gilbert-Lecomte, for example, declares: "The cinema does not exist: it must be born or it must die. At the moment it is no more than a shadow in a limbo of possibilities, a rag lying amongst the bric-a-brac in the junk-room of the human mind."[51] In "The Precocious Old Age of Cinema," Artaud similarly argues that cinema is "only a tentative sort of poetry, the poetry of what might have been."[52] He also claims that "[t]he world of cinema is dead, illusory and split up,"[53] and partially attributes this state of affairs to the inherent limitations of the photographically based, mechanically produced image:

> The lens that goes to the heart of objects, creates its own world and the cinema may put itself in the position of the human eye, think for it, sift the world for it, and, by this concerted and mechanical task of elimination, let nothing but the best subsist. The best, that is to say what is worth retaining, those shreds of things which float on the surface of the memory while the lens seems to filter their residue automatically.[54]

For Artaud, the film image is "definite and irrevocable, . . . it prevents the effect of the images from changing or surmounting itself. It is incontestable."

Thus, he concludes with disappointment: "Poetry did exist around the lens, but before being sifted, being inscribed on the film."[55]

Boully's own contribution to "Cinéma 33," a short text entitled "A.B.C.D . . .," shows obvious marks of Artaud's influence, including approving references to "The Theatre of Cruelty." All traces of Boully's earlier praise of cinema's "transcendental irrationalism" are now gone. Instead, the Yugoslav poet further develops Artaud's critique of the fixating, selective and, therefore, limited and limiting nature of the photograph, and he builds upon this critique a brief but precise theory of the Image as such. Boully defines the Image (capital "I") as "a primordial, creative image, lived in its interior reality and its existence. The Image is not an abstraction, but an ACT in which the individual spirit identifies with the universal one."[56] Mentally and sensually perceptible, but never properly reproducible (no matter how sophisticated the technology), possible to experience but impossible to materially duplicate, the Image is a state of being that all photographic and cinematographic images can only unsuccessfully aspire to attain:

> As the essential form of the illusion of movement, the Image cannot be captured by the mechanical eye. Beyond the rough information given to the naked eye, a visual apparatus in its own right, the Image is evoked or conveyed by the invisible side of the image perceived through the senses. As a physical perfector of the senses to which it addresses itself, film entirely fulfills its duty, just like the telescope, the microscope, the phonograph . . . do. It enriches our knowledge as it impoverishes our mind—film lets us see a lot, but badly.[57]

The dialectical relationship between the Image and the multitude of ("failed") photographic images is, Boully claims, the essence and the truth of cinema. The terms of this relationship are rigorously predetermined: "every film, no matter how beautiful, poetic, or touching" is, ultimately, only "a slave to the mechanically rendered image." This is why, according to the poet, even the greatest masterpieces of cinema—*The Battleship Potemkin*, Chaplin's early works, *Entr'acte*, *Un Chien andalou*, *L'Age d'or*—are only capable of "reaching the lower level of perfection."[58]

And what of the "upper level" of perfection? In a footnote to the text, Boully hints at abstract animation as possibly the cinematographic form that can be productively related to his notion of the Image. But the lasting impression "A.B.C.D . . ." leaves upon the reader is that it is, above all else, the experiential, sensorial, lived Reality that constitutes the proper realm of the Image—reality understood as an intense, affective, even trance-like state of the human being's immersion in the world. By extension, this position implies that Reality, at its most irrational and inconsistent, may also be identified as the ultimate, pure state of Cinema (a claim that, as we shall see in the next chapter, would become quite common among the postwar film avant-garde). And the written film-text becomes, then, the strut, the amplifier, of the reader's/viewer's existence in the world *qua* Cinematic Spectacle. No more camera, no more photographic image, no more reification of perception in the object-ness of the film. For the author of "Doctor Hypnison," the cinema is written as an elementary technique of living!

Chapter 4

Notes around General Cinefication

> *A polymorphous camera has always turned, and will turn forever, its lenses focused upon all the appearances of the world. Before the invention of still photography, the frames of the infinite cinema were blank, black leader; then a few images began to appear upon the endless ribbon of film. Since the birth of the photographic cinema, all the frames are filled with images.*
>
> *There is nothing in the structural logic of the cinema filmstrip that precludes sequestering any single image. A still photograph is simply an isolated frame taken out of the infinite cinema.*
>
> —Hollis Frampton

The earliest efforts to systematically investigate and promote cinema's relational character and meta-potential took place in the energized context of the 1920s Soviet avant-garde. A multitude of original, highly imaginative projects developed, which, hand in hand with an intense campaign to build the infrastructure of film distribution and exhibition across the country, bespoke a major push toward what may be understood as *general cinefication* of the newly established revolutionary society.[1]

Some conceptual aspects of the process of general cinefication—of reality at large being increasingly understood as a sort of "spontaneous" cinema—were, in fact, already being thought through in the theatrical realm of the prerevolutionary Russia. "As early as 1899," Yuri Tsivian asserts, "Stanislavsky was nurturing the idea of a new stage form that he jokingly called the 'cinematograph' [sinematograf]. In the vocabulary of the Moscow Art Theatre the word 'cinematograph' developed as the designation for a show that presented the audience with a sequence of fragmented excerpts instead of a single action."² In the 1910s, the rising popularity of Delsartean physiognomy and Dalcrozean "eurhythmics" (rhythmic gymnastics) led to the development of what Mikhail Yampolsky describes as "the new anthropology of the actor."³ Searching for ways to establish steady control over the actor's movements and gestures, and drawing inspiration from the natural sciences, technological research, and musicology, Sergei Volkonsky, Vladimir Gardin and, eventually, Lev Kuleshov theorized and practically engaged the cinematograph as an instrument for regulating the rhythms of the human body. "Anna Lee" (Anna Zaitseva-Selivanova) even proposed that the cranking mechanism of the film camera be used as a "corporeal metronome" of sorts. According to this line of thinking—typical, in Yampolsky's view, of the final days of the premontagist era of Russian cinema—the sounds generated by the camera during the act of filming could help coordinate the actor's body as it moved in front of the lens.

In the post-Revolutionary context, one of the best-known experiments indebted to the spirit of "general cinefication" was carried out by the members of Kuleshov's Film Workshop. Faced with a severe shortage of film stock, Kuleshov and collaborators staged their now legendary "films without film": theatrical performances presented as if for the eye of the camera, structurally organized according to the various parameters of shot succession, that is, montage.⁴ Around the same time, the "Blue Blouse" theatrical collectives were incorporating stroboscopic light designs—the "flicker effect" associated with the process of film projection—into some of their agit-performances. In the realm of visual arts, Kazimir Malevich and El Lissitzky were among the many who found inspiration in the possibilities suggested by the young medium of the cinema. Malevich produced an incomplete script for a (never-realized) Suprematist film, "Art and the Problem of Architecture." Lissitzky's *prouns* sought to extend the basic geometrical elements of Suprematism into the multiperspectival, three-dimensional space.⁵ In 1920, he created the *Story of Two Squares*, a children's tale which he designated a "bioscopic book." Its Suprematist narrative is organized as a sequence of six abstract visual constructions. "The Film of El's Life" is, on the other hand, the title of Lissitzky's written autobiographical sketch in which the artist declares: "My eyes—Lenses and eye-pieces, precision instruments and reflex cameras, cinematographs which magnify or hold split seconds, Roentgen and X, Y, Z rays have all combined to place in my forehead 20, 2,000, 200,000 very sharp, polished searching eyes."[6]

This type of aspiration toward a radical symbiosis of the human being and the film machine, common among the Soviet Futurists and the Constructivists (but also shared, as we have seen in chapters 1 and 2, by many Dadaists), reached its apex in the work of the filmmaker Dziga Vertov. His Kino-Eye (Film-Eye) method claimed the workings of the camera and the techniques of montage were superior complements to the faculty of human sight and, therefore, the foremost epistemological tools available to the modern, socialist subject. In the words of Annette Michelson: "The evolution of his [Vertov's] work renders insistently concrete, as in a series of kinetic icons, that philosophic phantasm of the reflexive consciousness: the eye seeing, apprehending itself as it constitutes the world's visibility: the eye transformed by the revolutionary project into an agent of critical production."[7]

In the spirit of the Marxist understanding of reality as always, inevitably, a social reality, and of the human agent as a being of *praxis*—actively involved in perceiving/deciphering and changing/constructing this reality—Vertov put filmmaking in the service of the "communist decoding of reality." It is crucial not to misread his aspiration to directly affect the world through a "montage way of seeing" as simply an instance of Revolutionary romanticism or idealism. Vertov developed his platform for the role of the filmmaker in the building of the Soviet society by following a scientifically and mathematically inspired line of thinking. At the origin of his cinematic pursuit of social truths and political knowledge is the presupposition that montage is the underlying principle of reality itself. While the filmmaker relies on the tools of editing to articulate a specific set of relations among the chosen "film facts" (captured by the camera), the reality at large is always already underwritten by an inexhaustive set of possible montage-patterns. "To find amid all these mutual reactions, these mutual attractions and repulsions of shots, the most expedient 'itinerary' for the eye of the viewer, to reduce this multitude of 'intervals' (the movements between shots) to a simple visual equation, a visual formula expressing the basic theme of the film-object in the best way: such is the most important and difficult task of the author-editor."[8]

Vertov's notion of the "interval," in some measure indebted to the unhinging of space and time set forth by Albert Einstein's theory of relativity, is particularly important to note here. As the mark of a momentary intersection of two or more "movements" of images and sounds—as, simultaneously, a confirmation and a negation of the spatiotemporal differences between a variety of visual and auditory stimuli—the "interval" is the elementary function of Vertov's thoroughly dynamic view of reality: reality as characterized by an incessant process of *structuration* (a "permanent structural revolution" of sorts). As Michelson put it, the "theory of intervals" enacts "a *displacement* of the principle of montage, which now governs not only the editing of all the visual parameters of the film text, but becomes the operative compositional principle invoked at every level or stage of the labour process. . . . Montage is a process now expanded well beyond the work at the editing table, no longer restricted to the composition of the image (or later to the soundtrack), but now governs all stages or parameters of production. Vertov's theorization of montage is, like that of Eisenstein, aimed toward the construction of a totalizing structural principle."[9]

Or, in Vertov's own words:

> By editing, artistic cinema usually means the *splicing together of individual filmed scenes* according to a scenario, worked out to a greater or lesser extent by the director.
>
> The kinoks attribute a completely different significance to editing and regard it as the *organization of the visible world*.
>
> The kinoks distinguish among:
>
> 1. *Editing during observation*—orienting the unaided eye at any place, any time.
>
> 2. *Editing after observation*—mentally organizing what has been seen, according to characteristic features.
>
> 3. *Editing during filming*—orienting the aided eye of the movie camera in the place inspected in step 1.
>
> Adjusting for the somewhat changed conditions of filming.
>
> 4. *Editing after filming*—roughly organizing the footage according to characteristic features. Looking for the montage fragments that are lacking.

5. *Gauging by sight (hunting for montage fragments)*—instantaneous orienting in any visual environment so as to capture the essential link shots. Exceptional attentiveness.

A military rule: gauging by sight, speed, attack.

6. *The final edit*—revealing minor, concealed themes together with the major ones. Reorganizing all the footage into the best sequence. Bringing out the core of the film-object. Coordinating similar elements, and finally, numerically calculating the montage groupings.[10]

Vertov's theoretical elaborations effectively convey his conviction that the global sweep of the film medium is rapidly giving rise to a new, technologically inspired but, ultimately, *trans-technological* condition: a meta-reality of the cinema in which, to use Timothy Murray's concise formulation, "*the specialized codes of cinema [are] themselves becom[ing], or always already are, 'naturalized' or 'cultural.'* In this sense, they 'return' to cinema not as 'specialized' but as cultural codes that function for the most part '*within* photographic and phonographic analogy.'"[11]

In his well-known 1930s essay, "The Work of Art in the Age of Its Technological Reproducibility," Walter Benjamin assumes a perspective akin to that of Dziga Vertov. He develops a complex theoretical speculation on the exact place and the role of film technology in the modern-day reality. "The shooting of a film, especially a sound film," writes Benjamin, "offers a hitherto unimaginable spectacle. It presents a process in which it is impossible to assign to the spectator a single viewpoint which would exclude from his or her field of vision the equipment not directly involved in the action being filmed—the camera, the lighting units, the technical crew, and so forth (unless the alignment of the spectator's pupil coincided with that of the camera)." In the process of shooting a film, Benjamin continues, "the apparatus has penetrated so deeply into reality that a pure ... equipment-free aspect of reality has here become the height of artifice, and the vision of immediate reality the Blue Flower in the land of technology."[12]

Reality is here understood as having become proto-cinematic because it had been irrevocably "infected" by the modern technologies of image production and reproduction. It is as if upon an infinite soundstage (a set) of sorts, the film of reality is now being shot! In the aftermath of the cinematograph's invention and the subsequent development of the film industry, to be inside a "pure," "equipment-free" reality—to experience the world as a technologically unmediated state of existence—is, therefore, predicated upon aligning one's perspective *with* the eye of the camera. Only then can one occupy the ground zero of what, in fact, is still a delusion of pure reality. In other words, that which in the age before film used to be understood as the state of "natural" existence in the world, can now be attained only through the sacrifice of one's awareness of such "extraneous accessories" as the camera, the lights, the sound equipment, and so on. If "nature is always second nature" (as Adorno claimed), we are dealing with a specific version of this proposition: reality is always a cinefied reality; it is thoroughly mediated by the all-subsuming dynamics of cinematography.

One lives without experiencing reality for what it *really* is or, to be more precise, for what it has become in the twentieth century: a technologically underwritten and inspired "spectacle" of shooting an infinite para-film in which we all appear as protagonists. Benjamin seems to be implying that the practice of filmmaking has turned the whole of reality into a technological-sensorial event. In the era of the technologically (re-)producible moving image, one's subjective field of vision, one's look, is almost *a priori* aligned with the kino-eye. In a way, one's naked eye *is* already the eye of the camera. However, the paradox of this dialectic between the human and the mechanical modes of looking is that recognizing reality for what it has become in the age of cinema—a state of existence contaminated, without a remainder, by the technologies of vision—is possible only if one assumes a borderline psychotic perspective. It is only possible if one experiences a cinematic delirium of the "making of" kind which, in the end, invariably spells a loss of any direct access to the "ordinary" reality. In the age of the moving image technologies, one is, therefore, either properly interpellated into the worldwide cinematic network that *is* (the new, the only) reality; or, one gives up one's "sanity" in the name of a critical consciousness of the fact that one is living the endless shoot of the Ultimate Film—of the ultimate "film without film" that life has become.

The manner of Benjamin's discussion of the "spectacle" of shooting a film anticipates some aspects of the postwar avant-garde's engagement with a fundamental new feature of the social reality. This feature is the emerging condition of *universal mediation*, brought on by the cultural ubiquity—the rapidly growing presence and the evermore encompassing "reach," as well as the public's seemingly insatiable consumption—not only of the cinema, but also of other technologies of vision and visualization, production and reproduction of moving images (first television, then video).[13] As we have seen in previous chapters, a substantial portion of the prewar avant-garde was eager to explore, as extensively as possible, not only the creative but also the emancipatory potential of the then young film medium. In this spirit, various modalities of "non-cinematographic cinema" were also nurtured as so many forms of opposition to technological determinism, teleology, and reification. Considered in the context of the 1920s and the 1930s, *cinefication* of reality—its growing contamination by both the technological features and the perceptual-aesthetic functions of the film medium (as diagnosed by Benjamin)—is to be understood simultaneously as the ultimate consequence of and a condition for the successful proliferation of the conceptual-materialist art of "cinema by other means." However, by the mid- and late 1950s, cineastes, artists, and all sorts of media practitioners and theorists increasingly began to take the generalized character of cinefication for granted, as a *fait acompli*. What is more, cinefication proper now became only a particular modality of a much more inclusive process of total media(tiza)tion which, according to its most radical critics such as Guy Debord, aligned the vast majority of the new image technologies and their accompanying industries with the late capitalism's ideological production and perpetuation of an all-subsuming "society of the spectacle."

In 1963, Yugoslav poet Oskar Davičo (an original member of the 1930s Belgrade Surrealist Group) published a collection of poems called *Shots*. Each poem in the collection functions as either a photographic snapshot, or as a film "take" of some uninterrupted duration: "A Shot of the Landscape of Danger, Day and Night"; "A Shot of the Landscape of a Shadow"; "A Shot of the Biographic Landscape"; "A Shot of the Landscape of Indeterminacy"; and so forth. A year earlier in 1962, Bora Ćosić, a representative of the younger generation of Yugoslav writers, published his study *The Visible and the Invisible Man: A Subjective History of Film*. In the opening pages of this book, Ćosić argued:

The tremendous psychological potential of film does not exhaust itself in ordering the worlds it has created, nor is it content with the superior role it plays in establishing the new relations among the elements of authentic life. Film does not leave its viewer in peace after it has permitted him to exit the theatre, and the multitude of images it bequeaths upon him during the screening continue to flow through the viewer's consciousness long after a particular cinematographic tale has ended. Film involves itself in man's private associations; it lends its shots to his dreams and his paranoid moments. It may boldly be claimed that over the course of the past sixty years, the inhabitants of the world have had their dreams enriched just as much as they have had their conscious visual experiences enhanced. The cinema did this. The habit of attending great many film projections has generated novel conscious and subconscious codes, established qualitatively new associations, helped facilitate new traumas and obsessions, and has significantly affected the structure of the modern novel. . . . Finally, for sixty years already dying man has also been taking to the grave those representations he'd acquired in the cinema. . . . [H]ow unpredictable are those bonds that tie the fictional world of film to the real circle of our existence; how drastic can be those associations which today make the two realms almost equal.[14]

Davičo's and Ćosić's are two related versions of the world understood as thoroughly *cinefied*. At stake for both authors is the meta-reality of the cinema: "the world is lost," as Gilles Deleuze put it more recently, "the world itself 'turns to film,' any film at all," and "images are already assembled without a camera."[15] But systematic exploration of both the psychodynamics and the far-reaching social consequences of this process of general cinefication had been under way since at least the mid-1950s, when Edgar Morin wrote his groundbreaking work, *The Cinema, or the Imaginary Man*. Proceeding along the path that likely would have also appealed to Benjamin, Morin's anthropological study focuses on the manner in which the technologies and the practices of mechanical image production and reproduction—the cinematograph (the machine), and the cinema (the medium, the art, the institution)—have irrevocably transformed the role of the imaginary in the social reality.

Morin's analysis revolves around the dialectical entwinement—the "circular dialectic"—between the cinema and the human mind, dream and technology, "reality and unreality." Driven by an undying "astonishment that the imaginary is a constitutive part of human reality,"[16] the book explores the complexities of how "*the cinema reflects the mental commerce of man with the world*": "This commerce is a psychological-practical assimilation of knowledge or of consciousness. The genetic study of the cinema, in revealing to us that *magic* and, more broadly, *magical participation* inaugurate this active commerce with the world, at the same time teaches us that the penetration of the human mind in the world is inseparable from an imaginary efflorescence."[17]

The imaginary, as understood by Morin, is a realm both of imagination and perception, of production and consumption of images, a realm of visual traffic between the subjective and the objective, between the human mind and the external material reality. The French scholar pays much attention to the fact that the cinema, that foremost medium of the imaginary, has effected a major cultural-anthropological transformation: in the modern era, magic and magical participation have "returned," recasting the imaginary as itself technological/mechanical/machinic. The cinema is thus not only structurally upheld through the human subject's mental activity and participation—it also insistently externalizes all the subjective labor that belongs to the imaginary. Writes Morin:

> The anthropology of the imaginary, then, leads us to the heart of contemporary problems. But let us remember that that is where it started. The cinema is a mirror—the screen—but it is at the same time a *machine*, a device for filming and projection. It is the product of a machine era. It is even in the vanguard of mechanization. . . . The cinema poses one of the key human problems of industrial mechanization. . . . It is one of those modern technologies—electricity, radio, telephone, record player, airplane—that reconstitute, but in a practical way, the magical universe where remote-controlled action, ubiquity, presence-absence, and metamorphosis reign. The cinema is not content with providing the biological eye with a mechanical extension that allows it to see more clearly and further; it does not only play the role of a machine to set intellectual operations in motion. It

is the mother-machine, genetrix of the imaginary, and, reciprocally, the imaginary determined by the machine. The latter has installed itself at the heart of the aesthetic that we thought reserved for individual artisanal creations. . . .[18]

In the history of art, Lettrism was probably the first movement to systematically and programmatically operate on the normativized presupposition of the general "cinematicity" of the world. In *Aesthetics of Cinema*, the cornerstone text of Lettrist film theory which appeared in 1952, Isidore Isou, the movement's founder and leader (and Morin's contemporary), explicitly aligns Lettrism with efforts to radically reconceptualize reality and human existence in the light of cinema's ubiquity:

> Even if nothing was any longer on the screen, and a man was to be seen walking between the rows [of theatre seats], his walk, as such, would not have any meaning if it did not express an **attitude toward a universe saturated with reproductions**.
> In the eyes of the savages, who never attended a screening, this walk would represent an entirely ordinary action.
> In the eyes of those who expected to witness a film presentation, it would acquire the significance of a sacrilege. The living being that would appear instead of the common, recorded images, would be surrounded with the aura of an entire mass of reproductions which usually emanate from the screen.[19]

Unlike the avant-garde film theorists of the 1920s and 1930s, Isou treats cinefication as an already accomplished, indisputable fact and, therefore, as a point of departure rather than an objective to strive for. For Isou, the cinema is a well-functioning spectacle. It is, to appropriate Yuri Lottman's precise formulation, already fully "given in the consciousness and the semiotic experience of the collective," as no less than a central feature of an effectively naturalized "habit of mediation."[20] The Lettrist leader, therefore, characterizes the film medium as, at its foremost, a strictly "relational function" and suggests *discrepancy* as the central operation of an elaborate program of "anti-cinema." "Who ever claimed that the cinema is the art of photography?" Isou complains:

> Take the photograph away and cinema becomes radio. It is like reading in a chair. Why not? Radio through television became a species of cinema. Why shouldn't cinema in turn become a species of radio? . . . There is a constant disestablishment of art. Poetry and painting have become music. Actually this signifies the enrichment of one art by another, or the abandonment of certain questions in favor of other arts. . . . Daniel [Isou's alter ego in the film] recalled how he always shuffled things. Music within poetry, painting within a novel, and now a novel within cinema. A novel recited by a reader to friends, squatting before the burning hearth of the silver screen, watching the sequences fall like logs and pass without hiatus from incandescence to ashes. But the significance of my deed stems precisely from the fact that what I'm doing is not cinema now, but shall henceforth, thanks to me, become cinema.

This passage makes obvious the fact that on one level, the Lettrist dynamic of discrepancy directly extends the logic of "retrograde remediation" already developed by the prewar avant-garde: to reinvent the cinema is to rematerialize the cinematograph, to convert film into other mediums. A trademark Lettrist technique such as *metagraphology*—creating visuals by mixing and superimposing letters and images—is thus to be understood as a distinctly cinematographic procedure. For example, in 1953 Isou made *Amos*, a narrative sequence consisting of nine photographs elaborately engraved with large amounts of written text. Frederique Devaux assessed its operative logic: *Amos* is "a sketch taking off from the idea that cinema no longer has to use the traditional supports or mechanisms and can use as images simple photographs whose chiselings constitute a complete text in super-writing or *hyper-graphics*."[21]

However, because Isou situated all contemporary attempts at redefining the film medium firmly *within* the framework of general cinefication, these efforts now, for the first time in the history of modern art, also began to show signs of a thorough and open disregard for the sovereignty of the cinematographic apparatus, for the norms of its technological and material specificity. That is, with the condition of universal mediation in effect, it increasingly appeared possible to Isou to orchestrate frictionless and instantaneous conversions of any and all signs into other signs, of any one medium into another. This led him to develop the notion of "imaginary aesthetics," which he grounded in the conviction that "one did not need to manipulate any real element to create art."[22] Jean-Paul Curtay elaborates: "[I]naudible phonemes could be composed in ways to realize imaginary sound works. The first silent poems were performed in 1959. Invisible signs (infinitely small or infinitely big), of course, could also be the material of imaginary visual works. Finally, Isou came to believe that anything which was not seen as a concrete sign but as a surrogate particle for imaginary or 'impossible' matter was entitled to represent the works of a fourth structure (after figuration, abstraction, and hypergraphy) in art: 'infinitesimal' or *esthapeirist* art (from *esth*, 'aesthetics,' and *apeiros*, 'infinite,' in Greek)."[23]

Applying the principles of infinitesimal art to film meant, essentially, triggering an unrestrained pursuit of the medium's dematerialization, backed by the conviction that the entire world had become an infinite sequence of latent, "pre-cameratic" moving images. Indeed, Isou is one of the first authors who very liberally separated the idea of cinema from the material of film (to recall Jonathan Walley's formulation, discussed in chapter 2) by treating the medium to the logic of general convertibility, restructuring, and realignment of signs (the same logic he had already applied to other art forms and media, including poetry, the novel, and painting). In short, starting from the presupposition that there no longer is any other reality but the one that is entirely mediated, Isou inaugurated a series of *purely conceptual shifts with which he granted each of the existing mediums the right to function as another*. In the final analysis, one no longer needed to do much more than to imagine remapping the set of relational functions characteristic of one medium across the technological apparatus commonly or normatively associated with another medium. "Take the photograph away and cinema becomes radio" is, thus, ultimately to be understood as the procedural logic justifying an even more straightforwardly declarative stance: "From now on, radio is (to be thought of/ understood as) cinema!"

The creative force released by Isou's disregard for the traditional notions of media sovereignty—epitomized in his carefree application of what are strictly conceptual shifts to the normative incarnations of a variety of artistic media—was tremendous. His own media inventions and interventions included establishing that "dialogue/discussion is cinema";

that paintings and environments can themselves function as novels; that, with only slight alterations, photographs become films, and so forth. In Isou's universe, practically all media—even those that are thoroughly technologically based—can easily be liberated from any and all dependence on technology!

Isou's motivation for elaborating and propagating the infinitesimal and imaginary aesthetics came from his desire to free both the artist and the audience to make a definitive leap beyond the concrete material properties of whatever medium they engaged. Roland Sabatier, a foremost representative of the second generation of Lettrist filmmakers, excelled in creating infinitesimal films. His first work in the genre was *Evidence* (1966) (fig.4.1). In it he simply exhibited a can of film, charging it with the task of inspiring a flow of images and sounds in the audience's sensory-mental apparatus.

Even more interesting is *Entrac'te*, made three years later (the title is a pun on Rene Clair and Francis Picabia's, *Entr'acte*, a classic of Dadaist cinema). This film—or "cinematographic séance," as Sabatier refers to it—consists of a single and static composite-image: a drawing of an empty frame or screen with a fragment of a photograph visible in its top left corner (color plate 7). The photograph depicts a car being driven through some sort of mountainous landscape, but in the context of Sabatier's "film," an unmistakable impression is created that the car is actually heading into the whiteness of the empty frame. At the bottom of the frame,

Figure 4.1 Roland Sabatier, *Evidence* (1966) © 2011 Artists Rights Society (ARS), New York / ADAGP, Paris; image courtesy of the artist

written in longhand, are the author's audio instructions: "The soundtrack is represented by the sum of noises, words, and thoughts produced by the spectators gathered around the image."

Inscription of desire into the visual and auditory fields—a technique which, as we have seen in chapter 3, distinguished some of the best Surrealist art—is at work again, engaged by Sabatier as the motor of his "cinema by other means." As the spectator mentally extends the image and the sound of the car moving across the empty frame, his/her desire literally turns *Entrac'te* into a "motion picture" evolving in time.

It is particularly interesting to consider the function of time in the Lettrist reformulations of the cinema. Stated most directly, the Lettrists were interested in establishing no less than cinematic eternity. Throughout the 1950s, Isou was developing a critique of time's subordination to representation in general and to the automatism of the mechanically produced, photographically based image in particular. Before all else, insisted Isou, film is a time-bound flow—"this is true *even when its content is reduced to a single, motionless image.*" Duration precedes the movement, or the lack thereof, associated with the film image. The Lettrist guru demonstrates an impressive awareness of the fact that every instance of perceptual privileging of a stable photographic image—or, of a series of intermittently moving and, therefore, representationally legible film frames—also inevitably endorses the cinema's "emplacement" of the temporal. (The same opposition—time versus representation—is also at the core of another notable Lettrist film, Gil J. Wolman's *L'Anticoncept*. The author designated this 1952 work "cinemato*chronic*" in order to differentiate its aims and techniques from those of cinemato*graphy*.)

Accordingly, Isou advanced the concept of "supertemporal settings" for art and cinema and argued in favor of such works that would achieve infinite duration by remaining unfinished, or rather, in a permanent state of becoming. "Supertemporal films"—the first of which was Isou's own *Sup Film or The Idiots Hall* (1960)—were to be produced and performed on an ongoing basis by the very audiences who came to "see" them. The audience's active, creative participation in the making of these films was, in turn, to be triggered each time by a set of parameters, a "frame," determined and provided by the filmmaker.[24]

Maurice Lemaitre, another seminal proponent and promoter of Lettrism (whose status in the movement was second only to Isou's), also turned his attention to the cinema early on. His 1951 work, *Has the Film Started Yet?* (Le Film est déjà commencé?), is one of the earliest instances of performative or "syncinema." Lemaitre proposed to drastically transform the film apparatus by extending its various components—technological, spatial, spectatorial—into "the cosmos of performance." He redefined the screen and the projection, as well as the consumption of images and sounds, as all on-site inventions—mobile, transformative, and in no small measure conceptually and practically articulated by the audience itself. In Frederique Devaux's concise summary of Lemaitrian cinematic innovations:

> It is not a matter of perfecting the screen but of making it the frame for the new esthetics. "The screen appears, draped in colored tapestries and hung with objects that stage hands will move around all during the film. At various moments heads, hands, and hats will be placed in front of the movie projector to veil the images." In addition, Lemaitre introduces for the first time in the history of cinema actors in flesh and blood in the movie theatre for a complete spectacle which inaugurates the syncinema show. From this point on spectators will be yanked out of their passivity, forced to act, no longer submitting to the hordes of images that conventional movies overwhelm them with. The role of the ticket seller is no longer just to sell admissions, he will now have the impromptu function of handing out our stupefaction; usherettes and sweepers have their lines too, as does the producer who used to stand out by his absence, and the director or film maker himself from now on is present on stage for his show.
>
> Another innovation not lacking interest is that Lemaitrian cinema can use the whole universe in putting together the cinematic spectacle that is renewed in this manner....
>
> Finally, and above all, *Is the Feature on Yet?* [sic] is also a film to read, a "take out" film, since it was published in the spring of 1952 by André Bonne, finally allowing purses to open up to the renewed art of the screen.[25]

The invention of the cinematographic apparatus, then, gave body to—and thus made visible—a set of dynamic relations that have all along constituted the formal design or the diagrammatic structure underlying the human subject's (psychophysiological) interaction with the world. In the postwar context, Isou and Lemaitre were among the first artists who dogmatically, unconditionally, insisted on this fact: that the invention of the cinematograph had irretrievably opened the door to the Cinema understood as a metalanguage, ineffable yet all-pervasive.[26] This "linguistic revolution" with respect to the cinema also explains the Lettrists' particular insistence on the significance of redefining (destroying, deconstructing, rebuilding) the screen. If the cinema is to function as a metalanguage, it will require a new, expanded space of application—the old "writing pad," the rectangular screen with its fixed placement in front of the rows of theatrical seats, will no longer suffice. No less than the entire world—the entire universe, the Lettrists would insist—would have to be cinematically rethought. Lemaitre therefore literally relocated the screen outside the theatre. He gave instructions for the placement of a portable screen in front of the theatre, in the darkness of the night, in order to "add relief" to the cinema, to stir its three-dimensionality, and to physically extend it into the screen's surroundings. Aleksandar Vučo's prewar fantasy of total cinema, developed in his written film *Crustaceans on the Chest* (discussed in chapter 3), thus became a postwar Lemaitrean reality.

Lettrist cinema took the critique of technological essentialism, determinism, and reification—which had already preoccupied the historical avant-garde—to its outermost limits. It did so, however, at the price of dissolving the dialectical procedure upon which the most complex among the prewar exercises in "cinema by other means" had rested. Man Ray's, Picabia's, Vučo and Matić's, or Hausmann's insistent re-materialization(s) of the cinematographic apparatus left no doubt that film technology and the practice of filmmaking may have been born of the idea of cinema, but that the latter was also constituted with full precision only retroactively, following the relational and structural patterns concretized in the production of actual films. Lettrism, however, for the most part pushed this dialectical circuit aside in favor of what is perhaps best understood as the practice of "medium-free media." By aiming to take various forms of art beyond their material realms and to rid the existing media of their technological specificity, the

Lettrists assumed a radically antireificatory stance. This stance demonstrated their keen awareness of the fact that modern society was mercilessly eliminating all potential for unmediated, direct communication and/or (political) action (if such "pure" communication and action had ever been possible in the first place). But this is precisely what, speaking from a properly dialectical point of view, also gave rise to the movement's most questionable principle. Can the practice of predominantly imaginary art establish a truly effective critique of technological determinism *under the conditions of universal/generalized mediation*? As Debord, the Situationist leader and a Lettrist renegade, asserts in the opening of his book, *The Society of the Spectacle*: "The spectacle is not [merely] a collection of images; rather, it is a social relationship between people that is mediated by images."[27]

To identify the cinema with the imaginary without dialectically relating it to its material base—to the technologies of image production and the dynamic structural patterns, processes, and operations that distinguish the work of the cinematographic apparatus—is to slide into extreme idealism. It is to hypostasize cinefication, that particular modality of the condition of universalized mediation, as an abstract ground upon which the total creative autonomy of the human subject is supposedly preserved. It is, ultimately, to perpetuate the society of the spectacle by naïvely assuming a superior and dismissive stance vis-à-vis the technological base of its production and maintenance. Paraphrasing Debord, one could say that the Lettrists erred insofar as they thought it possible to negate the cinematograph without realizing it, and to realize the cinema without negating it.[28] The two procedures are intricately intertwined and dependent upon each other.

But what exactly would an emancipatory dialectization of (the idea of) cinema and its physical/technological support entail in the age of universal mediation, in a world thoroughly cinefied? To begin with, it would entail a renewed emphasis on the material features of both the normative and the nonnormative forms of the cinematographic apparatus. Furthermore, it would entail a historical-materialist insistence on the fact that filmmaking in particular, and audiovisual labor in general, are first and foremost concrete instances of human praxis—and all this in order to curb and to counter the idealist overvaluation of the moving image's potential for virtualization (dematerialization). As the filmmaker and theorist Pier

Paolo Pasolini perceptively recognized: it is true that "the cinema is a corrective to the ... constrictions of 'film'"; but "film" must, at the same time, be appreciated "as a corrective to the limits of 'cinema.'"[29]

The remainder of this chapter will, accordingly, explore three distinct cases of theoretical or practical explication of the role and significance of filmic and para-filmic matter amid the late-twentieth-century logic of general cinefication—in a world in which, as Francesco Casetti put it, the cinema "no longer has its own place, because it is everywhere, or at least everywhere where we are dealing with aesthetics and communication."[30]

I will first elaborate some of the central tropes of Pasolini's unorthodox film theory. One of his key postulates, especially accentuated in his final writings from the early 1970s, is that Cinema is an inaccessible metalanguage of reality. This inaccessibility is, furthermore, understood as both generated by and generative of an unsurpassable, though constructive, structural incommensurability figuring between the abstraction that is Cinema and the concreteness of film. More precisely, having already in the mid-1960s posited cinema as "the written language of reality" and reality as, in turn, "an infinite long take," Pasolini drew a key distinction between the Cinema—an ineffable totality of reality expressing "itself with itself"—and the multitude of specific films (texts) in which this totality is given a concrete but, ultimately, always partial and, therefore, incomplete form.[31] Pushing this distinction to its limits in some of his last theoretical texts, Pasolini developed an entirely nonfigural, relational understanding of the Cinema: it constitutes the "rhythmeme," the "abstract and spiritual" *spatio-temporal code* of reality, which the cinematographic practice transcribes into the audiovisual language of films.[32]

Placing at the center of his analysis the elementary (hypothetical) situation of "a Woman looking at a Plain," the poet and filmmaker claimed: "If I were a computer I could make a chart—in which the spatial relationships are indicated by little squares and the temporal relationships are indicated by lines—in which it would be possible to represent graphically *the entire gamut of the semantic and expressive possibilities* of the narrative relationship of that Woman with that Plain."[33]

As the diagrammatic "code of reality," the Cinema, according to Pasolini, ciphers both

a) our psycho-physiological experiences of reality—for instance, one's perception of "a woman looking at a plain"; and
b) the cinematographic capture of reality—its presentation in a series of distinct film shots.

What is more, in both cases, the spatiotemporal relations contained in the Code of Cinema are converted into one and the same language of audiovisual representation. At the same time, however, without this language of audiovisual representation (shared by the cinematographic and the human psychophysiological apparatuses), there would be no Cinematic Code to begin with! This Code, while abstract, cannot exist without the material realm within which it is instantiated: the Code of Cinema, Pasolini claims, is a "concrete abstraction."[34] And it is precisely because of this concrete, material dimension of the Code of Cinema that a difference also becomes apparent which, in the end, does exist between our perceptual-sensorial experiences of the world and the cinematographic capture of reality.

This difference, Pasolini asserts, resides in the fact that the former (a. above) foregrounds the *relational indeterminacy* of the Cinema (the lack of directional precision associated with its diagrammatic nature), whereas the latter (b. above) eliminates ambiguity from the language of audio-vision. In films, editing "splices," or cuts, commonly intervene to distribute cinematic relations as relations between the included and the excluded, the present and the absent spatiotemporal entities. Being a direct incision into film matter, the cut is conceived as a particularly explicit manifestation of the act of filmmaking, which is understood as a techno-materialist practice par excellence. Cinema may be an ineffable metalanguage, Pasolini seems to be saying, and the splice, the cut, may be the marker of a "meaningful nonexistent."[35] But this fact cannot and should not prevent the human subject—the subject in and of language, the subject in and of cinema—from making films. Quite the contrary, it is only in an unconditional commitment to filmmaking, cast as a sociohistorical intervention against the background of the Cinema's auto-naturalizing and trans-temporal aspiration, that the human subject can secure for himself or herself the role of an active agent in charge of his or her existence. In Pasolini's own words: "[O]nly Films . . . exist in practice and concretely, while Cinema . . . does not exist; it is simply an abstract and normalizing deduction which has its point of departure in infinite films. . . ."[36]

In the late 1960s and the early 1970s, Pasolini's contemporary, the Hungarian director Miklós Jancsó, developed an original approach to filmmaking which similarly rested upon an understanding of the cinema as an abstract spatiotemporal code dialectically related to a multitude of concrete, material, cinematographic inscriptions. In a manner unique in film history, Jancsó composed and executed his trademark lengthy, continually moving sequence-shots, not simply according to the imperatives of the diegetic events they depicted, but according to the "content-less" patterns of camera movement, determined and rehearsed even before any particular action had been "assigned" to them. Having attended the production of Jancsó's *Electra, My Love* (1974), Gideon Bachmann instructively summarized the director's method: "[B]y the time he [Jancsó] shoots, the work of making the film has already been practically finished. Putting it on film and sticking it together is only a requirement of the commercial need to get it seen."[37] According to Bachmann, "[t]he actual preparations for the day's *kép* [image, shot] begin with the laying of the track. There is always a track, sometimes 60 or 70 feet long, curving in and out of the buildings, like a children's train set. But considering the complexities and acrobatics which the camera performs along its lines, these are remarkably simple, sometimes forming half an ellipse or the form of two 'J's, joined at the top and standing on each other, or just half or three-quarters of a slightly squashed circle."[38] Rehearsals would begin early in the day:

> It can take a whole morning, and sometimes a whole day, often leaving just enough time before the light goes out to shoot the take. The best description I can think of that might resemble the movements being rehearsed is a fish tank full of water, enormously enlarged to include the entire set with actors, camera, tracks and crew, with the camera representing a delectable lady-fish aimlessly

gliding about in her three-dimensional realm, pursued by every living thing in sight. *For despite the fact that ostensibly it is she, the camera, that observes what surrounds her and moves to do so, in reality every movement is being planned for her and every action exists only for her approval. Thus order is reversed: it is reality which is set in motion by deft manipulation in order to be at the right place at the right time.* As soon as she has passed them, actors jump up, throw off a costume or don another, run ahead of her along her planned path, and crouch down again ready for another fleeting close-up. . . . That is why the line of the track can be relatively simple: the major part of the movement is orchestrated for the camera in a ballet of calculated fabrication.[39]

During the shooting of a Miklós Jancsó film it is, then, the actors who follow the elaborate tracking choreographies performed by the camera, not the other way around. The camera never simply "covers" the events; rather, the protagonists' actions provide the content which is fitted into the already patterned movements of the filming apparatus. The tracks along which the camera moves outline, as if in a diagram, a nondeterminate dynamic structure: cinema as a relational "master code." The filming of actual actions fleshes out this abstract matrix, giving it a variety of particular audiovisual expressions. In films intent on exploring the class struggle throughout history (the master-theme of Jancsó's cinema, from *The Round Up* and *The Red and the White*, to *The Red Psalm* and *Electra, My Love*), the outcome of this approach is a sense of History as inherently, unavoidably dialectical: the human subject's mandate is to accept it as such, and to participate in it. In other words, Jancsó does not use the camera to interpret history dialectically—to detect, in different epochs and socioeconomic constellations, instances of an ongoing struggle between classes, between the oppressor and the oppressed. Instead, he creates filmed testimonies to his Marxist conviction that History, much like the Cinema, is an always already dialectical, though empty, structure. Actual historical praxis is, in turn, not unlike the practice of filmmaking: the specific manner in which the abstract "Code of Cinema" is actualized in individual films (giving rise to concrete filmic enunciations), is analogous to the manner in which the eternally dialectical structure of History is brought to life by the human protagonists' sociopolitical actions, undertaken in particular historical moments of their existence.

I conclude this chapter with a discussion of the Yugoslav poet, visual artist, and cineaste Ljubiša Jocić. His thoughts about the cinema, although not extensive, productively oscillate between the poles of idealism and materialism. On the one hand, Jocić theorized the cinema from within the framework of Signalism, a 1960s and 1970s Yugoslav literary and artistic movement which, not unlike Lettrism (from which it partially drew inspiration), generally favored a de-essentializing outlook on the new technological media. On the other hand, Jocić's writings also demonstrate a number of distinctly cinematographic insights and concerns. This is, no doubt, attributable to the fact that Jocić also had substantial experience as a filmmaker—between 1949 and 1971 he directed over a dozen films.

Founded by the poet Miroljub Todorović, Signalism was a movement driven by the idea of a creative synthesis between poetry, science, and mathematics. Internationalist in orientation, it set out to regenerate language and to explore the dynamic structures and the energetic currents, the "infinite potential of atomic energy,"underlying the modern world—the world of both computer- and consumer-culture. In the words of one Signalist, Žarko Djurović: "If thoughts are particles of a moment, and we think they are, then their multiplication and combinatory, mediated by the influx of fiction, give rise to a perception fertilized by the spirit—whatever it [perception] affects, it turns into flexible matter. Surrealism turns thought upside down; Signalism punctures it through estrangement, accumulating a number of media into a single system and integrating a number of conceptual vibrations into a rounded whole."[40]

The Signalists engaged and invented a variety of artistic forms and genres: statistical, visual, computer-generated, permutational, and quantum poetry; cybernetic and mail-art; ready-made writing; conceptual-linguistic machines (Fig.4.2), and so on. A former associate of the Surrealists (he published his first verse in the late 1920s), Ljubiša Jocić joined Todorović's movement in the mid-1970s. That year he published

GENERAL CINEFICATION

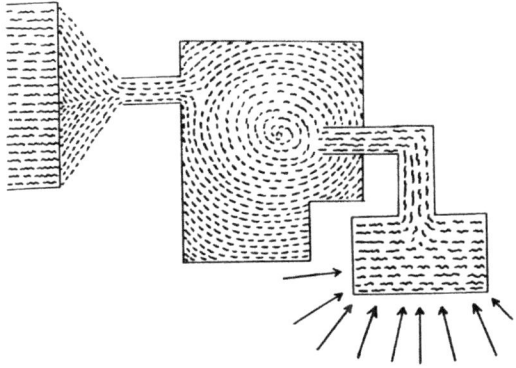

1. REČI SE ODABIRAJU I SKUPLJAJU U POSEBNOJ KOMORI. TU SU IZLOŽENE RAZNIM PRITISCIMA.
2. U SLEDEĆOJ FAZI ONE SE UBRZAVAJU. KREĆU SE SVE BRŽE I BRŽE U RASTUĆOJ SPIRALI. NJIHOVA ENERGIJA SE AKUMULIRA I ZNATNO POVEĆAVA.
3. KONAČNO PRI ODREDJENIM BRZINAMA REČI SE OTKIDAJU OD SVOJE SPIRALNE PUTANJE I ISPALJUJU NA OGROMNI EKRAN. NA EKRANU SE POSTEPENO FORMIRAJU SASVIM NEOČEKIVANE JEZIČKE I PESNIČKE TVOREVINE.

Figure 4.2 Miroljub Todorović, *The Language Machine* (1960s), courtesy of the author, reproduced from his book *Signalizam* (1979). Instructions under the Machine read: "1. Words are selected and collected in a special chamber. There they are exposed to various types of pressure. 2. In the next phase they are accelerated. They move faster and faster in a growing spiral. Their energy is accumulated and significantly increased. 3. Finally, at certain speeds, words break away from their spiral trajectory and are fired onto a gigantic screen. Entirely unexpected linguistic and poetic creations gradually form on the screen."

his first book of Signalist poetry, *Moonshine in a Tetra Pack* (Mesečina u tetrapaku). One of the distinguishing traits of this book is that it offers a sustained and insightful reflection on the media culture in the "global village." The protagonists of Jocić's poetry include Marshall McLuhan, Timothy Leary, Richard Nixon, Andy Warhol, and Leonardo da Vinci. His writing concerns events that take place in all corners of the world—

from Yugoslavia to Vietnam and Cambodia; from Paris to Washington DC to the Moon (at the time of the Apollo landing). The montage-poem bearing the title "A Collage of TV Information" is particularly illustrative in this respect:

> "Washington Post" takes body count as its chief
> measure
> of success whisky alcohol poisoning while a Vietnamese was
> whining
> at some creaky instrument and the sergeant's face on a round
> head
> seems to have been printed in the vermilion color Reuters
> reports they have
> found themselves
> in a whirlpool (of leeches or trumpets) of severe inflation the
> Congress
> is being
> asked to raise the level of national debt by 18 billion dollars . . .
> "make love not war" ain't that so Rockefeller
> "god why they are against the establishment" and you student with
> your hands
> raised on the frescoes a canonical wailer over the body of a dead
> student
> "God they are killing us"

In his programmatic theoretical writings, Jocić called on the Signalists "to make language transparent":

> Language clarifies things, puts them in proximity of each other, but it is also obfuscating and alienating because of the simple fact that it is symbolic, it tells of things which are not itself. A more transparent "language," a mode of communication which makes mind-reading possible—assuming that our brain is capable of functioning as a rapid electromagnetic emitter and receiver of thoughts, feelings, drives, and information . . . —would reduce the opacity of human

relations and would lessen the alienation (which, in any case, will not be fully eliminated any time soon).[41]

Taking his analysis beyond the questions of language and writing, Jocić aligned universal and transparent modes of communication with what is essentially a generalized process of *retrograde remediation* of the mass media. In this spirit, he anecdotally evoked an apparent "testimony of a missionary, as told by [the anthropologist] Levi-Bruhl: A tribesman was standing by a tree and talking. When asked what he was doing, the man replied that this is how members of his tribe communicate with each other, since they are too poor to afford the telephone." "Perhaps this is not a true story," Jocić acknowledged, "but such a fantasy could become reality. Why shouldn't humans discover the possibilities of the computer, of television, or of the telephone, within themselves. Once we have mastered these, we will find it strange that they have, in fact, always already been there for us to claim."[42]

"Retrograde remediation" is here pushed as far as it can go, resulting in a sweeping relocation of all media to their point of origin: the human subject's "initial," pure, *unmediated* engagement with the world. The fantasmatic directive underlying Jocić's position is unmistakable: completely dissolve the technological base of any and all media; this radical procedure will create the most direct channel of communication possible, a "medium without the medium."[43]

In the above respects, Jocić's argument is in line with the idealist tendency that we have already seen at work in the Lettrist reconceptualizations and transformations of language and various technological media, including film. At the same time, however, the Yugoslav poet's theoretical position is visibly marked by a desire to recuperate the specificity of the film medium through an insistence on what he describes as its "orthodialectical" nature. The truth of the cinema, claims Jocić, resides in the dialectic of the mind (understood as a primordial cinematic apparatus) and the cinematographic machine itself, the camera. In a manner that brings together lessons of the prewar avant-garde—one thinks of Hausmann, Gilbert-Lecomte, or Jean Epstein[44]—with Morin's and Pasolini's postwar explorations of the cinematic imaginary, Jocić writes:

> The filmmaker is a dreamer who transforms the world with the camera, that "hard philosophical eye." He creates an oneirism of the real. . . . What Bachelard said of the magnifying glass may also be said of the camera. To engage the camera means to be attentive, but does not being attentive already entail engaging a camera? In thinking about the cinema, the filmmaker is already attentive, he is holding a camera. By extrapolating from [the surrounding] space its own space of the film image, the camera is being attentive, and by being attentive it magnifies. Imagination, too, is exactly such a magnifying procedure—subsequently assumed by the camera.[45]

To film with the camera is, then, to affirm the fact that in a sense, one was always already filming without it. And, according to this "ortho-dialectical" logic of the cinema, the obverse of the relationship in question is just as important to note: in the twentieth century, the "century of the cinema," many of our common perceptual and mental experiences would seem to replicate the technologically grounded work, the features and the effects of the film apparatus, by nontechnological means.

Consider in this light Jocić's film-poem *Horror is a Bestseller*, which concludes his book *Moonshine in a Tetra Pack*. The moral of this Signalist text is that too much indulgence in the visual pleasures of commercial cinema and television inevitably results in libidinal thrombosis. For this profoundly disturbing assault on the industrialized mode of film practice and its commodification of all audio-visual enjoyment, Jocić chose as his point of departure William Friedkin's 1973 horror film, *The Exorcist*. In Friedkin's exploitative gender spectacle, the combined rampage of the libido, the Unholy spirit, and the bodily fluids turns the body of a pubescent girl (played by Linda Blair) into a diabolically malfunctioning Optophone. Recreating the spirit of *The Exorcist*, Jocić presents a detailed verbal depiction of the film-machine as itself a perverse and vulgar assemblage of libidinal protuberances holding together disparate fragments of significatory junk:

> Linda Blair L'Espresso reports it has become
> some sort of a ritual every night
> between assessing the Watergate Affair

and Henry Kissinger's travels all
American television networks bring
the latest on the film
"The Exorcist"
In a technological nightmare who can count the horrors
You play with stringed ears
tucked to a belt you rape and set on fire
you watch as it burns and folds in a cramp
the naked and bloody body of a girl
and you vomit
Television viewers the press reports have seen
the audiences running out of the theatre
before the film's end firmly holding hands
on their mouths and the theatre manager
distributing heaving bags the oral-anal tube
for gulping down fresh blood puss and vomited vomit
has been unclogged
...
Extended senses stuck in the tools of intercourse
at the door of the mortuary
the devil has claimed the burnt land
sterile from napalm priests and doctors
the civilized exorcise the devil from Linda Blair
they exorcise the souls of countless victims
to induce the viewers' vomit lying
in the fields are girls whose blood is spilled
and puss covers their faces Linda Blair is lying
with *help* written across her belly
and a crucifix between her legs
the underage Linda Blair masturbates with the crucifix
for thousands of viewers vomiting is a masturbatory
stimulant at the price of 50 dollars
the oral-anal tube is jerking still thirsty for horrors

Slobodan Škerović has recently offered the following Signalist diagnosis: "In an all-out movement of recycling, waste-words and waste-bodies attach themselves to and fall away from the living organism, the sole surviving carrier of the message."[46] This, precisely, is the process that Jocić's *Horror Is a Bestseller* may be said to trace in the realms of commercial cinema and popular culture. The restless libido has found a host in the body of L. B. (Linda Blair). Salvation of the cinematographic apparatus is sought in its re-materialization as writing. Not unlike what he had already done in his 1937 visual collage, *The Dada Machine* (see color plate 8), Jocić here replaces (film) technology with the corporeality of language. Cinema's *élan vital* is thus extricated from the abyss of mass-media consumerism and turned into a ready-made substance of transgressive poetry. For all these reasons, however, Jocić's Signalist text is also a truly equivocal object. It simultaneously comes across as a bizarre film-machine in its own right, and as the onslaught of imagery generated by this machine. *Horror Is a Bestseller* is, at the same time, a malfunctioning film apparatus whose material-libidinal excesses are rendered linguistically, in the form of a poem, and a proper "written film"—an instance of imaginary cinema, activated ("projected") at that point when the motion pictures begin to unfold in the reader's/viewer's mind.

Chapter 5

Whither the Imaginary Signifier?

A movie not imprinted on film doesn't exist.
—Michelangelo Antonioni

Initiated in the 1920s in such Dadaist and Constructivist undertakings as Man Ray's *Return to Reason* (1923) and Dziga Vertov's *The Man With a Movie Camera* (1929), exploration of film's material base became increasingly systematic in the post-World War II era. In the 1950s, it prominently manifested itself in the activities of the Lettrists in France, and during the 1960s became central to the work of the "structural" filmmakers in England and the United States, as well as Austria, Yugoslavia, Germany, and other countries.

The Lettrists explicitly announced that they intended to further radicalize the ideals and the forms once engaged by the Dadaists. Man Ray and his rushed improvisational style, which brought about *Return to Reason*, proved tremendously inspirational in this respect. Isidore Isou developed an entire theory of film as a debased audiovisual medium: an instrument not in the service of representation but, quite simply, of sending matter down the path of a-signification; a machine inherently indifferent about the symbolic value of the images and sounds it generates.

"Photography in the cinema bothers me," declared Isou in his feature-length film, *Treatise on Drool and Eternity* (1951). "I proclaim the manifesto of discrepant cinema! I call for a willfully lacerated film, a chiseled film." According to Isou, the cinema was to be reinvented in the process of "chiseling" the established material substance of film. A principal aim of this operation was to thoroughly dissociate the image track from the sound track and to submit the celluloid filmstrip to incessant scratching, scraping, and tearing. To chisel was to undertake a direct physical assault on Meaning: to engage film matter in the process of un-knowing itself; to liberate its energetic potential through designification.

However, as was the case with other aspects of their output, the Lettrist chiseling interventions into film matter seem, in fact, to have been in no small measure motivated by a nonmaterial(ist) outlook. Where the dialectic of film and cinema—the concrete and the abstract (as Pasolini would say)—is concerned, this precisely was also their limitation. For beyond the Lettrist celebration of meaningless film matter lay the ultimate goal of no less than total destruction of the celluloid filmstrip. Notwithstanding its other motivating impulses, chiseling was also a symptom of Isou's aversion to technology—an instrument in the service of film's transformation into an audiovisual "medium without a medium." Paradoxically, this means that in the end, chiseling was perhaps less an expression of Isou's desire to assert the dynamic materiality of film than a technique supposed to achieve a total dematerialization of both the film medium and its central function, the image. In this sense, Lettrist chiseling was, as Marx would have it, a materialist intervention that relapsed into idealism, or, to put it even more strongly, idealism disguising itself as materialism. Isou's "photography in the cinema bothers me" did not so much pertain to a critique of representation, of the specific forms of visual signification, or of the (frequently unquestioned) legibility of the image. Rather, it bespoke a more general attitude of "materiality in the cinema bothers me." The situation is not dissimilar in the case of Roland Sabatier's *Evidence*, conceived as an "infinitesimal film" (see chapter 4). The can of film Sabatier put on display epitomizes the material substratum of cinematography, which the author sought to leave behind, to transcend, in the name of a cinematic imaginary generated by the viewer's own mind.

In the 1960s, what Annette Michelson termed the "critique of cinematic illusionism" developed in the work of the so-called structural and structural-materialist filmmakers in the United States and Europe. Unlike the Lettrists, these cineastes and artists were concerned with filmic materiality more firmly within the framework of medium specificity. Among those who sought to problematize the legibility and the representational stability of the projected moving image and to examine the logic and the processes governing the work of the cinematographic apparatus were Kurt

Kren in Austria (*Experiment with Synthetic Sound (Test)*, 1957; *People Looking Out the Window, Trash, Etc.*, 1962); Tomislav Gotovac (*Direction, Circle*, both 1964) and Vladimir Petek (*Encounters*, 1963 [color plate 0]) in Yugoslavia; Stan Brakhage (*Mothlight*, 1963), George Landow (*Film in Which There Appear Edge Lettering, Sprocket Holes, Dirt Particles, Etc.*, 1966), Paul Sharits (*T,O,U,C,H,I,N,G*, 1968; *S:TREAM:S:S:ECTIONS:S:ECTION:S: S:ECTIONED*, 1970), and Hollis Frampton (*nostalgia*, 1971; *Special Effects*, 1972) in the United States; Malcolm LeGrice (*Little Dog for Roger*, 1966) and Peter Gidal (*8mm Film Notes on 16mm*, 1971; *Room Film 1973*, 1973) in Great Britain. In the hands of the structural/materialist filmmakers, all components of film technology and all aspects of film technique—all the codes of image-making that typically guarantee the spatiotemporal unity of the photographically based theater of representation—came under close scrutiny and were systematically analyzed: panning, zooming, the filmstrip's intermittent passage through the projector gate, the grain of the image, exposure and focal length, conditions of projection, splice marks, and more. On the other hand, the noncinematic "impurities"—fictional content, narrative structuring, and other elements of representation that do not specifically refer back to the cinematic/filmic codes—were rigorously purged. In Peter Wollen's words, the structural-materialist cinema immersed itself in "the conscious exploration of the full range of properties of the photo-chemical process, and other processes involved in filmmaking, in the interest of combating, or at least setting up an alternative to, the cinema of reproduction or representation, mimesis or illusion."[1]

However, as Peter Gidal has pointed out in his rigorously theoretical explication of the structural-materialist film practice, most frequently "[t]he assertion of film as material is, in fact, predicated upon representation, in as much as 'pure' empty acetate running through the projector gate without image (for example) merely sets off another level of abstract (or non-abstract) associations. Those associations, when instigated by such a device, are no more materialist or nonillusionist than any other associations. Thus the film event is by no means, through such a usage, necessarily demystified. 'Empty screen' is no less significatory than 'carefree happy smile.' There are myriad possibilities for co/optation and integration of filmic procedures into the repertoire of meaning."[2]

Gidal's claim is interesting for two reasons. First, it emphasizes the fact that structural-materialist film practice remained for the most part rooted in the projection-based types of representation. Second, Gidal acknowledges the decisive role played by the dynamics of the imaginary in what we commonly understand as the "cinematic experience." The cinematic signifier is constituted at the crossroads of the projected image (a technologically generated "ethereal" appearance) and the viewer's imaginarium (their perceptual-mental, conscious as well as unconscious activity). Edgar Morin was one of the first to theoretically develop this point, arguing that it is not so much the photographic base of the moving image, but rather its "imaginary projection" that is the essence of the cinema. It was, however, Christian Metz who most famously described the cinema's *imaginary signifier*: "What defines the specifically cinematic *scopic regime* is . . . the absence of the object seen." Film is "something in whose definition there is a great deal of 'flight': not precisely something that hides, rather something that *lets* itself be seen without *presenting* itself to be seen, which has gone out of the room before leaving only its trace visible there." Finally, "(i)n the cinema, as in the theatre, the represented is by definition imaginary. . . . But the representation is fully real in the theatre whereas in the cinema it too is imaginary, the material being already a reflection."[3]

The centrality of the imaginary in the cinema is, as Peter Wollen pointed out, what makes film, as if by definition, an "illusionist" medium.[4] The only way to effectively suspend this centrality and to literally avoid positing "imaginary substitutes for the real world" (to appropriate Wollen's own terms[5]), would be through direct physical assertion of film's material substratum. At the same time, however, "nonrepresentational" filmic interventions of this sort would also, inevitably, threaten the end of the cinema as we know it. Once it is deprived of the imaginary-projection complex, the cinema may become nonillusionist—but would it then still be . . . cinema? Gidal, for example, explicitly warns that although the image "is inseparable from the material-physical support . . . [t]his is in no way to say that what is materialist in film is what necessarily *shows*, or that it is camera, lenses, graininess, flicker *per se*, etc."[6] Gidal's warning notwithstanding, what interests me here is precisely this "eliminative" or "literal" materialist route: what is achieved when, seeking to complicate and problematize the cinema's imaginary function, a filmmaker decides to draw directly on the physicality of the film apparatus? Can film's physical-material support be used to generate productive, perhaps even enlightening, confrontations and collisions with the cinema's projected/imaginary signifier?

Perhaps the best way to broach these questions is to begin at the far end of "nonrepresentational" film practice—where physical assertion of the medium's material base does, indeed, seem to bring about an end of the cinema as we know it. Two examples immediately come to mind: William Raban's *Take Measure* (1973) and Nikola Djurić's *Remembrance* (1978).

Take Measure was a cinematic performance that redefined the event that is the film projection. Raban—who, like Gidal, was a member of the London Filmmakers' Cooperative—circumvented "le défilement" (Kuntzel), the process whereby a succession of photograms is "converted" into an unfolding sequence of fleeting on-screen images. He used an unspooled strip of film to measure the distance between the projector and the screen in a movie theatre—the distance typically travelled by the light beam cast by the projector. By stretching the filmstrip, the filmmaker thus "projected" his film without ever even threading it into the apparatus. *Take Measure* bespoke Raban's refusal to sacrifice the physicality of film to the conventions of the cinematic projection.

In its experimentally assumed negative attitude toward the production of the cinematic imaginary, *Take Measure* is one of the more radical examples of a tendency that developed at the London Filmmakers' Cooperative in the early 1970s and also included works such as Annabel Nicolson's *Slides* (1971) and *Reel Time* (1973); Raban's *2'45"* (1972); and Malcolm Le Grice's *Horror Film 1* (1970). In his pioneering historical study of avant-garde cinema, *Abstract Film and Beyond*, LeGrice describes this tendency as "treat[ing] projection as the primary area of film's 'reality.' For the film's audience, the only point of contact with cinema as a material reality comes through the actual time and space of projection. Film, as a photographic medium, presents to the audience an illusion of a time and space normally quite unrelatable to the time and space which they actually occupy whilst watching the film."[7] "Philosophically," continues Le Grice, such exercises in performative or "process" cinema may be understood "as attempts to establish for the film audience the primacy of current experience over the illusory or retrospective, and [are] consistent with the 'material' preoccupation of modern avant-garde film."[8]

In the late 1970s, in the context of the vibrant experimental film scene in the socialist Yugoslavia—which, since the 1960s, had been maintaining regular contact with its British, Austrian, American, and other counterparts[9]—Nikola Djurić took physical assertion of film matter beyond the pale. A representative of the Belgrade-based arm of the so-called "alternative film" tendency, Djurić (*The Raven*, *Vowels*, both 1973) filled up a transparent Plexiglas box (40 cm x 40 cm x 40 cm) with unspooled reels of both developed and "raw" 16mm film.[10] He thus created *Remembrance* (fig. 5.1), a film-object that bespoke his total renunciation of the (standard) cinematic experience. The celluloid filmstrip was, literally, all that could be seen here. The film (the series of images) inscribed on the strip would never unfold, for it remained forever trapped inside the box. Intended by the author as a definitive statement on and a farewell to the experimental film practice, *Remembrance* bestowed a forthright prohibition on both the imagery and the imaginary of the cinema.[11] Here was film, treated as debased and "unavowable" (Blanchot) matter. Film as the substance of anti-cinema. After Djurić's intervention, not only could film no longer anchor the projected image, but *Remembrance* also uncompromisingly dismissed all strictly idealist faith in the possibility of keeping the imaginary signifier of the cinema alive solely by stimulating the spectator's own, subjective imaginary.

This faith is exemplified in works such as Sabatier's already discussed *Evidence*, which advanced the premise that presenting the viewer with a can of film would suffice to trigger their "mental" cinema. And yet, despite their diametrically opposed perspectives and aims, it is hard not to notice that there really is no significant difference in the immediate appearance of *Remembrance* and *Evidence*: one is a box filled with film, the other a can of film. True, the former wants to subordinate cinema to film, idea to matter, while the latter seeks the obverse—to negate film in the name of the cinema, to assert the primacy of idea over matter. But the same belief in a self-sufficient and Absolute principle equally motivates Djurić's "vulgarly materialist" and Sabatier's "naïvely idealist" gestures. The search for the singularity of film and the search for the singularity of the cinema overlap in what amounts to a starkly similar appearance of the two works. Alain Badiou's words ring true here: "Absolute idealism and strict materialism are indiscernible as far as the real is concerned, being merely two designations for monism."[12]

Figure 5.1 Nikola Djurić, *Remembrance* (1978), courtesy of Akademski filmski centar, Dom kulture "Studentski grad," Belgrade

Take Measure and *Remembrance* are two examples of nonrepresentational, "physicalist" film experimentation. Both unmistakably make clear the extent to which what we commonly refer to as the cinematic experience depends on the logic of the imaginary and its technological grounding in the process of film projection. But direct, unmediated assertion of the materiality of the cinematographic apparatus need not necessarily result in a foreclosure of the imaginary-projection complex. Frequently, in fact, it is within the realm of projection itself that experimental filmmakers would stage and examine the tension, the clash, between the physical and the imaginary.

For instance, in Le Grice's *Castle 1* (1966), standard conditions of cinematic projection and spectatorship are altered by an added piece of technology called the "winker." It consists, quite simply, of a lightbulb hanging on an electrical cord and flashing at regular intervals. Placed, according to the filmmaker's instructions, at different points in front of and around the screen, "the winker" eliminates the darkness of the screening room. As it calls attention to itself, the "winker" also makes visible the texture of the screen surface upon which the film image is projected, as well as the physical space of the theater: walls, rows of seats, spectators' bodies, and their distance from the screen.

Castle 1's incorporation of the "winker" into the cinematic experience blatantly reminds the viewer that the moving images transpiring on the screen are part of a projected illusion. Still more important, the "winker" alerts the spectator to the fact that by the time *Castle 1* was made in the mid-1960s, the physical world—our living reality—had itself become thoroughly "contaminated" with moving image technologies. Accordingly, in Le Grice's film-event, the cinematographic apparatus's material substratum is no longer erased, repressed, during the act of projection. Instead, the filmmaker encourages the "hard matter" of the cinema to freely assert itself and actively share the stage with its imaginary counterpart, the projected image transpiring on the screen.

On the other hand, in Birgit and Wilhelm Hein's 1968 work, *Rohfilm* (Rawfilm), the imaginary and the physical/material components of the cinema are directly confronted, demanding each other's exclusion. Birgit Hein provides a detailed description of the series of procedures according to which *Rohfilm* was made:

> Particles of dirt, hair, ashes, tobacco, fragments of cinematic images, sprocket holes and perforated tape are glued onto clear film. This is then projected and re-photographed from the screen, since the conglomeration of strips and glue technically allow only one projection. During this process the original gets stuck now and then in the projector gate, so the same image appears again and again, or film frames melt under the excessive heat of the projector which is running at a very slow speed. The ensuing film is put through all kinds of reproduction processes, projected as video, appears on the editing board and on a movie-scope, and is filmed again in order to capture the specific changes engendered by the processes of reproduction. Other pieces from various positive and negative strips and from 8mm and 16mm strips with their different frame sizes are also glued together and re-filmed. 8mm film is run without a shutter through the viewing machine and re-photographed so that frame borders and perforations, in other words the film strip as material, become visible.[13]

The Heins, then, elicited the filmstrip's refusal of its automatic, naturalized "sublimation" into a series of projected images. *Rohfilm* was the outcome of the filmmakers' struggle to assert the primacy of the physical/material over the imaginary. This struggle manifested itself in a multitude of strategies devised for the purpose of thwarting film's smooth passage through the projector gate. However, what the audiences ultimately saw was not the original, "worn and torn" *Rohfilm*. What was presented to the viewers was not literally the piece of film that had been "scarred" (burnt, chewed up, and so forth) on its journey through the cinematographic machine, but a stabilized, fully projectable print of it—a copy. In the end, the spectators-consumers of *Rohfilm* still remained one step removed from the actual material friction, from the turmoil and the disintegration, by means of which the Heins initially sought to redefine the event that is the film projection.

Other European filmmakers have explored the physicality of their medium in similar ways, but without even (ultimately) subordinating real debasement or destruction of film matter to its representation. In the early 1980s, Miroslav Bata Petrović—a member of the same Belgrade-based "alternative film" circle that included Nikola Djurić—made *The Sketch for a Feature Length Film* (Skica za dugometražni film) by gluing variously sized fragments of 8mm and super 8mm film stock onto the surface of a 16mm strip. Attempts to publicly screen *The Sketch* regularly resulted in failure: the "fat film" (as Petrović liked to refer to his creation) would, as a rule, get jammed in the projector, for it just could not be properly "digested" by most of the machines that were available at the time. The sole exception turned out to be a locally made "Iskra" projector. Petrović's subsequent comparative analysis of film technology revealed that this was due to the fact that the "Iskra" had a wider than usual film gate.

When Petrović made *The Sketch*, he was quite possibly unaware of the Heins' work on *Rohfilm*. However, his practice (or the practice of Nikola Djurić, for that matter) was not without a proper historical grounding. To the contrary, it represented a rather conscious extension of the rich tradition of "pure" film, nurtured in Yugoslavia since the early 1960s. This radical branch of experimentation originally developed, like nearly all avant-garde film activities in the region, within the fervent network of amateur cine-clubs—in this case, most prominently, the cine-clubs in the cities of Zagreb and Split.¹⁴ It was then consolidated into a programmatic tendency within the framework of the Genre Film Festival (GEFF), held biannually in Zagreb between 1963 and 1970. The essence of GEFF was the notion of "antifilm," which evolved out of a series of animated theoretical discussions first organized at the cine-clubs and subsequently accompanying the Festival screenings. The leading figure of "antifilm"—its foremost theorist and promoter—was Mihovil Pansini.

Film scholar Hrvoje Turković has pointed out that the emergence and development of GEFF must be understood within a broader context of socialist modernity and artistic modernism: "The second half of the fifties and the entire decade of the sixties in Yugoslavia were marked by a pronounced modernist 'excitement' . . . . The initial debates about anti-film, which took place in the context of the cine-clubs and GEFF, developed under the influence of, and were programmatically modeled after, various modernist and avant-garde phenomena." Some of these phenomena were themselves found in the realm of the cinema: the French New Wave (Godard, Chabrol); the modernist sensibilities of Antonioni (*La Notte*, 1961) and Fellini (*La Dolce Vita*, 1960); the emergence of the New American Cinema (Cassavetes). But other, equally influential innovations were taking place

> "in poetry, theatre, the novel, music, and the visual arts"—as Pansini himself stated in his introductory remarks to the GEFF discussions. . . . The name "anti-film" was coined after the notions, at the time regularly evoked, of "anti-theatre" [Ionesco, Beckett] and "anti-novel" [Michel Butor]. . . . The Student Experimental Theatre was founded in Zagreb in 1956. . . . This was also the time of frequent visits [to Yugoslavia] by some of the most distinguished theatre troups from around the world (*Porgy and Bess Ensamble* from the U.S. in 1954; *Burgtheater* from Vienna in 1955; *Il Picolo teatro* from Milan in 1955; . . . *Théâtre National Populaire* from Paris, etc.).¹⁵

Turković maintains that "the strongest influence" on GEFF came from "the neo-avantgarde and 'abstract' tendencies in the visual arts." Programmatic activities of the local 1950s art groups, *EXAT 51* and *Gorgona*, and the rapid expansion, since the early 1960s, of the so-called New Tendencies in art "were at the root of Pansini's theses about 'anti-film.' The fifties also saw numerous large-scale and retrospective exhibitions of modernist art from the West (exhibitions of contemporary French art in 1952 and 1958; Henry Moore, 1955; contemporary American and Italian art, both in 1956; abstract art, 1957; and more)."[16] Finally, modernist tendencies in music were also "frequently mentioned in the 'anti-film' discussions, with explicit references made to the enormously important Music Biennale Zagreb (founded in 1961), which featured works and guest appearances by many of the foremost composers and performers of the period (J. Cage, M. Kagel, W. Lutosławski, O Messiaen, L. Nono, K. Penderecki, P. Schaeffer, K. H. Stockhausen, I. Stravinsky, and others)."[17]

Pansini's most rigorous practical undertaking in the realm of "antifilm" is *K-3 (Clear Sky without a Cloud*, 1963) (fig. 5.2), a short minimalist work in which the image is reduced to an empty screen, predominantly white with some color fluctuations. It is an experiment in filmic abstraction, borne of a Malevich-inspired desire to altogether abandon the field of representation. But *K-3* is simultaneously a peculiar exercise in cinematic community-building. Pansini intended his absence of filmic representation—his calculated "failure" to give rise to a conventional cinematic experience—to induce a series of first-degree social interactions in the space of the movie theater. The filmmaker explains: "*K-3* was a pun! ... At a scientific gathering an Italian was giving a medical lecture that was supposed to be accompanied by an 8 mm film.... But nothing appeared [on the screen], there was no film. Only empty black and white frames. Everyone was very cheerful about this. And I thought to myself, that's what antifilm is.... You wait to see a film, yet what you get is something that is not a film. Let's film that! So I shot an empty white screen in a film lab. But I wasn't entirely true to myself—I took a few gels and threw in some color a couple of times."[18]

K-3 sought to redefine film spectatorship as an intersubjective, communal activity. But the project of negating the illusionist, trance- or dreamlike conditions of the standard cinematic projection was more than anything motivated by Pansini's aspiration to establish the film apparatus as, in fact, a self-contained system, altogether independent from the activities of the human subject. Making use of a thoroughly reductive approach to filmmaking, *K-3* directly enacted some of the basic theoretical postulates

Figure 5.2 Mihovil Pansini, *K-3: Clear Sky without a Cloud* (1963)

of antifilm (defined at the first GEFF festival in 1963, the same year Pansini made his film): "Antifilm means precise execution, balance of ideas, maximal simplification of the work, abandonment of all traditional means of representation. Antifilm ceases to be a personal expression, an expression of some sensibility, it is nothing but a purely visual-acoustic phenomenon.... We are returning to the primordial aesthetic conditions. Antifilm is a state of existence unburdened by intentionality, by all a posteriori forms of reflection, it leaves no aesthetic traces, disappears as fast as it was produced. The object that is antifilm is free of all psychological, moral, symbolic meaning. If better care were given to film, there would be no need to talk about antifilm."[19]

GEFF's emphasis on formal and stylistic reduction, motivated by a desire to free the film medium, once and for all, of all traces of authorial and human intervention, further gave rise to a number of unusual experiments that were properly physical-materialist in nature. From a historical point of view, these were among the earliest cinematic exercises of this sort undertaken in the context of the postwar international avant-garde. Coinciding with the early developments of systems art, and slightly predating the consolidation of a distinct structural/materialist film tendency elsewhere in Europe and the United States, GEFF released a declaration in 1963 that included the following programmatic statement: "THE FILMSTRIP AND THE PROJECTOR POSSES UNLIMITED POSSIBILITIES WHICH STILL HAVE NOT BEEN STUDIED IN DETAIL. THESE VISUAL, KINETIC-OPTICAL, MECHANICAL, CHEMICAL, AND ACOUSTIC PHENOMENA FORM THE FIRST LARGE GROUPATION WITHIN THE FIELD OF GEFF'S INTERESTS."[20]

Of the GEFF films that pursued this line of inquiry, two are particularly interesting for the present text because of their uncompromising commitment to cinema's debasement, their piercing assertion of film's materiality by means of its blatant destruction. At the first GEFF, Milan Šamec presented *Termites* (1963), a conglomerate of stains laboriously created by spilling the liquid developer onto a strip of film. When the film was projected, these random stains "came to life" in a manner that reminded Šamec of termite ants moving across the screen—thus the film's title. Notably, the filmmaker made *Termites* seeking to oppose, not promote, the ideas of antifilm. Šamec was a representative of the "traditional" wing on the local amateur film scene. His creation was intended to demonstrate his critical position toward GEFF, according to which "anyone could make an antifilm." However, in an ironic and superbly dialectical turn of events, the jury of the festival awarded *Termites* the First Prize of GEFF in 1963.

Zlatko Hajdler's *Kariokinesis* (Kariokineza), performed at the second GEFF in 1965, was similarly inspired by its author's distaste for the ideas of antifilm. And like *Termites* two years earlier, it won the Festival's First Prize despite its original purpose and ideational background. In its method of realization, *Kariokinesis* was even more radical than *Termites*, for this time the apparatus of projection was itself put in the service of the filmstrip's destruction. Hajdler orchestrated a cinematic performance in which the speed of the film's passage through the projector was manually decreased, and the resultant burning of the celluloid strip by the projector bulb was cast onto the screen. Projection thus became, literally, the act of film's execution, the procedure whereby it is simultaneously realized and destroyed. Though still projected, the film image was, *pace* Metz, no longer defined by the absence but by the presence of both the represented (content) and the representation. What was represented here was film's own violent consumption by fire, a series of swelling stains occurring on the screen at exactly the same time as they were being created by the actual burning of the filmstrip in the projector (see color plate 9). Film matter died in Hajdler's hands. Its death resembled the bulging and the convolutions of the nucleus of a cell about to undergo the process of self-division—a process scientifically known as "kariokinesis."

In 1971, Paul Sharits "liberated" the filmstrip.[21] He removed the registration pin and the shutter mechanism from the film projector and, by operating this altered machine, produced a *non*intermittent cinematic flow that appeared on the screen as a continuous imagistic blur. Sharits termed this unrestricted passage of the filmstrip through the apparatus cinema's *Inferential Current*.

In the unbound movement of Sharits' filmstrip, pure materiality and pure time receive their cinematographic expression. That is, empty duration and matter deprived of recognizable meaning are granted autonomous existence, as the film-machine gives rise to an unstructured procession of photograms *without any concern* for the imperatives of representational/perceptual legibility (which depends on an "optimal" projection speed, oscillating between 16 and 24 frames per second). The film-machine has assumed the task of radically negating the normative representational illusion of continuous motion; all that it may now be said to represent is the debased materiality of the freely (nonintermittently) moving filmstrip.[22]

The notion of cinema's "inferential current" rests upon the premise already elaborated in chapters 1 and 2, in the context the discussion of the 1920s and the 1930s European avant-garde: at its most elementary, before functioning as an instrument of audiovisual expression and communication, the cinematographic apparatus is, not unlike the human body, a host to a network of energetic/libidinal currents. Sharits himself particularly praised Man Ray as a crucial historical precursor on this front. This claim seems entirely appropriate considering the fact that Man Ray's *Return to Reason*, made in the early 1920s, constituted one of the earliest attempts at avoiding the libidinal-material "congestion" that typically accompanies the onset of signification. In the cinema as elsewhere, meaning usually aims to subdue frenetic outbursts of senseless matter. In this respect, Man

Ray was (as we saw in chapter 2) quite critical of the general direction in which the noncommercial cinema was moving in the aftermath of Dada. The Surrealists, he thought, were pushing film's physiological and corporeal character and its status as an alternative to, rather than an extension of, the representational theater and the "retinal vision" (as Duchamp would have it) too far into the background. Breton and others sought too much contemplative involvement and too little self-sufficient kinetic frenzy; they pursued signification and stimulation of desire through the film apparatus, but paid too little attention to the cinematograph as a basic circulator of *acephalic* (Bataille) drives, both machinic and human.

A discovery made not too long ago revealed another materialist peculiarity of *Return to Reason*. Its rayographic content, it turned out, includes some "photographic negatives of a nude woman (presumably Kiki of Montparnasse) stretched out on a bed in a lascivious pose. Laid lengthwise along the filmstrip, these images are irrevocably indecipherable when viewed through the mechanism of a projector... even when projected at a frame-by-frame speed. The crystal-clear imprint of the substrate is physically invisible to the mechanical eye and can be seized *only by the human eye when the filmstrip is held in the hand* rather than projected."[23]

Materiality of the cinematographic apparatus is pushed into the extreme foreground, causing an alteration in its operational logic. Spectatorship is made dependent on one's tactile interaction with the static celluloid strip; projection is sidetracked as only one way to watch a film. In the postwar context, it was, once again, Sharits who systematically extended this line of investigation, insisting on the material presence and visibility of the filmstrip as a central organizing principle of the cinematic experience. In 1972, he quite directly reactualized Man Ray's distinction (see the opening of chapter 2) between the "permanently immobile," "concrete," and "static" works of art and the works with finite duration, "limited to a period of presentation." Sharits cast this distinction as that pertaining to film as an "all-at-once" mode, and film as a durational phenomenon:

> [M]ost critics and historians still regard the *tentative* experience of perceiving a film as "more real," in their definitions of cinema, than

holding in their hand a non-tentative strip of celluloid that has a measurable length and width and that has a measurable series of "frames," degrees of opacity, and so on.... (I)n film we have a case where we can experience both a changing and an enduring existence—we can look at the "same" film as an *object*, before or after projection (and it is not a "score"; it is 'the film'), and as temporal *process*, while it is being "projected" on the stable support of the screen. This equivocality of object/projection is further complicated when we admit that there are occasions when we are looking at a screen and we don't know whether we are or are not seeing "a film"; we cannot distinguish "the movie" from "the projection." Let us say that the room is dark and the screen is white; we may believe that the projector is simply throwing light on the screen, because there is no indication that a film is being shown; yet, in fact, the projector may be casting *images* of a succession of clear-blank frames onto the screen, projecting not "light" but a *picture* which represents motion (the motion of the strip of film being projected); so, unless we are in the projection booth and thus experience both the film as object and as projection this "viewing" would be incomprehensible.[24]

Sharits rigorously explored this "equivocality" or "apparent dualism" of film. The consistency with which he emphasized that film is always both an object and an experience—and that neither is entirely meaningful without recourse to the other—allowed him to successfully dialecticize the two modes of film's appearance. Sharits exhibited some of his films in gallery spaces as objects-strips placed between the sheets of Plexiglas: the "Frozen Film Frames." But this pursuit of the most direct ways of asserting film's materiality was not at all motivated by a desire to simply annul the cinema's projection-imaginary complex. The "Frozen Film Frames" were the "all-at-once" form of the works that Sharits simultaneously conceived and exhibited as "projected time-light experiences."[25] What The Frozen Film Frames were intended to convey was the manner in which the filmmaker was "mapping out ... [his] films in a way similar to musical scores and modular drawings.... [S]een as 'Frozen Film Frames'—wherein strips of the films are serially arranged side by side from beginning to end, from right to left, between sheets of Plexiglas—these structural strategies become transparent to even the most naïve viewer, thus enriching the understanding of a given work and emphasizing the basic structure and tangibility of film itself."[26]

In explaining the conceptual foundation of his experimental method, Sharits admitted to what he saw as a strong structural analogy, an operational proximity, between the cinema and the mind. He wrote: "Premise: there is the possibility of synthesizing various, even contradictory concepts of perception-consciousness/knowing-meaning into a unified, open (self-reorganizing), systems model, through a close analysis of the most fundamental levels of what I am calling 'cinema.' We have to look 'below' the usage level of cinema (its typical 'documentation' and 'narration' functions) to its infrastructures, to its elementary particles of signification. Films have to be made which amplify cinema's general infrastructures. . . . Two sub-premises are implied and they are cybernetically 'bound' together: first, that 'cinema' is a conceptual system; and, second, that there is a submerged meaning in the primary-material ('support') levels of the cinema apparatus."[27]

As his writing suggests, Sharits believed in the interdependence of "the material of film" and "the idea of cinema" (to again use Walley's terms). Sharits did not think that limiting his investigation of the cinematographic medium to the physical manifestations of its primary matter could ever suffice on its own. At the same time, he was far from advocating some sort of simplistically "dematerialized" understanding of the cinema as a conceptual system. This position is evident, for instance, in Sharits's interest in exhibiting the Frozen Film Frames *as well as* their corresponding scores, graph drawings, charts, and diagrams. He thus wanted to strengthen his invitation to the spectator to invest himself/herself in the films' dynamic existence "beyond" their material substratum. Simultaneously, however, he maintained that imagining the "higher" processes of film's "temporal abstraction"—mentally projecting its flow—would be entirely pointless if it involved downplaying the basic features of the cinematographic apparatus, those "elements that can be observed" and that therefore constitute a "fundamental frame of reference": "We can observe cameras, projectors, and other pieces of equipment and their parts and their parts' functions (shutters, numerous circular motions of parts, focus, and so on). We can observe the support itself, its emulsions before and after 'exposure,' sprocket holes, frames, and so on. We can observe the effects of light on film and, likewise, we can note the effects of light passing through the film and illuminating a reflective support. There is a remarkable structural parallel, which is suggestive of new systems of filmic organization, between a piece of film and the projections of light through it; both are simultaneously corpuscular ('frames') and wave-like ('strip')."[28]

In approaching the cinema as a conceptual-material art, a number of Sharits' prewar predecessors—from Man Ray and Raoul Hausmann to Aleksandar Vučo and Dušan Matić—demonstrated an interest in the medium's potential for "re-materialization." Sharits, however, was not in pursuit of this extraordinary capacity of the cinema to *assert* its medium-specificity by embodying itself in the materials *other* than the normatively cinematographic ones. In this respect, he was and remained a filmmaker proper. But Sharits did insist on exploring his medium in the realms of the projected and the nonprojected image alike. Furthermore, in the latter ream, he staged a separation of cinema and film into graphs and drawings on the one hand, and the Frozen Film Frames on the other hand. He did so in order to explore the extent to which certain aspects of the former concept/idea/experience (cinema) are traceable within the primary materials of the latter (film), *even before these are assembled into a functioning cinematographic apparatus.* And this is why, in the final analysis, Paul Sharits is a truly materialist filmmaker. For him, film *qua* matter is, ultimately, all that exists. But this exclusivity of matter can be properly upheld only with a dialectical "detour" through the idea and the experience of the cinema. Paraphrasing Alain Badiou, we could say that here "film names being" while cinema names "its order—an order whose being lies in a vanishing nominal overhaul."[29]

A commitment to the physical-material dimension of the film medium is also at the core of the experimental practice of the Yugoslav director Slobodan Šijan. To begin with, some interesting parallels may be drawn between the two filmmakers' creative trajectories. Like Sharits, Šijan studied art and was a painter before he turned to filmmaking. The psychedelic culture of the 1960s had a significant influence on both artists. Also, each began making films with structural concerns in the late 1960s and early 1970s (Sharits: *Ray Gun Virus*, 1966; *T,O,U,C,H,I,N,G*, 1968; Šijan: *Structures*, 1970; *Handmade*, 1971). Finally, both Šijan and Sharits have cultivated a substantial investment in the questions of cinematic pedagogy and education.

Despite some parallels, however, the two filmmakers' overall cinematic "profiles" are considerably different, not the least because they were formed in starkly dissimilar historical contexts. Sharits belonged to the US counterculture and spent his years working entirely outside the realm of commercial cinema (the center of which is, of course, Hollywood). He is a foremost representative of what became known in the 1960s as the New American Cinema: an increasingly organized network of film production, distribution, and exhibition, completely independent from the industrial mode of filmmaking. A substantial segment of this postwar cinematic avant-garde developed within a broader context of advanced modernist art. Sharits' committed study of what he termed "cinematics"—an integrated theoretical-practical investigation of the cinema, partially defined by analogy with linguistics[30]—reflected the general aesthetic and theoretical climate of Conceptualism, Minimalism, and Post-Minimalism, which decisively shaped the modern art scene at the time.

On the other hand, Slobodan Šijan is best known as one of the most important feature film directors in the socialist Yugoslavia in the 1980s, and the author of some critically celebrated and audience-adored black comedies, such as *Who Is Singing over There* (1980) and *The Marathon Family* (1982). His eclectic taste betrays a genuine enthusiasm for the most diverse types of cinema. Šijan is a fan and a tireless promoter of both Hollywood (classical and contemporary) and European films, of "art" and "trash" alike—from King Vidor and Howard Hawks to Richard Sarafian and Walter Hill; from Robert Bresson to Michelangelo Antonioni and Lucio Fulci. But Šijan is also an experimental artist who, since the late 1960s—initially in the context of the so-called "new art practices" in the socialist Yugoslavia—has been exploring the cinematic potentials of painting, drawing, photography, and writing. He is thus, at the same time, a foremost representative of mainstream Yugoslav cinema and an author whose creative output equally belongs within the framework of the local neo-avant-garde (conceptual, intermedial) art scene.

GEFF was an important point of reference for Šijan. But his cinematic sensibility was above all shaped through his creative interactions and friendship with Tomislav Gotovac. As one of the most accomplished experimental filmmakers, conceptualists, and performance/body artists in 1960s and 1970s Yugoslavia (who entertained an uneasy relationship with GEFF and Pansini), Gotovac embodied the impossibility of separating art from life, "high" from "low" culture, and advanced modernist sensibilities from the popular ones. In the realm of the cinema, Gotovac swiftly moved back and forth between structural/ontological experimentation on 16 mm and 8 mm film (*The Morning of a Faun*, 1963) (fig. 5.3); "expanded cinema"-type performances and production of film-objects that posed questions about the political economy of institutionalized cinema (*CinemaTickets*, 1964) (color plate 10); spectatorial infatuation with and active promotion of Hollywood classics (Lewis Milestone's *All Quiet on The Western Front*, George Stevens' *A Place in the Sun*, and so on); and sexually explicit home movies (one of these, the *Family Film* of 1973, was shot by Šijan). "Tom was a sort of film guru for my generation," recalls Šijan. "His charismatic personality contagiously spread a passion for film. His adoration of the commercial American cinema, combined with the extremely hermetic, minimalist experimental films which he himself was making, made his views and ideas original and convincing. . . . His taste was almost impeccable and, like some enamored devotee who was soliciting accomplices for a marvelous crime, he revealed to us the treasury of the world cinema."[31]

One of the axioms of Gotovac's artistic and living practice alike was a firm belief in the omniscience of the cinema. He has claimed: "As soon as I open my eyes in the morning, I see film." In the same spirit, he repeatedly asserted: "It's all a movie." Art historian Ješa Denegri perceptively explains: "[F]ilm experience is crucial for the entirety of Gotovac's work; as an artist, in an expanded sense of that term, he was brought up and formed by the cinema; film is not only the basis but also the leading thread, the very essence, of even those among his works that are not directly realized in the cinematographic medium." In support of this claim, Denegri evokes the example of Gotovac's early photographic sequence, *Heads* (1960). Having had no opportunity in the early 1960s to shoot his own films, Gotovac

Figure 5.3 Tomislav Gotovac, *The Morning of a Faun* (1963)

decided to "satisfy his longing" by "directing a series of five photographs—close-ups of his own face in different poses, situations, and states. Although realized in the medium of photography, *Heads* is actually an imagistic series at the foundation of which is the language of cinema . . . . As the author himself confirmed, this work is, at its basis, a reflection on the nature and the meaning of the cinematographic shot in Robert Bresson's *A Man Escaped*." Denegri concludes that "Gotovac here used photography as a substitute for film" and that the series of images he produced represents an instance of "micro-directing by photographic means," existing against the background of "the absent . . ., the unavailable, and the unrealizable macro-directing in/of the cinema."[32]

"It's all a movie." A hypothetical visual ground zero of this dynamic may be located in Ivan Posavec's 1979 photograph, which shows Gotovac standing in front of an empty screen (fig. 5.4). One could imagine just about any movie being projected onto this screen. For cinefication of the

Figures 5.4 and 5.5 "It's all a movie." Tomislav Gotovac in front of an empty screen (Ivan Posavec, *Untitled* (1979), courtesy of Hrvatski filmski savez, Zagreb); and a frame from Weekend Art's "Body Film Essay," *She Wore a Yellow Ribbon/Stars and Soldiers* (2002)

everyday, as Gotovac understood well, is subject to neither quantitative nor qualitative limitations—"art" films qualify just as much as the "trashy" ones; Bresson just as much as, say, George Pal (Gotovac appropriated the soundtrack of Pal's *The Time Machine* (1960) in one of his structural films); equally acceptable are all films already shot, all films that will be shot, and even all films that ought to be shot. Thus for instance, most recently (2002–2004), Gotovac and two collaborators, Aleksandar Battista Ilić and Ivana Kesser, decided to demonstrate the process of reality's cinefication in the form of a collective performance for which they chose as central points of reference two films, one by John Ford and one by Miklós Jancsó (fig. 5.5). The three artists staged what they called a "Body Film Essay" by executing a series of elementary physical actions—walking, undressing, lying down, singing, and so on—in front of a movie screen onto which were projected various scenes from Ford's *She Wore a Yellow Ribbon* (1949) and Jancsó's *The Red and the White* (aka *Stars and Soldiers*, 1967). (The choice of Jancsó's work for the realization of this project is particularly apt, considering the unique value of his own directorial approach for our understanding of the logic and mechanisms of "general cinefication"—the point I discussed at length in the previous chapter).

"As soon as I open my eyes in the morning, I see film." Gotovac's credo—another symptom of everyday reality having been thoroughly subordinated to cinephilia—effectively condenses those aspects of his aesthetic philosophy that also strongly inspired Slobodan Šijan at the critical time when his own pursuits in the realm of "cinema by other means" were germinating. In his "Film Manifesto" from 1972, Šijan wrote: "Film is a wedding: the object and the subject realize that they are one." And further: "The one who knows how to watch a film also knows how to make it." Years later, in the 1990s, he still acknowledged that "the possibility of directly entering the filmic reality" is a key question that has persistently motivated his work.

In 1970, having earned a degree in painting and having already made some experimental films, Šijan enrolled in the Belgrade Film Academy (FDU) as a student of directing. This was the tail end of the period often characterized as the "golden age" of Yugoslav cinema. At FDU, Šijan was taught by some of the most accomplished filmmakers of the time. His mentor was Živojin Pavlović, the author of such acclaimed films as *The*

Rats are Awakening (1967), *When I am Dead and Pale* (1969), and *The Ambush* (1969). Marshalling a distinct style of raw cinematic realism, these works had earned Pavlović the status of one of the most uncompromising critics of the Yugoslav socio-political everyday. In the early 1970s, however, as Šijan was beginning his education as a professional filmmaker, major controversy erupted. An ideological campaign was mounted by the cultural watchdogs and the political apparatchiks of the state-socialist system, against what became known as the Black Wave: the "negative," "socially destructive," and even "counter-revolutionary" tendencies that have supposedly developed in contemporary Yugoslav cinema, most obviously in the works of Pavlović, Aleksandar Saša Petrović, Dušan Makavejev, Želimir Žilnik, and Lazar Stojanović. A number of films were eventually censored while Stojanović, a graduating senior at the FDU, even served a three-year prison sentence for his thesis film (starring Tom Gotovac), *Plastic Jesus* (1971), which meddled with the personality cult of the Yugoslav President Josip Broz Tito. Saša Petrović (Stojanović's mentor) and Pavlović were both forced to step down from their professorial posts at the Academy.

When he was a student at the FDU, Šijan, then, witnessed a dramatic change affecting the Yugoslav cinema. An atmosphere of unbound creativity, artistic experimentation, and free sociopolitical engagement was interrupted by the repressive methods of the political bureaucracy. The immediate future did not seem particularly encouraging, and a young director-in-the-making would have doubts about whether he would be given an opportunity to make films professionally. Šijan recalls:

> Before [the purge at the FDU], the atmosphere among the students of film directing was fantastic, there was incredible enthusiasm and belief in the future of Yugoslav cinema. . . . (M)uch was expected from the new films being made by Žilnik (*Kapital*), Joca Jovanović (*Young and Fresh as a Rose*) and Lazar Stojanović. Makavejev had already finished his *WR: Mysteries of the Organism* and, generally speaking, at that moment Yugoslav film was the 'new thing' in European cinema. We [students] completely felt ourselves to be part of this cinema. . . . The ensuing purge, which halted that vertiginous rise of Serbian cinema for several years, had severe consequences for my entire generation. For a long time, students of film directing

from the Belgrade Academy for Theatre, Film, TV and Radio, were treated as the "black sheep"—those who, as the saying went, "planted the plastic bomb." Very few of my colleagues managed to make films in the coming years. But there was something else . . . . We grew up in an atmosphere of creative freedom promoted by Saša Petrović and Živojin Pavlović. It was hard for us to get used to the new rules of the game, to become the harmless "good kids" . . . . We wanted to crush all obstacles in our way, much like our predecessors did. But there was no longer any room left for that. And there was no light on the horizon either. After the cinematic "Black Wave," we plunged into a still darker reality. We became a Garbage Dump.[33]

Throughout the 1970s, Šijan conducted numerous unconventional experiments "around film" (as they would subsequently become known). His artistic background and interest in the mixed-media notwithstanding, these exercises were to a certain extent also symptomatic of a specific creative need—an urge to produce something *distinctly filmic* amid the trying atmosphere of ideologically recalibrated standards of cinematic expression. It is as if faced with the uncertainty of its future development, the practice of filmmaking underwent in Šijan's hands a process of thorough dispersal into its constitutive components—a process which, in turn, gave rise to multiple novel and often highly unusual trajectories of filmic/cinematic engagement. To practice cinema literally came to mean "making films by any and all means possible." Šijan conducted, with equal zeal, both the rigorously immaterial and the intensely material exercises "around film," all of which partook of the same project of discovering valid and constructive alternatives to filmmaking proper. Purely conceptual scripts for unrealizable, "centuries-long" films (*Outline for a Family Film*, 1976) took turns with graphic poems that traced similarities and differences between individual filmmakers, such as Federico Fellini and Vincent Minnelli (*Vincentefederico*, 1979); while the melodramatic *Kitsch-sequences* (1977–1978), compiled from postcards depicting idealized scenes of family life, shared the stage with the comic strip-based cinematic ready-mades, such as *The Sketch for a National Cinema* and *My Adventures at the Cinematheque* (both from 1979; in the latter (fig.5.6), the filmmaker appropriated some frames from an enormously popular Italian comic book, *Alan Ford*).

Figure 5.6 Slobodan Šijan, *My Adventures at the Cinematheque* (1979), courtesy of the artist

All of these works were also, in one capacity or another, related to Šijan's master-project at the time: his continual production, from 1976 to 1979, of the single-page, double-sided fanzine called the *Film Leaflet*. In the forty-three realized issues of this do-it-yourself serial "paper movie," Šijan inventively combined text and image—fan writing, drawings, photography, critical analyses of films and filmmakers, appropriated newspaper clippings, poetry, storyboards, and much more. One of the most interesting projects developed across a number of issues of the *Leaflet* was the "In the Rhythm of . . ." series. It was composed of a variety of hand-drawn graphs and diagrams—continuous and discontinuous lines, checkerboards, wavelike formations, and so on—which sought to capture the characteristic rhythms of intra- and inter-shot progression in the films of Howards Hawks, John Ford, Alfred Hitchcock, Robert Altman, and others (figs. 5.7, 5.8).

Each of the cinematic diagrams in question presents an abstract matrix, a cinematographic Code of sorts (a Rythmeme, as Pasolini would call it). Šijan aimed to distill in these Codes some elementary information pertaining to the patterns of audiovisual movement in the works of the aforementioned film directors. But what makes these cine-rhythmic diagrams truly special is the implication that they might also be put to practical use. The spectator could, for instance, select any one of Šijan's extrapolated matrices and attempt to "apply" it to various aspects of reality itself. The spectator-become-filmmaker would thus find himself/herself in the midst of producing a "living cinema" environment. That is, by endeavoring to activate some of Šijan's Codes amid an array of everyday occurrences, the spectator would temporarily assume the task of "directing" life *in the rhythm of* Howard Hawks, John Ford, or Alfred Hitchcock.

In the 1990s, Šijan further advanced precisely this line of thinking as he devised additional strategies of comprehensive immersion into Hitchcock's cinematic universe. He visited the Northern Californian locations for Hitchcock's 1958 film *Vertigo* and shot dozens of photographs there (see color plate 11). He subsequently organized these into the cinematically inspired sequences of three images (some of which, incidentally, bear a striking structural resemblance to Vučo and Matić's also tripartite Surrealist assemblage, *The Frenzied Marble*, discussed in chapter 2). At the time, Šijan also began to write a serial poem in which he pondered

Figure 5.7 Slobodan Šijan, *In the Rhythm of John Ford* (1974), courtesy of the artist

the complexity of the relationship between reality, fantasy, and the recording eye of the camera. The outcome of this multileveled (conceptual, geographic, aesthetic) exploration was a book, which itself bore the title *Vertigo* (Vrtoglavica). It forcefully conveyed Šijan's infatuation with Hitchcock's film, but also his passion for the genre of "written cinema"

IMAGINARY SIGNIFIER

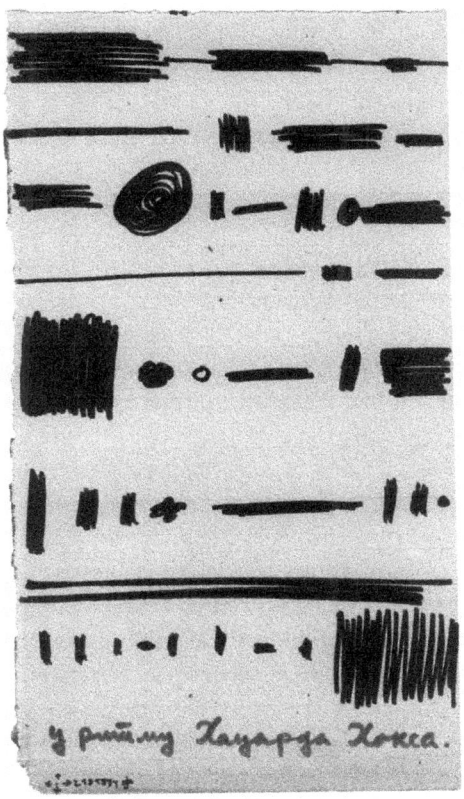

Figure 5.8 Slobodan Šijan, *In the Rhythm of Howard Hawks* (1974), courtesy of the artist

(the book is dedicated to Boško Tokin Filmus, whose own cinematographic poems (see chapter 1) had already been reproduced in an early issue of the *Film Leaflet*).

Šijan's diverse para-cinematographic activities also uniquely advanced the project of "intensification of [film's] materiality" (as Sharits would say), and it is to this dimension of his work that I now wish to turn.[34] Through a series of metonymic displacements, Šijan propelled film matter—specifically, the filmstrip's celluloid base—in pursuit of its sturdier and longer-lasting replacements. Inspired by the aesthetics of the garbage dump, as theorized by the Yugoslav 1950s and 1960s artist Leonid Šejka, the director utilized a variety of waste materials as the new physical support for his "films." He literally drew frames and images, indicated shot transitions, and wrote instructions for camera movements on the pieces of refuse he collected. Notable among these works are *Bag-film* (1974, color plate 12) and *Onto a Double Perforated* . . . (1974, color plate 13), produced on bags in which film laboratories at the time used to ship reels of processed film (color plate 14), as well as a series of storyboards developed on the randomly gathered bits of old paper (including a set of visual notes for a projected cinematic ode to Šejka). Šijan even fashioned a "Manifesto of the Film Garbage-Man" (1978, fig. 5.9), which consisted of a single photograph of him standing in front of a vast pile of junk, camera in hand.[35]

What seems to be resonating in the background of these "garbage-works" is Šijan's concern with the crisis that was affecting the Yugoslav cinema at the time. Filmmaking as a form of wasteful expenditure, the garbage dump as a substitute for the studio set! By cultivating the decay of meaning, but (much in the spirit of Leonid Šejka) also the possibility of its regeneration, Šijan in a sense demanded of cinematic practice—whatever the means of its execution—to become political in a very specific way: to offer "equivocation of matter" as a rejoinder to the unreasonable pressures exercised by the ideological apparatus of the state. Such was this filmmaker's creative call for the Yugoslav cinema's "return to reason."

Šijan's interest in aesthetics of cinematic decay continued throughout the 1980s and the 1990s, even after he had successfully established himself as a director of feature-length films. At the end of his second feature, *The Marathon Family*, undifferentiated film matter "pierces" through the diegetic content/representational illusion and gradually overtakes the entire screen. The face of the central narrative protagonist, Mirko, the youngest in a family of morticians, unexpectedly freezes in the midst of a violent spasm. A growing stain emerges from the depth of the image, rapidly consuming Mirko's stilled, half-lit close-up. The film seems to have jammed in the projector; the celluloid strip is burning under the heat of

Figure 5.9 Slobodan Šijan, *Manifesto of the Film Garbage-Man* (1978), courtesy of the artist

the light-bulb (color plate 15). Mirko's face is assaulted. His eye, in particular, is visibly deformed. Eventually, his entire face is obliterated, consumed by the ever-expanding burn, which effortlessly extends the affective charge of the man's ecstatic body.

Given its "funerary" content—the hilarious misadventures of five generations of gravediggers in 1930s Serbia—it is entirely appropriate that *The Marathon Family* end by bringing together human flesh and primary film-matter in an act of common decay. An instance of Šijan's long-standing exploration of what he has called "media suicide" (technologies of image production and reproduction succumbing to auto-destructive impulses), this event of combined carnal and celluloid disintegration also invites a comparison between the dynamics of cinematic spectatorship and the process of mortification.[36] This problematic is most extensively developed in Šijan's aforementioned book of cinematographic poetry and photo-sequences, *Vertigo* (inspired by Hitchcock's own masterpiece of "funerary" and "necrophilic" cinema). Consider the following verse from the opening section of the book, called "Darkness":

> The lights are turned off.
> During those few moments
> between the two lights,
> he'd always feel the cold firmness
> of the wood in the rear of his head.
> The stench of the grave,
> for he was six feet under,
> was warning him of the true nature of the place
> he'd come to occupy.
> But this would happen only during the few
> moments of complete darkness.
> One illusion was disappearing while,
> in the dark, he was anticipating the onset of another.
> . . .
> He would relax,
> expecting the beam of light to cut the
> darkness in two,
> the interior and the exterior part.
> Then these split parts would strive to unite,
> to join each other again
> in a ceremony of sorts, which he used to call a wedding
> while others referred to it as
> film.

Employing the medium of written language and the form of prosodic poem, Šijan presents the movie theater as a liminal zone. Figuring "between two illusions," between two adjacent realms of light, the theater is an *interstitial* space that makes possible the transition from the living reality to the reality of the silver screen. As we have seen in chapter 3, Breton and the Surrealists conceived of the movie theater as a space of "deracination," and on occasion evoked its similarity with the womb. In the hands of the Constructivists, such as Dziga Vertov, the screen in the theater at times seemed to function as if by analogy with the iconostasis in the Orthodox church.[37] In Šijan's poem, however, the transitory darkness of the movie theater is identified as, before all else, grave-like. After the lights in the theater have been turned off, but the projector still has not cast any images onto the screen—during this interregnum when reality is already "suspended," but the cinematic illusion has not yet begun to unfold—the spectator is temporarily left without any "suturing" points of reference. That is, under the conditions of the physical world's visual inaccessibility, the spectator, as described in "Darkness," becomes acutely aware of his/her carnal, libidinally underwritten existence. In the space of the darkened movie theater, Šijan insists, one finds oneself in a ditch! In lieu of all representations, all illusions, all external images of any kind, the flesh is given an opportunity to reassert itself by recalling to mind the fact that it never stops rotting.

Chapter 6

The "Between" of Cinema

There would never have been an "art" of cinema had there not been many different hypotheses about montage, *many different ways of forbidding oneself to pass from A to B, without some underlying theory of editing that "insured" the transition.*

—Serge Daney[1]

Throughout this book I have been discussing works which in a variety of ways demonstrate that, *in extremis*, cinematic desire, desire of the cinema, can be successfully reproduced even under the conditions other than those of watching an actual film. Examples abound among the historical avant-garde—Raoul Hausmann, Man Ray, Marko Ristić, Monny de Boully, Max Ernst, and more—as they do among the postwar experimental filmmakers and artists—from Roland Sabatier to Ljubiša Jocić to Slobodan Šijan. Despite their often substantially different aesthetic, philosophical, and political orientations, all of these authors effectively demonstrated that static, originally *non*cinematographic mediums can be successfully engaged to generate the effects of filmic seriality and movement.[2] When properly stimulated, the mind will itself perform an ersatz cinematographic synthesis, stitching together and animating disparate imagistic fragments it encounters. The decisive role montage plays in this process was identified early on by the 1920s Soviet filmmakers and theorists, Sergei Eisenstein and Dziga Vertov. In chapter 4, I already addressed the key aspects of Vertov's position on this matter. Now I will briefly turn to Eisenstein.

Using the example of Leonardo da Vinci's detailed written notes for a projected painting of The Deluge ("a certain remarkable 'shooting-script'"), Eisenstein points out that the distribution of details in a picture on a single plain also presumes movement—a compositionally directed movement of the eyes from one phenomenon to another. Here, of course, movement is expressed less directly than in the film, where the eye *cannot* discern the succession of the sequence of details in any other order than that established by him who determines the order of the montage.

Unquestionably though, Leonardo's exceedingly sequential description fulfills the task not of merely listing the details, but of outlining the trajectory of the future movement of the attention over the surface of the canvas. Here we see a brilliant example of how, in the apparently static simultaneous "co-existence" of details in an immobile picture, there has yet been applied exactly the same montage selection, there is exactly the same ordered succession in the juxtaposition of details, as in those arts that include the time factor.[3]

Next, Eisenstein turns to elaborating the spectator's own vital contribution to the production of meaning in a montage-based work: "The strength of montage resides in this, that it includes in the creative process the emotions and mind of the spectator. The spectator is compelled to proceed along that selfsame creative road that the author traveled in creating the image. The spectator not only sees the represented elements of the finished work, but also experiences the dynamic process of the emergence and assembly of the image just as it was experienced by the author."[4] One of the conclusions Eisenstein ultimately draws from this is "that the montage principle in films is only a sectional application of the *montage principle in general*, a principle which, if fully understood, passes far beyond the limits of splicing bits of film together."[5]

Consider, in light of Eisenstein's generalization of the montage principle—which, nonetheless, retains film as its central point of reference—the medium of comics. The space between consecutive frames—known as the "gutter"—is, by definition, structurally repeated across a chain of images. As such it stimulates both the actual movement of the reader's eye along this chain and an imaginary effect of movement within the space of the image(s). It was precisely this preponderance of activity triggered by the naturalized textual fissures that once prompted Jean-Luc

Godard—himself, like Eisenstein and Vertov, also an advocate of an inclusive understanding of montage—to claim that "the découpage of comic strips is aesthetically years ahead of film découpage."[6]

An illuminating example of the convergence between the comic-strip and the filmstrip is found in the eight-frame-long cartoon bearing the title "A French Nurse's Dream." (fig. 6.1). Sigmund Freud originally used this cartoon (discovered by Sandor Ferenczi in a Hungarian newspaper) to describe a fundamental mechanism of dreaming: the dreamer's wish to continue dreaming. He wrote:

> The drawings bear the title "A French Nurse's Dream"; but it is only the last picture, showing the nurse being woken up by the child's screams, that tells us that the seven previous pictures represent the phases of a dream. The first picture depicts the stimulus which should have caused the sleeper to wake: the little boy has become aware of a need and is asking for help in dealing with it. But in the dream the dreamer, instead of being in the bedroom, is taking the child for a walk. In the second picture she has already led him to a street corner where he is micturating—and she can go on sleeping. But the arousal stimulus continues; indeed, it increases. The little boy, finding that he is not being attended to, screams louder and louder. The more imperiously he insists upon his nurse waking up and helping him, the more insistent becomes the dream's assurance that everything is all right and that there is no need for her to wake up. At the same time, the dream translates the increasing stimulus into the increasing dimensions of its symbols. The stream of water produced by the micturating boy becomes mightier and mightier. In the fourth picture it is already large enough to float a rowing boat; but there follows a gondola, a sailing ship and finally a liner. The ingenious artist has in this way cleverly depicted the struggle between an obstinate craving for sleep and an inexhaustible stimulus towards waking.[7]

Structurally, the wish to continue dreaming bespeaks the desire to be, to remain, "sutured" into the signifying network at hand. In the cartoon, diegetic elimination of the persisting threat of the dream's cessation has its

THE "BETWEEN" OF CINEMA

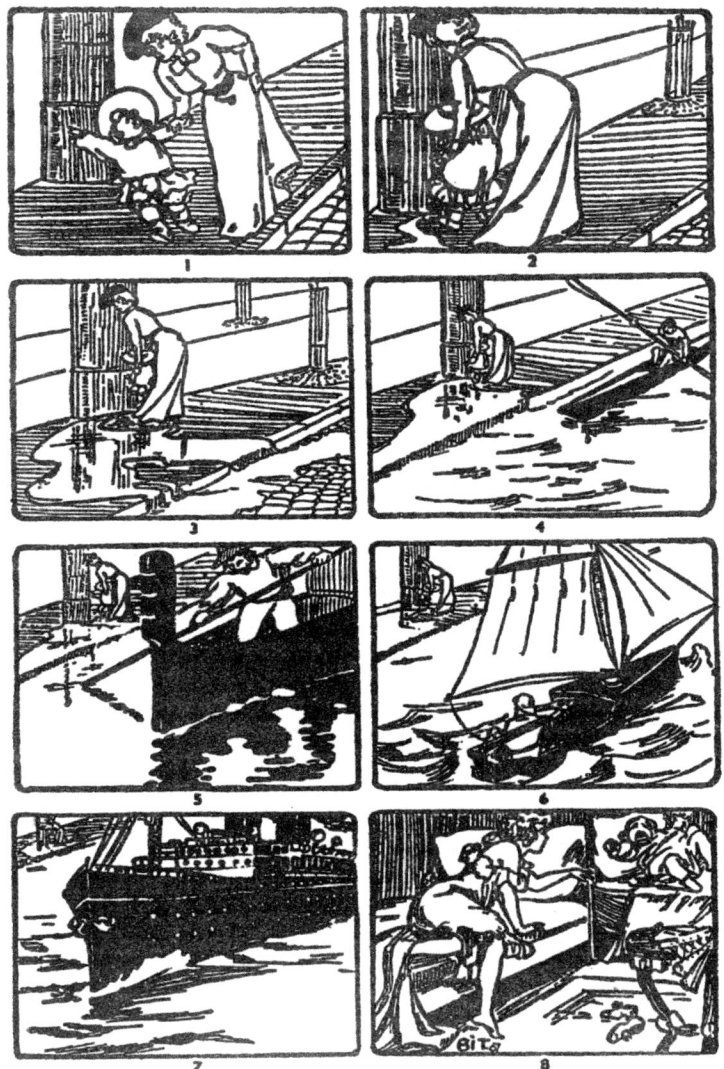

Figure 6.1 "A French Nurse's Dream"

formal expression and support in the artist's act of making visible, from one frame/drawing to the next, ever more offscreen space. But what especially interests us here is the fact that, although presented in a series of distinct static images, the struggle at the core of the dream narrative generates a cumulative (proto-)cinematic effect of enduring movement (within as well as between images). The tension between the wish to continue dreaming and a disruption in the form of an external stimulus motivates not only the content and the mise-en-scène of the comic strip (the nurse taking the boy to the street corner, where he can micturate), but also the *framing* of the event that brings together the actual fragmented (montage-based) layout of the cartoon, and the reader's/spectator's impression of an ongoing, uninterrupted *tracking shot*. The more intense the external disruption (the boy who awoke is crying), the further the "imaginary camera"—which provides the reader's point of view on the entire incident—seems to dolly out. As it "moves," without any change of angle, from the original full shot (the first drawing) to an extreme long shot encompassing not only the boardwalk but also the surrounding water and the huge ship passing nearby (the seventh drawing), it effectively bridges (diegetically conceals, one could say) the textual breaks—the "gutter"—evident in the cartoon's paper layout. This is precisely what the (psychoanalytic) logic of "suture" entails: maintaining spectatorial desire, like some sort of incessant, discretely sensed tracking shot, through perpetual negotiations between the on- and the offscreen space, between images and the innumerable fissures, ruptures, and voids that traverse them.

Significantly, the impression of the "camera's" movement in the French nurse's "dream" would seem to rest on a paradox. The camera reveals the space around the nurse and the boy—the water and all the vessels in it: a canoe, a gondola, a sailboat, a liner—*only insofar as this initially offscreen space is constituted by the micturating boy himself*. It is as if his action within the frame actually makes possible an extension of the diegetic reality beyond the frame. Only after it has been properly summoned into existence by the on-screen events can this reality be incorporated inside the frame. Here we encounter a version of what Lacan, in his "return to Freud," designated the "effect of retroversion": the cause functioning as the consequence of its own effects.[8] The camera dollies out to reveal more space, but this space is, to begin with, generated by the camera's movement. Do the passing vessels increase in size because of the boy's incessant micturation, which enlarges the surface of the water? Or, is his persistent micturation ("the dream's assurance," in Freud's words, "that everything is all right") actually stimulated by the ever larger vessels passing him by (symbols of the growing external pressure to stop dreaming)? In a sense, the answer is . . . both. The dreamer's/spectator's desire for an uninterrupted drift along the chain of images—the wish to continue dreaming, to continue watching the film—directly stimulates an ongoing production of the signifying chain. In the words of Serge Daney: "The brain functions as a second projector allowing the image to continue flowing, letting the film and the world continue without it."[9] Understood in this light, filmmaking is not unlike the process of mutual adjustment between a dream, or a hallucination, and the format of the comic strip.

There is something inherently equivocal about the cinematic cut. It brings two shots together while setting them apart. It plays an important role in the constitution of the film's meaning, but can also function as its limit—as a trace of the failure of discursive and perceptual totalization. The cut simultaneously conceals and asserts the space, the crevice, that figures between images.

For its part, this crevice is the necessary though commonly disavowed foundation of every cinematic series. It is the point of departure for the aforementioned operation of *suture*: the zero that ensures continuous textual signification by maintaining spectatorial engagement with the flow of images. The notion of suture (which reached the peak of its theoretical popularity in 1970s film theory) originated in Jacques Lacan's teaching, but it was Jacques-Alain Miller who, in 1966, elevated it to the status of a theoretical concept in its own right. Emphasizing its general character, Miller defined suture in terms of formal logic as the operation that joins the subject to the signifying chain and as the "relation in general of the lack to the structure of which it is an element, in as much as it implies position of a taking-the-place-of."[10]

For the film scholars who follow Miller's original account, suture is the operation that ties the subject to the cinematic discourse—*not* (as has sometimes been wrongly assumed) by simulating closure, but rather by effecting the impression that there is always more than meets the eye, that there is an excess beyond the frame of the image: *an impression that closure is never total*.[11] It is, then, through *inscription* of lack in the audiovisual field, rather than its concealment, that the subject is "stitched" into the discourse. Anticipation of the absent audiovisual content—the "more" to be seen and heard—is encoded into the cinematic chain, and this anticipation operates as an exciter of the spectator's desire. In a sense, suture may be said to bespeak the subject's endless affirmation, through the signifying chain, of his/her desire to desire (to use that famous phrase).

The spectator desires the totality of the image, of the visible and its meaning. Although according to psycho-semiotics, *suture* pertains to the human subject's *general* acquisition of meaning, the institution of cinema—because of the specific manner in which it relates time to the image; because of the way it, by definition, *passes* time through a series of signifiers—provides a particularly valuable point of reference where understanding the dynamic of this acquisition is concerned. In the cinema, the spectator's desire "to see more" is structurally upheld, normativized as a desire for an ongoing flow of images—a desire for a film to "take place." Mechanisms of this cinematic desiring are, on the other hand, most directly revealed—and, potentially, most radically upset—in films built on the principles of fragmentation, elliptical structuring, and disjunctive montage—films that highlight the existence of crevices, holes, and precipices in the fabric of their images. As we shall see below, the cinema of Jean-Luc Godard is a case in point.

When the cinematic cut foregrounds its crevicular properties, it begins to function, in Gilles Deleuze's words, as a montage *interstice*. The French philosopher identifies the interstice thus:

> [T]he question is no longer that of the association or attraction of images. What counts is on the contrary the *interstice* between images, between two images..., Given one image, another image has to be chosen which will induce an interstice *between* the two. This is not an operation of association, but of differentiation, as mathematicians say, or of disappearance, as physicists say: given one potential, another one has to be chosen, not any whatever, but in such a way that a difference of potential is established between the

two, which will be productive of a third or of something new.... It is not a matter of following a chain of images, even across voids, but of getting out of the chain or the association.... It is the method of BETWEEN, "between two images".... It is the method of AND, "this and then that," which does away with all the cinema of Being=is.[12]

In the interstice—the cinematographic relative of the "gutter" in the comics—the distance between two images is forever preserved. Although it cannot entirely terminate the operation of suture, this separation or differentiation among images does have the power to temporarily suspend it—at the price, however, of simultaneously intensifying the desire for its restitution. The interstice represents a liminal cinematic structure, open and indeterminate. It is a paroxysmal manifestation of the cut's ability to make two shots both attract and repel each other. For this reason, the interstice can also function as a powerful instrument of political filmmaking.

Instances of interstitial use of montage can be found scattered throughout the history of cinema. Its origins are probably in the age of Dada, in works such as Man Ray's *Return to Reason*. Deleuze, however, notes that the interstice becomes particularly prominent in the cinema after the second World War, and that this tendency reaches its peak during the highly politicized late 1960s and the early 1970s. Deleuze is thinking first and foremost of Jean-Luc Godard, especially his *Ici et ailleurs* (Here and Elsewhere), a project begun in 1970 with Jean-Pierre Gorin under the aegis of the Dziga Vertov Group (and originally titled *Jusqu'à la victoire*) and finished in 1975 with Anne-Marie Miéville.

In this piece of radical film *praxis* (commissioned by Al Fatah), the possibility of developing a revolutionary propaedeutic is critically examined in the context of the 1970–1971 Palestinian Revolution, through a superimposition of, on the one hand, dialectical materialism, and, on the other hand, semiotic analysis of the cinema, in no small measure carried out in the register of *cinema by other means*. The filmmakers explicitly posit the cut as an index of auditory and visual separation, as a marker of spatial and temporal, as well as political, differences between Western Europe (the passivity of "here") and the Middle East (the struggle waged "elsewhere"), between "Arab Revolution and French Revolution," "Foreign and National," "Victory and Defeat," "Dream and Reality." At the same time, the authors also acknowledge that the cut, this elementary feature of film language, is typically concealed by the naturalized movement of images. Godard's voice-over declares early on: "Death is represented in this film by a flow of images.... A flow of images and sounds that hide silence.... A silence that becomes deadly because it is prevented from coming out alive."

The possibility of eroding the classically constructed film text—of replacing a stable and nonporous "big picture" with a variety of uprooted, free-floating image-bits, and thereby foreclosing (if only temporarily) the subject's effortless insertion into the signifying chain—has permeated Godard's cinema since its inception. Already in his first films, Godard sought to problematize, by way of the spatiotemporal caesurae created through jump-cuts (*A bout de souffle/Breathless*, 1959) and narrative chapters (*Vivre sa Vie/My Life to live*, 1962), the normative, seemingly "self-evident," mechanisms of textual causation used to transform lively multiplicities of images into homogeneous units of meaning. By the mid-1960s, his analysis of different modes of spectatorial engagement by the variously fragmented cinematic structures had clearly become intertwined with, on the one hand, linguistic and semiotic concerns and, on the other hand, Marxist critique of ideology. Endless reflexive layering of sounds over images, images over images, and sounds over sounds in the 1966 work *Deux ou trois choses que je sais d'elle* (including the director's own whispering voice, questioning the validity of the film's diegesis), and the commanding, even suffocating, presence of the textual citation in *Weekend* of 1967 (Buñuel, Dumas, Saint-Juste, Brontë, Engels, Carroll, Mozart, the International, and much more), corresponded with the contemporary structural-Marxist (Althusserian) accounts of the all-pervasive character of ideology and the dynamics of "interpellation."[13] On the other hand, in *La Chinoise* (also made in 1967, before *Weekend*), Godard explicitly took his exploration of the cinematic sign along the path of Maoism. Famous for its "anticipation" of the 1968 student rebellion, the film advanced a sustained critique of representational realism (by drastically reducing the depth of compositional space and saturating images with written text, thus complicating the indexicality of the profilmic event with the symbolic valence of the political slogan), but it also concluded with an equivocal stance toward the necessity of revolutionary violence (a stance also assumed in *Weekend*).

Weekend proclaimed "Fin de cinema"—a claim that may be understood as both a call to bring about the end of the mainstream commercial cinema and a diagnosis of the future of the medium as such, if it were to remain rooted in capitalist modes of production and bourgeois ideological values. In the spirit of this proclamation, in 1968, *Le Gai Savoir* staged a Godardian experiment in total suspension of suture, diegetically motivated by "Patricia Lumumba" and "Émile Rousseau's" youthful revolutionary desire to *impose* the *tabula rasa* and strategically undo the meaning of all images and sounds before reconstituting them on entirely new ideological grounds.[14] *Le Gai Savoir* was to clear the way for the future of radical filmmaking—the future the shaping of which would begin with the activities of the Dziga Vertov Group (*British Sounds, Pravda, Vent d'est, Lotte in Italia, Vladimir et Rosa, Jusqu'à la victoire, Tout va bien, Letter to Jane*).[15]

Creating cinematic fissures was defined as an elementary objective of the Dziga Vertov Group. The interstice—commonly evoked through the use of the black screen—became an expression of the Group's desire to enact a political demystification of the cut in a thoroughly *cinefied* world, a world that had become, in Victor Burgin's words, "the *negative* of the film, . . . a space formed from all the many places of transition between cinema and other images in and of everyday life."[16] The theoretical rationale behind this strategy was given one of its clearest expressions in *Vladimir et Rosa* (1971): "What's this black section mean? . . . We've been toting those black frames around for ever so long, since May, 1968, to hide a bladeless knife without a handle. At first, these black frames were shots we couldn't shoot, we'd say they belonged to CBS, and we couldn't afford them, so . . . we'd put black leader instead. Then we realized those black frames were shots we didn't know how to shoot: shots of bourgeois ideology and imperialism and they weren't even black, they were colored, like in any James Bond movie. So we started looking for black images, production relationships, images defining relationships. Our problem is to show colors different from those in bourgeois and imperialist films."

In the case of *Jusqu'à la victoire*, however, efforts to promote "different colors" led to a serious creative and ethical crisis. Could a group of French filmmakers credibly speak in the name of the Palestinian people by shooting footage of the fedayeen in Jordan, Lebanon, and Syria, and then returning to Western Europe to edit these images in the commodified comfort of their "home"? The pertinence of this question was made disturbingly obvious by the fact that most of the guerrillas whom the Dziga Vertov Group filmed between February and July of 1970 had been killed shortly afterward in Amman, in the events of the Black September. Were their images, nonetheless, still to be used? Were they still to appear as actors in a film made by and belonging to someone else? Godard and Miéville eventually decided to build these concerns into the very foundation of the film's structure. Some five years after the original filming took place, *Ici et ailleurs* found a way to speak about the armed struggle in the Middle East by simultaneously engaging in an unsparing auto-critique, confronting the filmmakers' desire to use moving images to simulate life where there was now only death. In Daney's excellent formulation, "What Godard says, very uncomfortably and very honestly, is that the real place of the filmmaker is in the AND."[17] Between "here" and "elsewhere," *in* the interstice.

The true brilliance of *Jusqu'à la victoire/Ici et ailleurs* stems from the fact that its authors discovered the tools with which to most adequately render this "between" separating one film image from the next—life from death, fact from fiction—in the realm of "cinema by other means," immersed in the visual economy of static images "wishing to be more" (a "wish" already apparent in the French Nurse's Dream, in Eisenstein's theoretical observations on The Deluge, but also in a number of Godard's earlier films, such as *Les Carabiniers* (1963), *Made in USA* (1966), and *One Plus One* (1968)). Three slide-viewers are lined up by Godard and Gorin. Each lights up when an image is inserted into it: Adolf Hitler, an advertisement for Israel, Richard Nixon, military aircraft, fedayeen, Golda Meir, Leonid Brezhnev. . . . (see figs. 6.2, 6.3). The pattern of insertion, constituting the movement from one static image to the next, is arbitrary:

1–2–3	1–3–1	1–1–(complete elimination of the 2nd image)–3
1–3–2	1–3–3	. . .
1–3–3	1–2–3	

THE "BETWEEN" OF CINEMA

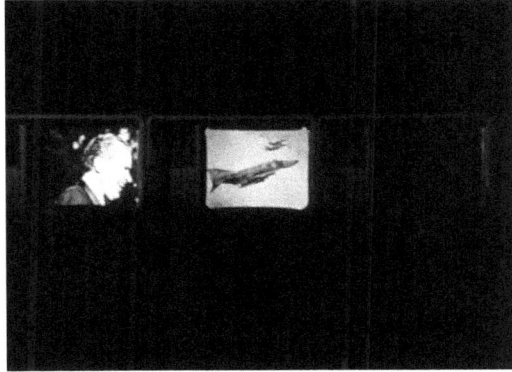

Figure 6.2 *Ici et ailleurs*, Jean-Luc Godard, Jean-Pierre Gorin, Anne-Marie Miéville (1975)

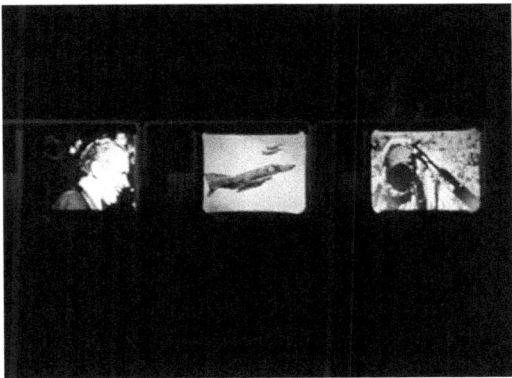

Figure 6.3 *Ici et ailleurs*, Jean-Luc Godard, Jean-Pierre Gorin, Anne-Marie Miéville (1975)

The apparatus the filmmakers created for this paratactic sequence was inspired by the amateur cinematic practice of a Jordanian doctor. Gorin explained: "In Palestine, during the shooting of the film . . . we discovered a doctor in the south of Jordan who was making films with stills. Each week he received some stills from Amman, from El Fatah, edited them, put black spaces into them, made his own commentary in front of the people. He was a real film-maker."[18] A real anti-illusionist filmmaker, more specifically, is what Gorin seems to have meant. For by including a replica of the doctor's home cinematograph into their own film, the Dziga Vertov Group effectively *overlap the space and the function of the interstice with the dynamic of intermittent movement*. By filming in a single shot, in an uninterrupted stretch of cinematic duration, a tripartite sequence of motionless but changing slides, the authors "give us," as Rosalind Krauss would have it, "the moment of [analytic] reflection without destroying its object; . . . at one and the same time the abstract components of film and the reality of its experience."[19] Godard and Gorin invite a structural analogy between the process of filmic signification—specifically, production of meaning through montage: interaction of the psycho-semiotic sewing machine that is the human subject (filmmaker, spectator) with the dispersed "patches" of visual text (shots)—and the manner in which the cinematographic technology transforms the discontinuous passage of serial photograms (the filmstrip) through the projector gate, into an impression of continuous on-screen movement.[20]

What is more, the multiple ruptures inherent in the structure of the film are not only made visible—they are also explicitly identified as essential sites of cinematic labor. In Godard and Gorin's "self-conscious" paracinematographic apparatus, the darkness and the emptiness of the space separating the three slide-viewers coincide with the "emptiness" (direct experience) of the time required to accomplish the transition from one image to the next, the time required to *perform* the interstice. As a barely visible hand maintains the visual flow by changing slides, the linking of images is prevented from dissolving into "invisible" cuts. That is, the cut here does not function as a mere trace of the "*abstracted* labor-time" (Marx) needed to produce it. Instead, each edit figures as a transparent, dereified (and demechanized) set of material relations—a process of unique duration demanding a specific type of work. In the hands of the Dziga Vertov Group, a dynamic sequence of photographic slides has become a means to enact a return of the ordinarily "repressed" cinematic time.[21] This time—the time of the cut (of the "splice," as Pasolini put it)—in turn permits the filmmakers to reflexively expose all cinematic pleasures as inherently ideological: determined by the particular mode of human interaction with film technology.

THE "BETWEEN" OF CINEMA

By the time *Ici et ailleurs* was completed in the mid-1970s, Godard's optimism about the possibilities of direct political action through alternative types of cinematic *praxis* had clearly declined. The Dziga Vertov Group's perspicacious diagnosis of the intersection of desire, labor/production, and ideology in the sphere of cine-economy had acquired a tenor of fatality that was not originally there. Symptomatic in this respect is the film's follow-up to the sequential (dis)ordering of images along the horizontal axis established by the three slide projectors. Godard and Gorin next decided to significantly increase the number of slides/images on display by introducing a rectangular 3 x 3 formation (fig. 6.4).

The outcome of this procedure is a perceptually uncontainable barrage of multiple and thoroughly discontinuous pictures. Contrary to the cinematic effect of movement, of a drift along a singular visual chain—achieved by manipulating the tripartite linear structure of static images—the pictures in this new formation are all unmistakably motion-*less*: experienced by the viewer as permanently static. By initiating a quantitative assault on

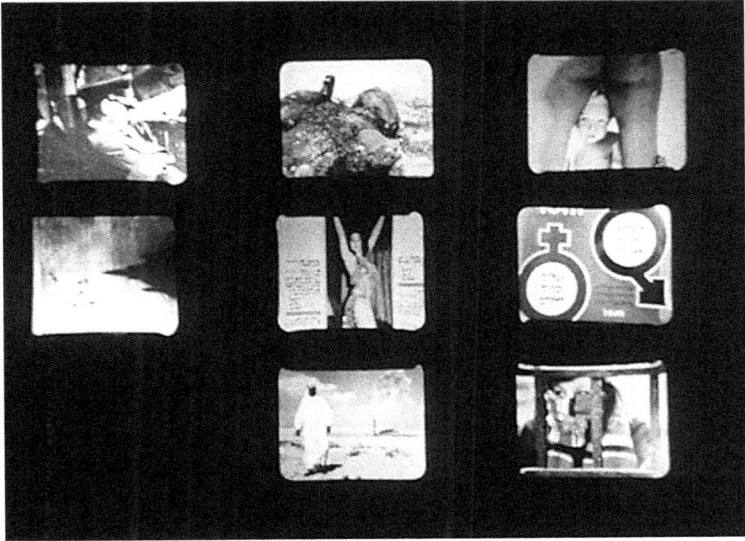

Figure 6.4 *Ici et ailleurs*, Jean-Luc Godard, Jean-Pierre Gorin, Anne-Marie Miéville (1975)

perception (and, consequently, on cognition), the filmmakers have summoned the threat of an effective suspension of suture. In the process, they have also rendered Time heterogeneous. Fully divorced from its former function as an instrument of both kinesis and signifying coherence, time has been permitted to flow on its own terms. Each still image has, therefore, become an index of an entirely autonomous, inassimilable temporal zone. Excluded from this seemingly chaotic signifying polyphony—deprived of the crutches of chronology yet acutely aware of the irretrievable passage of his/her "own" subjective time—the (centered) spectator, too, has become disoriented: a witness to the paralysis of his/her omniscience.[22]

The properly political background of this staging of spectatorial paralysis was lucidly assessed by Daney:

> In 1975, *Ici et ailleurs* came off as either a caprice or a gag. Yet the film spoke of how difficult it had become to intervene—from a militant point of view—with images. Though sympathetic to the Palestinian cause, Godard couldn't find an organizing principle for the images he had shot in the camps. He lacked a *movement* to structure the images. So, as always in such cases, he traded the question for the same question squared: "Why can't I show these images?" I believe this was the last time a great filmmaker joined forces with a political cause (and organization). A long chapter in film history came to a close.[23]

The crisis of the image revealed itself as both a cause and an effect of the crisis of political agency. Godard the *cinéaste*, Godard the *zoon politikon*: clearly, the two names signify only one struggle—the one and only—to define, claim, and uphold an active and responsible subjectivity in the age of "generalized visualization," in the midst of the process of sweeping "amplification" of "optical density of the appearances of the real world."[24] "[T]he film that is, on the whole, a chain-work of images," laments the filmmaker in *Ici et ailleurs*, "renders good account, through this series of images, of my double identity, space and time chained one to the other, as two workers on the assembly line, where each is at the same time the copy and the original of the other.... As a matter of fact, it is likely that a chain also consists in arranging memories, chaining them in a certain order which will get everybody to find one's place on the chain again, that is, to rediscover one's own image. . . . OK, but then: how does one find one's own image in the other's order or disorder? With the agreement or the disagreement of the other? And then: how to construct one's own image?"

"Film is a way to disconnect the normal links of the reality we're subjected to," claimed Gorin in the early 1970s.[25] Thirty-something years later, in works such as *Notre musique* (2004), the relationship between montage, (film) matter, and meaning still appears crucial for Godard. In this Dante-inspired triptych composed of the "Kingdoms" of Hell, Purgatory, and Heaven, the focus is once again on the relationship between cinema and politics, alterity and violence. The stigmatized "other" is identified, as in *Ici et ailleurs*, as a fantasized image of the non-Occidental subject: the Native American, the Palestinian, and, as of recently, the Bosnian Muslim who, with the eruption of the war in the former Yugoslavia, came to play the role of Europe's "internal other" within the mainstream Western political discourse.

As if adhering to a generalized logic of "retrograde remediation" (see chapter 2), *Notre musique* locates the building blocks of contemporary cinema among the ruins of the Old Bridge in the town of Mostar. Destroyed during the 1990s war in Bosnia and Herzegovina, the Bridge (designed in 1566 during the Ottoman Empire) gave way to a void between the two banks of the Neretva River. The work on rebuilding it—piece by piece, stone by stone—began in the late 1990s (fig. 6.5). Numerous stones were retrieved and then labeled according to the positions they once occupied in the overall structure of the bridge (fig. 6.6). Instead of the dismantling movement of *Ici et ailleurs*, a reconstitutive pattern is now sought: how to put all the pieces of the puzzle together again?

The set of stones/numbers is:

37 . . . 40 . . . 42 . . . 7–8 . . . 48 . . . 52 . . . 54 . . . 50 . . . 44 . . . 47 . . . 7 . . . 19 . . . 31–32 . . . 42–43 . . . 45–46–47–48. . . .

How to complete the sequence? How to order it into a meaningful whole? A voice laments over the visual matter Godard's camera encountered in "Purgatory," on the banks of the Neretva:

Figure 6.5 *Notre musique*, Jean-Luc Godard (2004)

Figure 6.6 *Notre musique*, Jean-Luc Godard (2004)

It's not a question of re-establishing tourism between the banks of the Neretva. We must at once restore the past and make the future possible. Combine the pain and the guilt. Two faces and one truth: the bridge. . . . The relationship between me and the Other isn't symmetrical. At first, the Other matters little with respect to me. That's his business. For me, he's the one I'm responsible for. Here, a Muslim and a Croat. . . . The stones were salvaged in two phases. In June 1997 and August 1999. Each stone was identified on a card on which each detail was noted. Its position in the water, its position in the structure, and a description of each face on which clamps were attached. It was like rediscovering the origin of language. You know that before writing was invented at Sumer, they spoke of the past using the word "after" and for the future the word "before."

"It was like rediscovering the origin of language." Rebuilding the Bridge—retracing all the steps of its elaborate montage—is also not unlike mastering Time. But Godard knows too well that this mastery could never entail an easy temporal reversal or a simple erasure and rewriting of the past. Indeed, for every piece of the original that was successfully retrieved from the Neretva, many more new stones had to be cut and fitted into the structure. Inevitably, then, to resurrect the Bridge is, as Philip Rosen would have it, "to construct, on the shell of the old, a modern ideal substitute of an ancient thing."[26] At most, it is to "restore the past" and "make future possible" at the price of assuming the burden of responsibility for the Bridge's destruction in the present. For the rebuilt bridge can always only be the New Old Bridge: a flawed replica of itself,[27] a discomforting object of dubious authenticity somehow out of sync with its "own" time—a sort of social incarnation of the Tauskian "delusion of reference."[28] (Godard's position may, therefore, be directly contrasted with the truly diabolical fantasy about the power of montage to altogether invalidate time, entertained by the same military leaders who ordered the bombing of the Bridge. Seeking to appease the upset public in the wake of their destructive act, these soldiers vowed to build another bridge which, in their own words, was to be "not only bigger and more beautiful," but also— "*older!*"[29])

Godard has claimed: "The history of cinema is first linked to that of medicine. Eisenstein's tortured bodies, beyond Caravaggio and El Greco, speak to Vesalius' dissections.... Since it wanted to imitate the movement of life, it was normal, logical that the film industry first sell itself to the death industry."[30] In Mostar—as well as in Srebrenica, Sarajevo, Vukovar, and other war-torn towns of the former Yugoslavia—the *corps morcellé* became the iconic image of the 1990s. The country's disintegration along its ethnic stitches gave rise to numerous eyewitness, photographic, filmed, and televised accounts of widespread massacres, of bodies torn apart. In 1993, *Je vous salue, Sarajevo*, Godard's video-letter to the inhabitants of the besieged Bosnian capital, addressed exactly this point. Stylistically evocative of Eisenstein's theories of montage within a singular static image, the two-minute exercise in textual dismemberment presented a documentary photo of a Bosnian war atrocity as an accumulation of corporeal fragments: a series of close-ups of the depicted soldiers' and their victims' heads, boots, hands, weapons....

Montage as butchery. Such is the primal scene of film editing, the fantasy of cutting as always already a direct (more or less sanitary) intervention into the flesh.[31] It is from this fantasy of origin that montage has historically drawn its enormous potential to critically reflect on the massive social violence frequent in the twentieth century—from Eisenstein and Buñuel to Hitchcock and Kubrick; from Pasolini and Makavejev to Conner and Sharits.[32] For in the space of the interstice—between two images, in the realm of the cinematic unconscious—there is no distinction between assembly and fragmentation, life and death instincts, reality and artistic imagination.[33]

This point is further developed in *Notre musique*. The film opens with an elaborately edited humanitarian critique of warfare through the ages: costumes, locations, and sets may change, but carnage remains a defeating constant. Godard constructs his "Kingdom of Hell" (as this section is called) by freely mixing countless documentary and fictional images of extermination: Griffith's *Intolerance* (1916) and Eisenstein's *Battleship Potemkin* (1925) and *Alexander Nevsky* (1938) with news reports from Vietnam and Bosnia; Bondarchuk's *War and Peace* (1968), Kurosawa's *Ran* (1985), and Coppola's *Apocalypse Now* (1979) with Nazi propaganda films, footage of concentration camps, and Palestinian guerrilla fighters;

Hollywood cowboys and Indians, with monkeys and penguins struggling amidst natural catastrophes. "They're horrible here with their obsession for cutting off heads," a female voice declares, "It's amazing that anyone's survived."

Significantly, as this carefully paced series of violent images unfolds, its editing seams become progressively looser. "Hell" is, ultimately, revealed as a rather fragmentary collage in which the depicted atrocities are separated by empty intervals of black screen (a technique once favored, as noted earlier, by the Dziga Vertov Group). George Baker has recently argued that "[s]uture is ruptured, but in this rupture it will also be redeemed, perhaps reborn. New connections will be forged out of disconnection.... [R]edeemed suture will foreground lack—create it—posing a connection or relation that is only made possible by absence."[34] Redemption through rupture—this unorthodox designation of suture, equally concerned with the ethical as with the structural dimension of the operation, also accurately sums up the central function of montage in *Notre musique*. What is at stake is no longer the cinematic articulation of a radical political stance inspired by the theoretical lessons of Marxist antihumanism—as was the case with the projects of the Dziga Vertov Group. Rather, it is the possibility of a political revalorization of intersubjectivity that motivates *Notre musique*. Montage here enacts, on the level of form, Godard's search for reserves of solidarity among the shreds of the fabric of humanity.

In "Purgatory," the film's second Kingdom, the filmmaker theoretically elaborates the crevicular structure of his critique of cruelty and its representational fetishization. In a lecture staged for the film (and inspired by an actual lecture Godard delivered in Sarajevo in 2003), he declares: "Yes, the image is joy. But beside it lies the void. All the power of an image can only be expressed through it." He then reflects on the fact that "language arbitrarily divides up things in reality." As if the still visible marks of the wartime devastation of the Bosnian capital had somehow inspired him to pay another tribute to the artisanal magic of the Jordanian doctor-turned-filmmaker (or, for that matter, to the découpage of the comic strip), Godard seeks to convey the violence of this destabilizing partition into sets of twos by engaging yet another modality of "cinema by other means": he shows his audience a sequence of paper-based photographic images paired in his hands (fig. 6.7). Focusing on film language, he emphasizes: "The shot and counter-shot are basics of film grammar.... it's the same thing twice.... Shot and counter-shot, shot and counter-shot...." This binary structure was established early on as "the principle of cinema." As such, asserts Godard, it affirmed and extended our propensity for producing never ending series of signifying differences. Thus: "A man [Cary Grant] and a woman [Rosalind Russell] in a Hawks movie [*His Girl Friday*]," but also the equally cinematic (real? fantasized?) binaries of "Jew and Muslim," "Israeli and Palestinian," "Kosovo and Egypt," "certainty and uncertainty"....

The self and the other, here and elsewhere ... time and again. The "and" is the crevice, but also the stitch.[35] It is the void of the unconscious, as well as the substance of fantasy, of desire, rising from its depths. While they are always marked by particular historico-political circumstances and by different ideological struggles, the desire to build cinematic bridges (like the one intended to reconnect the Muslims and the Croats in Mostar)

Figure 6.7 *Notre musique*, Jean-Luc Godard (2004)

and the desire to uphold cinematic gaps (like the one separating France from Palestine) stem from the same, recurring structural pattern of presence and absence—they are but the two faces of the suturing relation.

The "and," the interstice—the gutter!—is the engine of the cinematic imaginary. It is where the filmmaker *and* the spectator reside. Such is the active principle of cinema—whatever the state of its being, whatever the concrete, material (always material) means of its execution.

> *I have become what I was when I first started*
> *being interested in cinema. I am a nothing which*
> *you throw into the gutter.*
>
> —Jean-Luc Godard[36]

"To be making a film is the same as watching a film and vice versa."
—Slobodan Šijan

"Things can only act on the mind through a certain state of matter...."
—Antonin Artaud

Plate 0   Vladimir Petek, *Encounters* (1963)

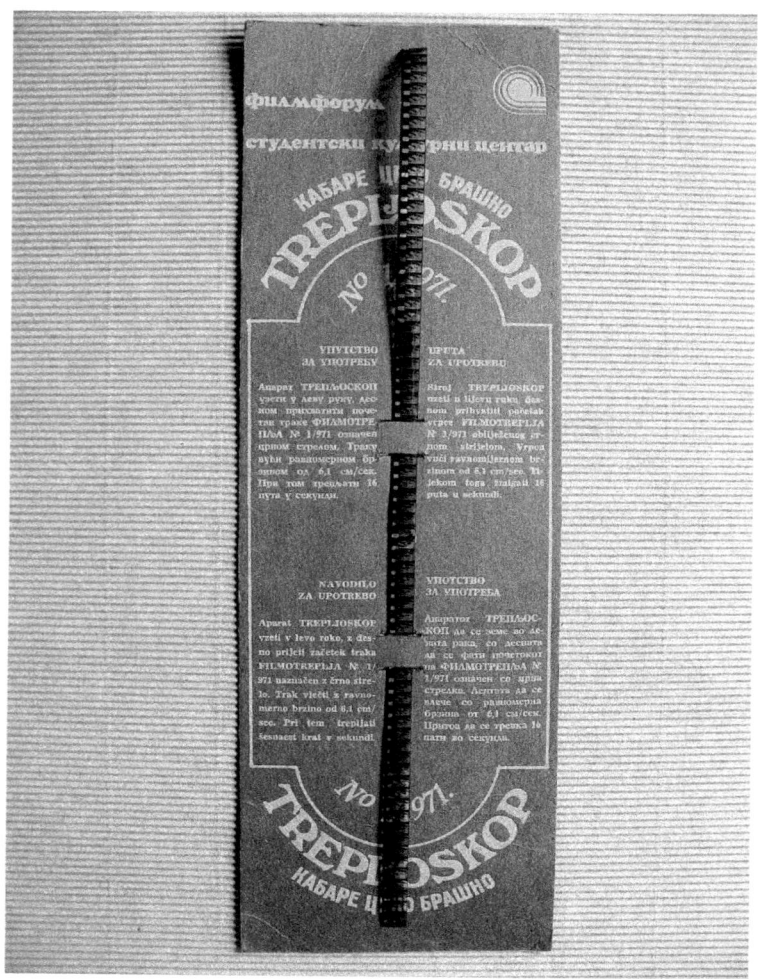

Plate 1   Milenko Avramović & Miša Jovanović, *Blink-O-Scope* (1971), courtesy of Akademski filmski centar, Dom kulture "Studentski grad," Belgrade

Plate 2 Kurt Schwitters, *Construction for Noble Ladies* (1919) © 2011 Artists Rights Society (ARS), New York / VG Bild-Kunst, Bonn; photo: Erich Lessing / Art Resource, NY

Plate 3 Boško Tokin, *Leave Your Prejudice Behind* (1929), courtesy of Marinko Sudac (Marinko Sudac Collection)

Plate 4 Radojica Živanović Noe, *Curtain at the Window* © Museum of Contemporary Art, Belgrade

Plate 5 Aleksandar Vučo and Dušan Matić, *The Frenzied Marble* (1930) © Museum of Contemporary Art, Belgrade

Plate 6 Raoul Hausmann, *The Self-Portrait of the Dadasoph* (1920) © 2011 Artists Rights Society (ARS), New York / ADAGP, Paris

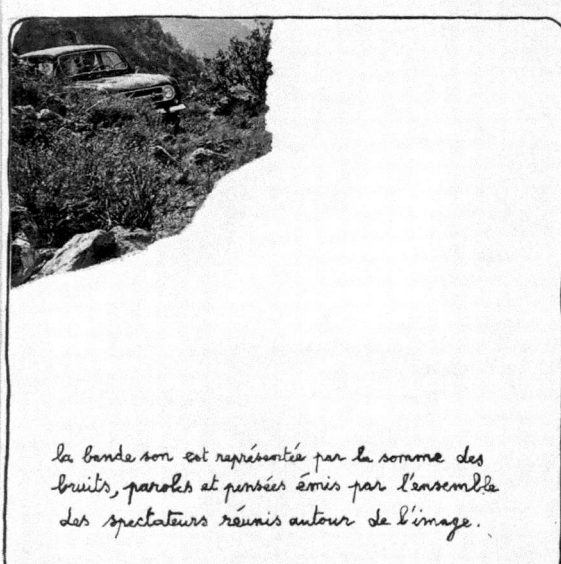

Plate 7 Roland Sabatier, *Entrac'te* (1969) © 2011 Artists Rights Society (ARS), New York / ADAGP, Paris; image courtesy of the artist

Plate 8 Ljubiša Jocić, *Ljubiša Jocić, aka Ljuba the Miraculous, Feeding the Dada Machine* (1937), courtesy of Marinko Sudac (*Marinko Sudac Collection*)

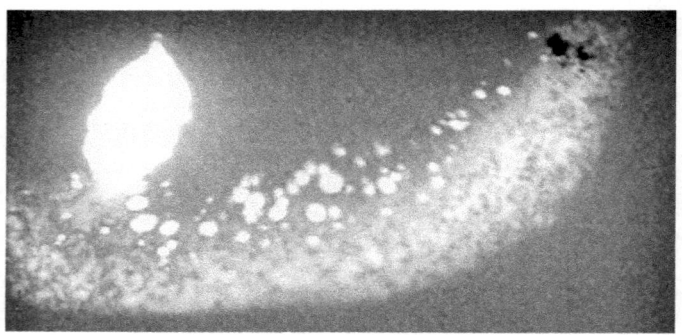

Plate 9 Zlatko Hajdler, *Kariokinesis* (1965)

Plate 10 Tomislav Gotovac, *Cinema Tickets* (1964), courtesy of Marinko Sudac (*Marinko Sudac Collection*)

Plate 11 Slobodan Šijan, *900 Lombard, San Francisco* (1998), from the series *Vertigo*, courtesy of the artist

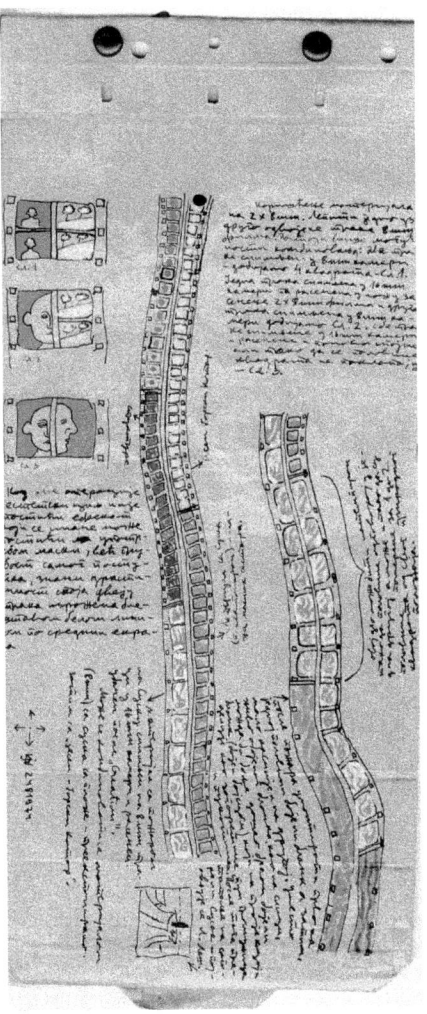

Plate 12 Slobodan Šijan, *Bag-Film* (1974), courtesy of the artist

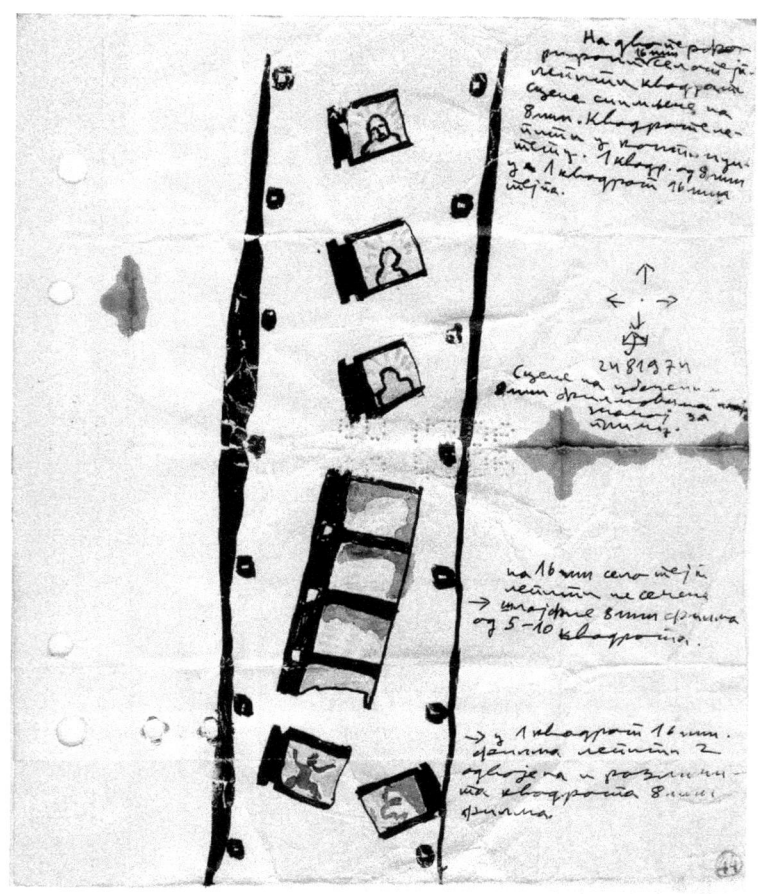

Plate 13 Slobodan Šijan, *Onto Double-Perforated…* (1974), courtesy of the artist

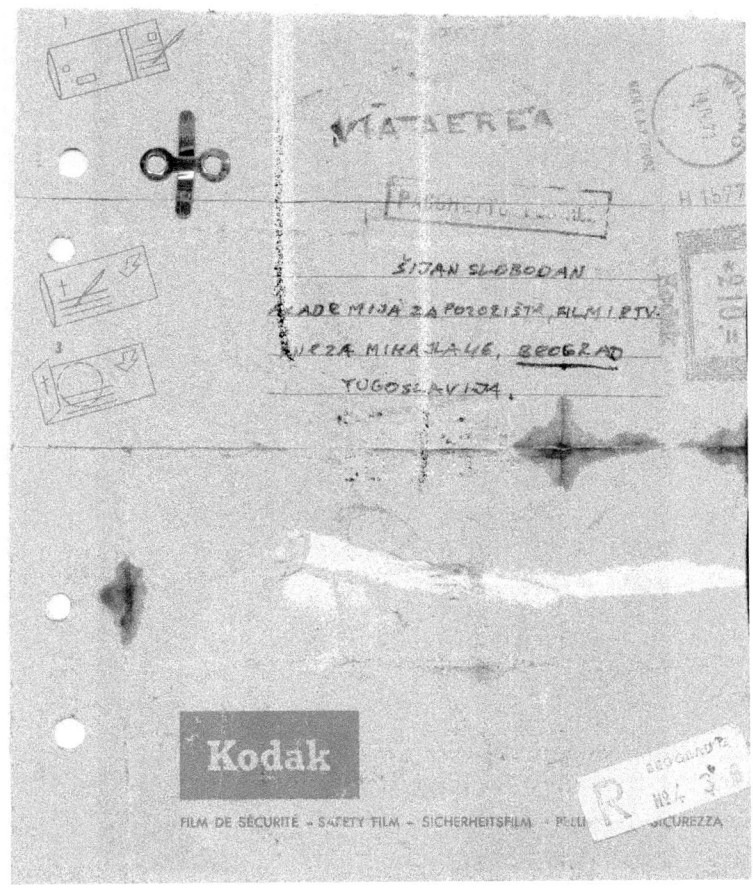

Plate 14 Bag for shipping film, used by Slobodan Šijan to produce the work in color plate 11 (photo courtesy of the artist)

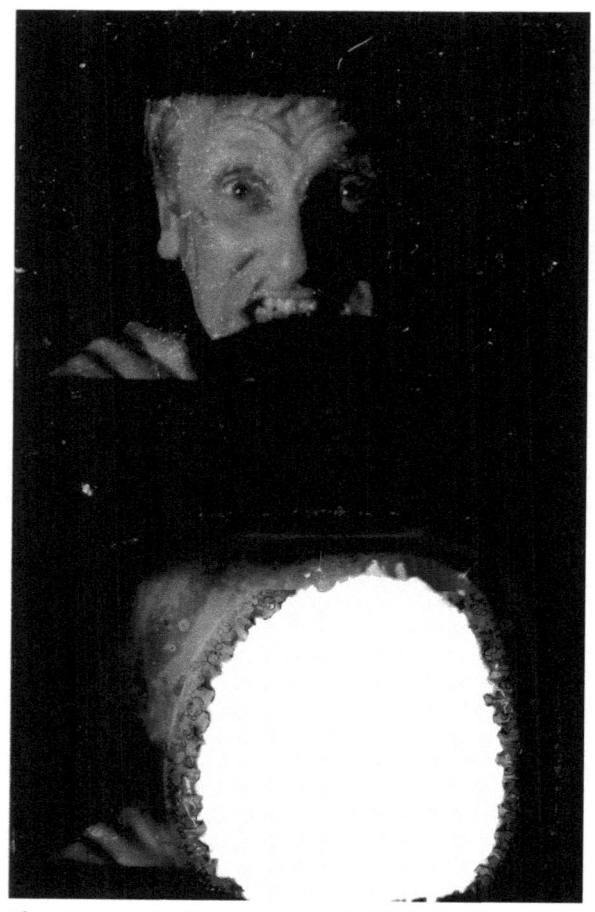

Plate 15 Burning frames at the end of Slobodan Šijan's film, *The Marathon Family* (1982); experiment also known as *Media Suicide, Investigation No. 4—Film, 1981* (courtesy of the artist)

NOTES

Preamble

1. Laurent Mannoni, *The Great Art of Light and Shadow: Archaeology of the Cinema* (Exeter, UK: University of Exeter Press, 2000), 467.
2. "Around film" is a phrase I borrow from the filmmaker Slobodan Šijan, whose non-cinematographic film works I discuss in chapter 5.
3. Miroslav Bata Petrović, *Alternativni film u Beogradu od 1950 do 1990 godine* (Beograd: Dom kulture Studentski grad, 2008), 301.
4. Philippe Dubois, "Photography Mise-en-Film: Autobiographical (Hi)stories and Psychic Apparatuses," *Fugitive Images: From Photography to Video*, ed. Patrice Petro (Bloomington: Indiana University Press, 1995), 154.

Chapter 1

1. I borrow this formulation from Denis Hollier, *Against Architecture: The Writings of Georges Bataille* (Cambridge: MIT Press, 1989), 28.
2. Georges Bataille, "Base Materialism and Gnosticism," *Visions of Excess* (Minneapolis: University of Minnesota Press, 1985), 50–51.
3. Stephen Kovács, *From Enchantment to Rage* (Rutherford: Farleigh Dickinson University Press, 1980), 116–117.
4. László Moholy-Nagy, "Production Reproduction," *Painting, Photography, Film* (Cambridge: MIT Press, 1987), 30–31.

5. Tristan Tzara, "Manifesto on feeble love and bitter love," *Dada Painters and Poets: An Anthology*, 2nd ed., ed. Robert Motherwell (Cambridge: Belknap Press of Harvard University Press, 1981), 92.
6. Barbara Rose, "Kinetic Solutions to Pictorial Problems: The Films of Man Ray and Moholy-Nagy," *Artforum* 10, no.1 (1971): 70.
7. Jean-Francois Lyotard, *Libidinal Economy* (Bloomington: Indiana University Press, 1974), 26.
8. Lyotard is quoted from Allen S. Weiss, *Perverse Desire and the Ambiguous Icon* (Albany: SUNY Press, 1994), 64–65. See also Lyotard, *Libidinal Economy*, 25.
9. Valentine de Saint-Point, "Futurist Manifesto of Lust," *Futurist Manifestos*, ed. Umbro Apollonio (Boston: MFA Publications, 1973), 71.
10. See Marcel Duchamp, "The Green Box," *The Writings of Marcel Duchamp*, ed. Michel Sanouillet and Elmer Peterson (New York: Da Capo Press, 2005), 39, 42–43.
11. Monny de Boully, "Iksion" in *Dve avanturističke poeme* (Belgrade: Biblioteka Hipnos, 1926).
12. Ljubomir Micić, "Zenitozofija ili energetika stvaralačkog zenitizma," *Pisci kao kritičari posle prvog svetskog rata*, ed. Marko Nedić (Novi Sad: Matica srpska, 1975), 524.
13. Ibid., 525.
14. Ibid., 526.
15. Micić, "Kategorički imperativ zenitističke pesničke škole," *Pisci kao kritičari*, 521.
16. Ljubomir Micić, "Reči u prostoru 15" *Zenit* 9 (November 1921): 12.
17. Boško Tokin, "Evropski Pesnik Ivan Goll," *Zenit* 1 (February 1921): 8.
18. Boško Tokin, "Kinematografske pesme," *Antologija pesništva srpske avangarde, 1902–1934*, ed. Gojko Tešić (Novi Sad: Svetovi, 1993), 218.
19. Micić, "Kategorički imperativ zenitizma," *Pisci kao kritičari*, 530.
20. André Breton, "Manifesto of Surrealism," *Manifestoes of Surrealism* (Ann Arbor: University of Michigan Press, 1972), 26.
21. Dawn Ades, *Dada and Surrealism* (Woodbury, NY: Barron's, 1978), 37.
22. See Georges Bataille, "Formless," *Visions of Excess*, 31. See also Yve-Alain Bois and Rosalind Krauss, *Formless: A User's Guide* (New York: Zone Books, 1997), esp. 15, 21–40, 235–252; and Pierre Fédida, "The Movement of the Informe," *Qui Parle* 10 no. 1 (Fall/Winter 1996): 49–62.
23. This, of course, is a variation on Marshall McLuhan's well-known thesis (developed in the 1960s): in the beginning and in the end, "the medium is the message." See Marshall McLuhan, "The Medium is the Message" in *Understanding Media* (Cambridge: MIT Press, 1994), 7–21.
24. Dragan Aleksić, "Dadaizam," *Pisci kao kritičari*, 543–544. As the quote makes clear, Aleksić was particularly fond of Schwitters's brand of Dadaism. As a result of the carelessness of the post-World War II Yugoslav cultural institutions, after

Aleksić's death in 1958, his entire archive of Yugo-Dada was irretrievably lost. It was discarded as refuse—buried under heaps of waste at Belgrade's central garbage depository.

25. Jacques Lacan, *Seminar XX* (New York: W. W. Norton, 1995), 49. In her essay "De Stijl, Its Other Face: Abstraction and Cacaphony, or What Was the Matter with Hegel?," Annette Michelson terms sound poetry "cacaphony" (after "caca," the word used by children to refer to excrement, waste).
26. Friedrich A. Kittler, *Discourse Networks* (Stanford: Stanford University Press, 1990), 212.
27. Marcella Lista, "Raoul Hausmann's Optophone: 'Universal language' and the Intermedia," *The Dada Seminars*, ed. Leah Dickerman with Matthew S. Witkovsky (Washington: The National Gallery of Art, 2005), 93.
28. Dragan Aleksić, "Tatlin. HP/s + Čovek," *Zenit* no. 9 (November 1921): 8.
29. Ibid., 8–9.
30. Dragan Aleksić, "Beograd, film, filmski Beograd i beogradski film," *Beogradski filmski kritičarski krug I (1896–1960)*, ed. Ranko Munitić (Niš: NKC Art Press, 2002), 77–78.

Chapter 2

1. Man Ray, *Self Portrait* (Boston: Little, Brown and Company, 1963), 232.
2. See Louis Aragon, "On Décor," and André Breton, "As in a Wood," in *The Shadow and Its Shadow*, ed. Paul Hammond (San Francisco: City Lights Books, 2000), 50–54, 72–77.
3. Kovács, *From Enchantment to Rage*, 151.
4. Man Ray, "Cinemage," *The Shadow and Its Shadow*, 133.
5. Jonathan Walley, "The Material of Film and the Idea of Cinema: Contrasting Practices in Sixties and Seventies Avant-Garde Film," *October* 103 (Winter 2003): 18.
6. Walley, "The Material of Film," 26. Filmmaker and theorist Alexander Kluge made a related claim in the late 1970s: "[F]ilm takes recourse to the spontaneous workings of the imaginative faculty which has existed for tens of thousands of years. Since the Ice Age approximately (or earlier), streams of images, of so-called associations, have moved through the human mind, prompted to some extent by an anti-realistic attitude, by the protest against an unbearable reality. They have an order which is organized by spontaneity. Laughter, memory, and intuition, hardly the product of mere education, are based on this raw material of associations. This is the more-than-ten-thousand-year-old-cinema to which the invention of the film strip, projector and screen only provided a technological response. This also explains the particular proximity of film to the spectator and its

affinity to experience." Alexander Kluge, "On Film and the Public Sphere," *New German Critique* 24/25 (Fall/Winter 1981–1982): 209.
7. Walley, "The Material of Film," 23.
8. Notably, Walley too seeks support for his "dematerialization" thesis in some of Sharits' work.
9. Walley, "The Material of Film," 24.
10. László Moholy-Nagy, *Painting, Photography, Film*, 26.
11. Moholy-Nagy, *Painting, Photography, Film*, 27. Around 1921–1922, Russian avant-gardist Velimir Khlebnikov similarly wrote: "Art habitually makes use of desire in the science of wielding power. I have a desire to take something before I actually take it. He said that art had to achieve the same status as science, and industry, Technology with a capital T. But a thousand years before the invention of the airplane, wasn't there the magic carpet? And the Greek Daedalus two thousand before? Captain Nemo in Jules Verne's novel sailed in a submarine a half a century before the Germans' mighty victory at the . . . islands. Wells's invention of the time machine. If an artist must take a back seat to science, life, events, then how is he supposed to foresee, foretell, forewill?" Velimir Khlebnikov, *Letters and Theoretical Writings, Collected Works*, vol.1, ed. Charlotte Douglas (Cambridge: Harvard University Press, 1987), 409.
12. Moholy-Nagy, *Painting, Photography, Film*, 122.
13. Moholy-Nagy, *Painting, Photography, Film*, 44.
14. See Raoul Hausmann, "Optophonetik," *Sieg Triumph Tabak mit Bohnen: Texte bis 1933*, vol. 2 (Munich: Edition Text + Kritik, 1982), 53. The English translation of the German text is from Jacques Donguy, "Machine Head: Raoul Hausmann and the Optophone," *Leonardo* 34, no. 3 (2001): 218.
15. See Edgar Morin, *The Cinema, or the Imaginary Man* (Minneapolis: University of Minnesota Press, 2005), 34, 41. Written in the mid-1950s, Morin's book has only recently been translated into English. It represents a crucial, direct link (a long-standing "missing link," where English-language readership is concerned) between Bazin's elaboration of film's ontological realism and the 1970s psychoanalytic theories of the medium. For a perceptive summary of Morin's central argument, see Soyoung Yoon's review of *The Cinema* in *Film Quarterly* 60, no. 3 (Spring 2007): 94–95.
16. Raoul Hausmann, "Filmdämmerung," *Sieg Triumph Tabak mit Bohnen: Texte bis 1933*, vol. 2 (Munich: Edition Text + Kritik, 1982), 119.
17. Quoted from Timothy O. Benson, *Raoul Hausmann and Berlin Dada* (Ann Arbor: UMI Research Press, 1987), 144. In the mid 1920s Hausmann intended to make a film on Hanns Hörbiger's World Ice Theory (Welteislehre). See Bernd Stiegler, "Raoul Hausmanns Theorie der Optophonetik und die Erneuerung der menschlichen Wahrnehmung durch die Kunst," *Hofmannsthal-Jahrbuch. Zur Europäischen Moderne* no.10 (2002): 342.

18. Benson, *Raoul Hausmann and Berlin Dada*, 144.
19. Morin, *The Cinema, or the Imaginary Man*, 203.
20. Milanka Todić, *Nemoguće: Umetnost nadrealizma* (Belgrade: Muzej primenjene umetnosti, 2002), 193.
21. See Raoul Hausmann, "Optophonetik," in *Sieg Triumph Tabak mit Bohnen: Texte bis 1933*, vol. 2, 51.
22. Stephen Heath, *Questions of Cinema* (Bloomington: Indiana University Press, 1981), 224.
23. Walter Benjamin, "The Work of Art in the Age of Its Technological Reproducibility," in *The Work of Art in the Age of Its Technological Reproducibility, and Other Writings on Media*, eds. Michael W. Jennings, Brigid Doherty, and Thomas Y. Levin (Cambridge: Belknap Press, 2008), 35.
24. I partially draw here on Edwin T. Layton, Jr.'s thesis about design as the structural pattern of technology and as "an attribute of a human being which may be expressed in an object but which is not identical with the object itself. At the outset, design is an adaptation of means to some preconceived end. This I take to be the central purpose of technology. The first stages of design involve a conception in a person's mind which, by degrees, is translated into a detailed plan or design. But it is only in the last stages, in drafting the blueprints, that design can be reduced to technique. And it is still later that design is manifested in tools and things made. Design involves a structure or pattern, a particular combination of details or component parts, and it is precisely the gestalt or pattern that is of the essence for the designer." Edwin T. Layton, Jr., "Technology as Knowledge," *Technology and Culture* 15, no.1 (January 1974): 37–38.
25. Barbara Rose, "Kinetic Solutions to Pictorial Problems: The Films of Man Ray and Moholy-Nagy," *Artforum* 10, no. 1 (1971): 69.
26. Gilles Deleuze, *Foucault* (Minneapolis: University of Minnesota Press, 1988), 35.
27. This is perhaps an aspect of what Rosalind Krauss has in mind when she writes of "the idea of a medium as such, a medium as a set of conventions derived from (but not identical with) the material conditions of a given technical support, conventions out of which to develop a form of expressiveness that can be both projective and mnemonic." See Rosalind Krauss, "Reinventing the Medium" *Critical Inquiry* 25, no. 2 (Winter 1999): 296.
28. George Baker, "Entr'acte" *October* 105 (Summer 2003): 160.
29. In 1966, American avant-garde filmmaker Hollis Frampton entirely based his short work *Information* on precisely such an elementary definition of the cinema. In this film, traces/circles of light—which could easily have been cast by a flashlight like the one seen in *Portrait of Max Jacob*—incessantly move across the screen. In Frampton's own words, *Information* is: "Hypothetical 'first film' . . . constructed from scratch on reasonable principles, given: 1) camera; 2) rawstock; 3) a single bare light bulb."

30. For a detailed account of Picabia's involvement with the cinema in general and his role in the making of *Entr'acte* in particular, see Kovacs, *From Enchantment to Rage*, 65–113.
31. For an informative overview of the activities of the Blue Blouse theater collectives, see František Deák, "Blue Blouse (1923–1928)," *The Drama Review: TDR* 17, no. 1 (March 1973): 35–46.
32. Francis Picabia, "The Law of Accommodation Among the One-Eyed," *I Am a Beautiful Monster: Poetry, Prose, and Provocation* (Cambridge: MIT Press, 2007): 331.
33. See Baker, "Entr'acte," 165. See also "Intermission: Dada Cinema," chapter 5 in Baker's book *The Artwork Caught by the Tail: Francis Picabia and Dada in Paris* (Cambridge: MIT Press, 2007), 289–348.
34. Jay David Bolter and Richard Grusin, *Remediation: Understanding New Media* (Cambridge: Massachusetts: MIT Press, 2000), especially 6–9 and 45–48.
35. Bolter and Grusin recognize that "[o]ur culture conceives of each medium or constellation of media as it responds to, redeploys, competes with, and reforms other media. In the first instance we may think of something like a historical progression, of newer media remediating older ones and in particular of digital media remediating their predecessors. But we are offering a genealogy of affiliations, not a linear history, and in this genealogy, *older media can also remediate newer ones*." Bolter and Grusin, *Remediation: Understanding New Media*, 55 (emphasis added). However, none of the examples offered by the authors are strongly marked by the sense of inherent "failure" evident when the cinema is presented in the form of a sculptural assemblage (Vučo and Matić), a diagrammatic drawing (Picabia, Man Ray), or a theatrical performance (Picabia). Bolter and Grusin speak of television "refashion[ing] itself in the image of the World Wide Web," and of "film incorporat[ing] and attempt[ing] to contain computer graphics within its own linear form"—on a strictly practical level, both of these are entirely possible: television can, indeed, refashion itself in the image of the World Wide Web, and film is capable of incorporating computer graphics.
36. Walter Benjamin, "The Work of Art in the Age of Its Technological Reproducibility," *The Work of Art in the Age of Its Technological Reproducibility, and Other Writings on Media*, eds. Michael W. Jennings, Brigid Doherty, and Thomas Y. Levin (Cambridge: Belknap Press, 2008), 38.
37. Benjamin, "The Work of Art," 52n30.
38. In Benjamin's case, it is his emphasis on obsolescence and restitution—prominent in such essays as "Paris, Capital of the Nineteenth Century" and "Surrealism"—that complicates a possible charge of technological essentialism. For an extensive discussion of Benjamin's investment in the dynamics of restitution, see Susan Buck-Morss, *The Dialectics of Seeing* (Boston:

MIT Press, 1991), especially chapter 5 ("Mythic Nature: Wish Image"). For a canonical critique of technological essentialism/determinism in the media, see Raymond Williams's study, *Television* (London: Routledge, 2003), 4–7, 129–138.

39. Thomas Elsaesser, "Dada/Cinema?," *Dada and Surrealist Film*, ed. Rudolf E. Kuenzli (Cambridge: MIT Press; 1996), 21.
40. Rosalind Krauss, "Reinventing the Medium," 292.
41. In 1919, Viktor Tausk's study of persecutory delusion in schizophrenia introduced the notion of the "influencing machine"—a concept based on a multitude of patients' disturbing accounts of the fantasmatic apparatuses experienced as manipulating and overtaking their minds. It is interesting to note that Tausk's study was written the same year Man Ray painted his *Admiration of the Orchestrelle for the Cinematograph* and Hausmann made *Gurk* and *Synthetic Cinema of Painting*. See Viktor Tausk, "On the Origin of the Influencing Machine in Schizophrenia," *Sexuality, War and Schizophrenia* (New Brunswick: Transaction Publishers, 1991). See also Allen S. Weiss's inspiring discussion of "influencing machines" in *Breathless* (Middletown, CT: Wesleyan University Press, 2002), 99–103.

Chapter 3

1. Monny de Boully, "Doktor Hipnison ili Tehnika Života," in *Avangardni film 1895–1935*, vol. 2, ed. Branko Vučićević (Belgrade: Dom Kulture-Studentski Grad, 1990), 12.
2. "Paper movie" is Branko Vučićević's term, from his book *Paper Movies* (Zagreb, Belgrade: Arkzin & B92, 1998).
3. See Richard Abel, "Exploring the Discursive Field of the Surrealist Scenario Text," in *Dada and Surrealist Film*, ed. Rudolf E. Kuenzli (New York: Willis Locker & Owens, 1987), 58.
4. See Christian Janicot, *Anthologie du cinéma invisible* (Paris: Éditions Jean-Michel Place/ARTE Éditions, 1995).
5. Gojko Tešić, "Kontekst za čitanje pripovetke srpskog modernizma i avangarde," *Antologija srpske avangardne književnosti*, ed. Tešić (Novi Sad: Bratstvo jedinstvo, 1989), xv.
6. Ibid.
7. Branko Vučićević, ed. *Splav meduze* (Ljubljana: Viba film; 1980), no pagination.
8. Although written in 1921, Khlebnikov's "The Radio of the Future" was first published in 1927 in *Krasnaia nov'*, n8. The English translation of the text can be found in Velimir Khlebnikov, *Letters and Theoretical Writings, Collected Works*, vol. 1, 392–396.

9. On this point, see Aleksandar Flaker, *Ruska avangarda* (Zagreb: SN Liber & Globus, 1984), 443–445.
10. Flaker, *Ruska avangarda*, 450.
11. In 1930, the Constructivist aspiration toward a total synthesis of sound and image and of radio and the camera-based media (apparent also in Khlebnikov's writings) became a *cinematic reality*. That year, Dziga Vertov made his first sound feature—*the* radio-film if there ever was one: *Enthusiasm: The Symphony of the Donbass.*
12. Marko Ristić, *Uoči nadrealizma* (Belgrade: Nolit, 1985), 289.
13. Louis Aragon, *Le Paysan de Paris* (Paris: Éditions Gallimard, 1926).
14. Monny de Boully, *Zlatne bube* (Belgrade: Prosveta, 1968), 127.
15. André Breton, "The Mediums Enter," *The Lost Steps* (Lincoln: University of Nebraska Press, 1996), 91.
16. Boully, *Zlatne bube*, 135.
17. Paul Hammond, ed., "Off a Tangent," *The Shadow and Its Shadow* (London: BFI, 1978), 5.
18. Hal Foster, *Compulsive Beauty* (Cambridge: MIT Press, 1993), 59.
19. Milanka Todić, *Nemoguće: Umetnost nadrealizma* (Belgrade: Muzej primenjene umetnosti, 2003), 69.
20. Marko Ristić, "Prve beleške of filmu," *Beogradski filmski kritičarski krug I*, 52.
21. Ristić, *Uoči nadrealizma*, 123.
22. Breton's written elaboration of the notion of "cinematic displacement" (*dépaysement*) appeared only in 1951 in a text called "As in a Wood" ("Comme dans un bois," *L'Âge du cinéma*, nos. 4–5 [August–November 1951]). For an informative discussion of this text, see Steven Kovács, *From Enchantment to Rage*, 36–38.
23. Vučićević, *Avangardni film 1895–1935*, vol. 2, 11.
24. Ibid. Arato, of course, was not alone among the 1920s avant-gardists in inventing nose-art. In the 1921 "PREsentist" manifesto, Raoul Hausmann made a claim for the scientifically grounded arts of "haptism" and "odorism." In his praise of "the radio of the future," Khlebnikov imagined a long-distance transmission of scents by means of radio waves. One of the projected functions of these scents would have been to physiologically stimulate the listener's gastronomic fantasies. Italian Futurist Carlo Carrà and the Czech avant-gardist Karel Teige also experimented with the "art of scents."
25. Boully, *Zlatne bube*, 145.
26. Ranko Munitić, *Alisa na putu kroz podzemlje i kroz svemir* (Belgrade: Dečje novine, 1986), 18.
27. Allen S. Weiss, "Between the Sign of the Scorpion and the Sign of the Cross: *L'Age d'or*," in *Dada and Surrealist Film*, ed. Rudolf E. Kuentzli (New York: Willis Locker & Owen, 1987), 164.
28. Jacques Baron, "Crustaceans," in Georges Bataille, Michel Leiris, et al., *Encyclopaedia Acephalica* (London: Atlas Press, 1995), 38–40.

29. The genre of "visual literature," popular at the time, was most substantially theorized by Moholy-Nagy and Karel Teige.
30. Todić, *Nemoguće*, 59.
31. Todić, *Nemoguće*, 60.
32. Neil Baldwin, *Man Ray: American Artist* (Da Capo Press, 2000), 136. See also Man Ray, "Cinemage," *The Shadow and Its Shadow*, 133.
33. On the associative and transformative powers that the Surrealists attributed to the spoon, see André Breton, *Mad Love* (Lincoln: University of Nebraska Press, 1987), 30–34.
34. Aleksandar Vučo, "Ljuskari na prsima," *Nemoguće* (May 1930): 68.
35. Morin, *The Cinema, or the Imaginary Man*, 42.
36. In "The Jesuve" and "The Pineal Eye," George Bataille's discussion of evolution and of human and animal anatomy persistently aims at *debasing* the eye by aligning it with the anus and other lower body parts. See Georges Bataille, *Visions of Excess*, 73–90.
37. Koča Popović, "Prodana sudbina," *Nadrealizam i postnadrealizam* (Belgrade: Prosveta, 1985), 19.
38. In "The Outline for a Phenomenology of the Irrational," a major theoretical text by the Yugoslav Surrealists, Koča Popović and Marko Ristić elaborate the paranoiac method of interpretation as the most extreme form of anti-idealist dialectical abstraction; they call this type of multiperspectivalist destabilization of vision "dialectical polyscopia." See Koča Popović and Marko Ristić, *Nacrt za jednu fenomenologiju iracionalnog* (Belgrade: Prosveta, 1985), 16–17, 37–40.
39. Popović, "Prodana sudbina," *Nadrealizam i postnadrealizam*, 19–20.
40. On the notion of "extimacy" see Jacques Lacan, *The Seminar, Book VII, The Ethics of Psychoanalysis, 1959–1960* (New York: W. W. Norton, 1992), 139.
41. Guillaume Apollinaire, "The False Messiah, Amphion," *Selected Writings of Guillaume Apollinaire*, trans. Roger Shattuck (New York: New Directions Books, 1971).
42. Apollinaire, "The New Spirit and the Poets," *Selected Writings*, 228, 237.
43. Abel, "Exploring the Discursive Field," 59.
44. Abel, "Exploring the Discursive Field," 60.
45. Abel, "Exploring the Discursive Field," 60.
46. See Peter Christensen's highly informative essay "Benjamin Fondane's 'Scenarii intournables,'" in *Dada and Surrealist Film*, 72–85.
47. Christensen, "Benjamin Fondane's 'Scenarii intournables,'" 72.
48. Benjamin Fondane, *Écrits pour le cinema*, ed. Michel Carassou (Paris: Plasma, 1984), 20.
49. Alain and Odette Virmaux, *Le Grand Jeu et le cinéma* (Paris: Paris Experimental, 1996), 114–117.
50. Virmaux, *Le Grand Jeu et le cinema*, 115–116.

51. Virmaux, *Le Grand Jeu et le cinema*, 116. English translation by Phil Powrie, "Film-Form-Mind: The Hegelian Follies of Roger Gilbert-Lecomte," *Quarterly Review of Film and Video* 12, no. 4 (1991): 19.
52. Antonin Artaud, "The Precocious Old Age of Cinema," *Collected Works*, vol. 3 (London: Calder & Boyars; 1972), 79.
53. Ibid., 77.
54. Ibid., 76.
55. Ibid., 77–78.
56. Monny de Boully, "A.B.C.D ...,"*Avangardni pisci kao kritičari*, ed. Gojko Tešic (Novi Sad: Matica srpska; 1994), 275.
57. Ibid.
58. Boully, "A.B.C.D ...," 274.

Chapter 4

1. In this book I use the term "cinefication" in an expanded sense—to refer, beyond the development of a network of film distribution and exhibition in a given society (the term's original meaning, initiated in the Soviet Union of the 1920s), to a variety of avant-garde theoretical and practical models that conceive of reality itself in pronouncedly cinematic terms. For historical accounts of "cinefication" in the Soviet Union see Richard Taylor, *The Politics of the Soviet Cinema 1917–1929* (Cambridge: Cambridge University Press, 1979), 87–88; Peter Kenez, *Cinema and Soviet Society from the Revolution to the Death of Stalin* (London: I. B. Tauris, 2001), 73–84. For a more expanded use of the term (related to my own), see James Goodwin, *Eisenstein, Cinema, and History* (Urbana: University of Illinois Press, 1993), 31–32.
2. Yuri Tsivian, "Early Russian Cinema: Some Observations," in *Inside the Film Factory*, eds. Richard Taylor and Ian Christie (London: Routledge, 1991), 9.
3. Mikhail Yampolsky, "Kuleshov's Experiments and the New Anthropology of the Actor," *Inside the Film Factory*, 31–50.
4. See *Kuleshov on Film: Writings of Lev Kuleshov*, ed. Ronald Levaco (Berkeley: University of California Press, 1974), 10. See also Jay Leyda, *Kino: A History of the Russian and Soviet Film* (Princeton: Princeton University Press, 1983), 159–160.
5. In the inscription written in the back of his 1920 work, *Proun AII*, Lissitzky claims: "To understand the infinity of the world which surrounds us, we enclose it in the space of the circle, in which all the elements are in a state of balanced rotating motion."
6. El Lissitzky, "The Film of El's Life," *El Lissitzky: Life, Letters, Texts*, ed. Sophie Lissitzky-Kuppers (Greenwich, CT: New York Graphic Society Ltd., 1968), 325.

7. Annette Michelson, "Introduction," *Kino-Eye: The Writings of Dziga Vertov* (Berkeley: University of California Press, 1984), xix.
8. Dziga Vertov, "From Kino-Eye to Radio-Eye," *Kino-Eye: The Writings of Dziga Vertov*, ed. Annette Michelson (Berkeley: University of California Press, 1984), 91.
9. Annette Michelson, "The Wings of Hypothesis," *Montage and Modern Life 1919–1942*, ed. Matthew Teitelbaum (Cambridge: MIT Press, 1992), 72–73.
10. Vertov, "From Kino-Eye to Radio-Eye," 72–73.
11. Timothy Murray, *Like a Film* (New York: Routledge, 1993), 3.
12. Walter Benjamin, "The Work of Art in the Age of Its Technological Reproducibility," 34–35.
13. In the early 1960s, William S. Burroughs took the conditions of general cinefication and universal mediation to their paranoid extremes. In his 1962 "cut-up" novel, *The Ticket That Exploded*, he wrote: "The film bank is empty. To conceal the bankruptcy of the reality studio it is essential that no one should be in position to set up another reality set. The reality film has now become an instrument and weapon of monopoly. The full weight of the film is directed against anyone who calls the film in question with particular attention to writers and artists. Work for the reality studio or else. Or else you will find out how it feels to be *outside the film*. I mean literally without film left to get yourself from here to the corner." Some pages later, Burroughs outlines the basics of what in his next cut-up work, *The Nova Express* (1964), he will explicitly develop as the notion of the "biologic film": "Take a talking picture of you. Now stop the projector and sound track frame by frame: stop. go go go. stop. go go. *Stop*. When the sound track stops it stops. When the projector stops a still picture is on screen. This would be your last picture the last thing you saw.... Death is the final separation of the sound and image tracks." William S. Burroughs, *The Ticket That Exploded* (New York: Grove Press, 1967), 151, 160. Throughout the 1960s, Burroughs also made a number of cut-up films.
14. Bora Ćosić, *Vidljivi i nevidljivi čovek* (Zagreb: Stvarnost, 1962), 12–13.
15. Gilles Deleuze, "Letter to Serge Daney: Optimism, Pessimism, and Travel," *Negotiations 1972–1990* (New York: Columbia University Press, 1990), 76. Consider in this light also the case of the Film Information Center, founded in the early 1970s by two multimedia artists and pioneers of video art in Yugoslavia, Ana Nuša Dragan and Srečo Dragan. Originating in the city of Ljubljana, but with branches also in Zagreb and London, the Film Information Center was motivated by the desire to explicitly (re-)cast the processes of communication in cinematic terms. In Bojana Piškur and Jurij Meden's concise description of the Center's activities: "This could take the form of a film screening, a discussion about film, a poster providing space for disseminating information; in short, a kind of cinematic social network enabling new forms

of socializing and working, direct contact with the audience, exchange and acquisition of all manner of (new) information about film and other forms of artistic expression." Jurij Meden and Bojana Piškur, "A Brief Introduction to Slovenian Experimental Film," in the catalogue for the exhibition *This is all Film!* (Ljubljana: Moderna galerija, 2010), 27.

16. Morin, *The Cinema, or the Imaginary Man*, 221.
17. Ibid., 206. In his explication of the complexities of the imaginary, Morin is at times willing to grant it a phylogenetic dimension (the imaginary as a "placental secretion" antedating subjectivity) and to bypass the ideological implications of its objectivization and universalization (the "anthropo-cosmomorphic" character of the imaginary). See 206–210, 214–216, as well as 226–227.
18. Ibid., 212–213.
19. Jean Isidore Isou, *Esthétique du cinema* (Paris: Ur, 1953), 48.
20. Yuri Lottman, *Semiosfera*, (Beograd: Svetovi, 2004), 183, 190.
21. Frederique Devaux, "Approaching Lettrist Cinema," *Visible Language* (special issue, "Lettrisme: Into the Present") 17, no. 3 (Summer 1983): 52.
22. See Jean-Paul Curtay, "Super-Writing 1983—America 1683" and "Rhythms," *Visible Language* (special issue, "Lettrisme: Into the Present"), 32, 83.
23. Curtay, "Super-Writing," 32.
24. Clearly, "supertemporal" films are among the precursors of the conceptual films made in the 1960s and the 1970s by the Fluxus artists. One thinks, for instance, of Yoko Ono's Fluxus film no. X (which consists only of a brief written instruction stating: "XYZ.").
25. Devaux, "Approaching Lettrist Cinema," 50.
26. The situation is not unlike that which, according to Jacques Lacan, pertains to the relation between a (mathematically) formalized metalanguage and a common, familiar language through which this formal language is "motivated": without "assistance" provided by the latter, the former remains impenetrable and indecipherable. As Andrew Cutrofello explains in his reading of Lacan's famous claim (put forth in the Seminar XX) that "there is no metalanguage": "To formalize a language would be to translate its terms into a set of fixed symbols and to specify a finite number of axioms that would govern the production of sentences in language. Such a formalized language would itself be a matheme—that is, a discourse that could serve as the repository of a mathesis universalis.... To say that there is no such thing as a metalanguage is to say that the task of constructing such a universal discourse could never be completed. At a minimum, Lacan suggests, it would always be necessary to motivate the metalanguage through some other discourse. Thus the attempt to translate everything into a formal discourse is subject to either of two possible failures: on the one hand, the translation is completed, with the result that the symbols become hermetically inscrutable; on the other hand,

one retains a discourse that can motivate the symbols, in which case the translation is never completed." See Andrew Curtofello, "The Ontological Status of Lacan's Mathematical Paradigms," *Reading Seminar XX*, eds. Suzanne Barnard and Bruce Fink (Albany: State University of New York Press, 2002), 142.
27. Guy Debord, *Society of the Spectacle* (New York: Zone Books, 1995), 12.
28. Debord, *Society of the Spectacle*, 136.
29. David Ward, "'Film' and 'Cinema' in Pasolini's Film Theory," *Pier Paolo Pasolini: Contemporary Perspectives*, eds. Patrick Rumble and Bart Testa (Toronto: University of Toronto Press, 1994), 140.
30. Francesco Casetti, *Theories of Cinema 1945–1995* (Austin: University of Texas Press, 1999), 316.
31. See Pasolini's essays "The Written Language of Reality," "Observations on the Sequence Shot," and "Res Sunt Nomina," in *Heretical Empiricism* (Washington, DC: New Academic Publishing, 2005).
32. Pasolini, "The Theory of Splices," *Heretical Empiricism*, 284–285.
33. Ibid., 287.
34. Ibid., 284.
35. Ibid., 287.
36. Pasolini, "Living Signs and Dead Poets," *Heretical Empiricism*, 250.
37. Gideon Bachmann, "Jancsó Plain," *Sight & Sound* 43 (Autumn 1974): 217.
38. Ibid., 220.
39. Ibid. (emphasis added).
40. Žarko Djurović, "Signalizam—Kreativna renesansa," *Gradina* 10 (2005): 90.
41. Ljubiša Jocić, "Signalizam i jezik," *Ogledi o signalizmu* (Beograd: Miroslav, 1994), 30.
42. Ljubiša Jocić, "Signalizam (II)" *Avangardni pisci kao kritičari*, ed. Gojko Tešić (Novi Sad: Matica Srpska, 1994), 349. Although its accuracy is questionable, this particular anthropological example does seem directly indebted to Lucien Levy-Bruhl's "law of participation"—the notion the French anthropologist situated at the core of animistic perceptions of the human subject's relation to, and communication with, the world. According to Levi-Bruhl, mystical participation is the belief that "objects, beings, phenomena can be, though in a way incomprehensible to us, both themselves and something other than themselves. In a fashion which is no less incomprehensible, they give forth and they receive mystic powers, virtues, qualities, influences, which make themselves felt outside, without ceasing to remain where they are." Lucien Levy-Bruhl, *How Natives Think* (Princeton: Princeton University Press, 1985), 76–77.
43. Thus also Jocić's utopian Signalist proclamation (reminiscent of Velimir Khlebnikov), that the day will come when "Man will be thinking in thunders." Jocić, "Signalizam (II)," 350.

44. In 1921, Epstein wrote: "The Bell and Howell [camera] is a metal brain, standardized, manufactured, marketed in thousands of copies, which transforms the world outside it into art." Jean Epstein, "The Senses 1(b)," *French Film Theory and Criticism, 1907–1939*, ed. Richard Abel (Princeton: Princeton University Press, 1988), 244.
45. Jocić, "Ortodijalektika filma," *Avangardni pisci*, 335. Jocić developed a similar argument regarding the importance of abstract painting. For him, abstract art is the true avant-garde of the natural sciences: it intuitively establishes the kinds of relations the sciences subsequently postulate as the nonarbitrary, objective features of the natural world. See Jocić, "Skriveni svetovi," *Avangardni pisci*, 328–333.
46. Slobodan Škerović, "Signalizam kao umetnički metod," *Gradina* 10 (2005): 106.

Chapter 5

1. Peter Wollen, "'Ontology' and 'Materialism' in Film," *Readings and Writings: Semiotic Counter-Strategies* (London: Verso, 1982), 194.
2. Peter Gidal, "Theory and Definition of Structural/Materialist Film," *Structural Film Anthology*, ed. Gidal (London: BFI, 1976), 2–3.
3. Christian Metz, *The Imaginary Signifier* (Bloomington: Indiana University Press, 1982), 61, 63, 67.
4. Wollen, in *Readings and Writings*, 195.
5. Wollen, in *Readings and Writings*, 205.
6. Peter Gidal, *Materialist Film*, (New York: Routledge, 1989), 16.
7. Malcolm Le Grice, *Abstract Film and Beyond* (Cambridge: MIT Press; 1977), 143.
8. Le Grice, *Abstract Film and Beyond*, 144.
9. The historical film avant-garde (primarily French and Soviet) was known to the first generation of the postwar Yugoslav cinephiles through the screenings regularly held in the Yugoslav Cinematheque. In 1954, Henry Langlois presented an exhaustive program there, "Fifty Years of French Cinema," which also included many avant-garde classics (Rene Clair, Luis Buñuel, Germaine Dulac, Jean Epstein). In 1967, P. Adams Sitney toured Yugoslavia (Belgrade, Sarajevo, Zagreb, Ljubljana) with his selection of postwar avant-garde films from the United States. These works from the American "underground" were received with much enthusiasm in the circles of Yugoslav modernists, which by now included the first as well as the second generation of experimental filmmakers. Nikola Djurić, whose own engagement with the cinema was just beginning at the time, is one of the many who attended these screenings. In the late 1960s and throughout the 1970s and the 1980s, many more

filmmakers and theorists of the avant-garde regularly visited Yugoslavia—Carolee Schneemann, Peter Wollen, Malcolm LeGrice, Jon Jost, Kurt Kren, Werner Nekes, to name but a few.

10. For an informative interview with Nikola Djurić, see the chapter "Sećanje" in Miroslav Bata Petrović's anthology *Alternativni film u Beogradu od 1950 do 1990 godine*, 150–157. A useful text about various alternative currents in the Yugoslav cinema is *Alternative film 1982*, ed. Miodrag Milošević (Belgrade: Dom kulture "Studentski grad," 1983).

11. Like Rabaan's *Take Measure*, Djurić's *Remembrance* thoroughly negated the process of cinematic *défilement*, theorized by Thierry Kuntzel thus: "From the film ('the strip of film') to the film ('the projected image'), 'a continuous and moving image is substituted for a series of still and separate perceptions': *the code of movement* 'intervenes in the cinematographic apparatus at the exact moment when the photogram flicks from stillness to its negation; this negation is its end, its specific work.' . . . *Défilement* lends itself to the same operation as 'erasing' because it means, in the vocabulary of cinema, 'progression, the sliding of the film-strip through the gate of a projector . . . .'" Thierry Kuntzel, "*Le Défilement*: A View in Close Up," *Apparatus*, ed. Theresa Hak Kyung Cha (New York: Tanam Press, 1908), 233, 238.

12. Alain Badiou, *Theory of the Subject* (London: Continuum, 2009), 192.

13. Birgit Hein, *Film im Underground* (Franfurt: Verlag Ullstein, 1971), 149. The English translation of the original German text is from: Christine Noll Brinckmann, "Collective Movements and Solitary Thrusts: German Experimental Film 1920–1990," *Millenium Film Journal* (Fall 1997): 30–31.

14. Since its inception in the 1950s, the cine-club culture flourished in the socialist Yugoslavia. The clubs played a major role in providing the aspiring cineastes with the equipment, the technical know-how, and the creative environment (less burdened by either commercial or ideological concerns) within which to develop their filmmaking skills and try out diverse ideas. A number of directors who, in the late 1960s and the 1970s, established themselves as the major auteurs of the Yugoslav cinema—Dušan Makavejev, Živojin Pavlović, Lordan Zafranović, Karpo Godina, to name but a few—came to professional filmmaking from the cine-club culture. They brought experimental interests and sensibilities into the cinematic mainstream. But other currents of amateur-led experimentation (those discussed here) continued to develop autonomously, without (or without decisive) cross-pollination with the professional, industrial types of film practice. On this topic see Jovan Jovanović, "Od amaterskog do alternativnog filma 1950–1993," in Petrović, *Alternativni film u Beogradu od 1950 do 1990 godine*, 24–29.

15. Hrvoje Turković, "Filmski modernizam u ideološkom i populističkom okruženju," *Hrvatski filmski ljetopis* 59 (2009): 92–106.

16. Turković, ibid.

17. Turković, ibid.
18. Pansini is quoted from the documentary film *Mihovil Pansini: Brodovi ne pristaju*, dir. Milan Bukovac (Hrvatski filmski savez & Autorski studio FFV, 2008).
19. *Knjiga Geffa 63*, eds. Mihovil Pansini et.al. (Organizacioni komitet geffa, 1967), 84
20. Ibid., 91.
21. Paul Sharits, "Words per Page," *Film Culture*, no. 65–66 (1978): 36.
22. This is perhaps as close as film practice would come to fulfilling Félix Guattari's theoretical fantasy about film as, before all else, an "a-signifying semiotic chain of intensities, movements and multiplicities," anterior to the "signifying grid that intervenes only at a second stage, through the filmic syntagmatic that fixes genres, crystallizes characters and behavioral stereotypes homogeneous to the dominant semantic field." Félix Guattari, *Soft Subversions*, ed. Sylvère Lotringer (New York: Semiotext(e), 1996), 161.
23. Deke Dusinberre, "La Retour à la raison: Hidden Meanings," in *Unseen Cinema*, ed. Bruce Posner (New York: Anthology Film Archives, 2005), 67.
24. Sharits, "Words Per Page," 35. See also Paul Sharits, "Exhibition/Frozen Frames (Regarding the 'Frozen Film Frame' Series: A Statement for the '5th International Experimental Film Festival,' Knokke, December 1974)," in *Paul Sharits*, ed. Yann Beauvais (Dijon: Le presses du reel, January 2008), 81.
25. Sharits, "Exhibition/Frozen Frames," 81.
26. Ibid., 81–82.
27. Paul Sharits, "Cinema as Cognition: Introductory Remarks," *Film Culture* no. 65–66 (1978): 76.
28. Sharits, "Words per Page," 35, 37.
29. Alain Badiou, *Theory of the Subject* (London: Continuum, 2009), 193.
30. Sharits, "Words per Page," 32.
31. Slobodan Šijan, *Filmski letak* (Belgrade: Glasnik, 2009), 101–102.
32. Ješa Denegri, "Pojedinačna filozofija Tomislava Gotovca," *Tomislav Gotovac*, eds. Aleksandar Battista Ilić and Diana Nenadić (Zagreb: Hrvatski filmski savez, Muzej suvremene umjetnosti, 2003), 4–5.
33. Šijan, *Filmski letak*, 150.
34. Sharits, "Words per Page," 30.
35. Years earlier, in 1970, Šijan had already made a student documentary about Belgrade's central garbage depot. It includes memorable images of a pig chewing on a strip of film. Some of the footage shot at the garbage depot is also incorporated into Šijan's rigorously materialist 8mm film, *Handmade*, from 1971.
36. "Media Suicide" was a project begun by Šijan in 1976. Using photography, photocopy machines, film, and video, he conducted a series of experiments revolving around the following thesis: "Imperfections in the reproductive system of a medium accumulate as fresh reproductions continue to be successively

reproduced, resulting in a total exhaustion of the medium's reproductive powers." The experiment with the burning film frames from *The Marathon Family* was the fourth in the series, and it bore the title *Media Suicide, Investigation No. 4—Film, 1981*. Šijan, *Filmski letak*, 64.

37. See Annette Michelson, "The Kinetic Icon and the Work of Mourning: Prolegomena to the Analysis of a Textual System," *October* 52 (Spring 1990): especially 24–28.

Chapter 6

1. Serge Daney, "From Projector to Parade," *Film Comment* 38, no. 4 (July/August 2002): 37.
2. Ernst's "picture-book," *Une semaine de bonté* (1934), quite literally gave rise to cinematic desire: it inspired a short film called *Desire*, coauthored by Ernst and Hans Richter (and included in Richter's 1947 multipart feature, *Dreams That Money Can Buy*).
3. Sergei Eisenstein, "Word and Image," *The Film Sense* (New York: Harcourt, Brace & World, Inc., 1947), 30.
4. Ibid., 32.
5. Ibid., 35–36. For a detailed discussion of the epistemological functions of Eisenstein's disjunctive montage, see Annette Michelson, "Camera Lucida Camera Obscura," *Artforum* 11, no. 5 (January 1973): 30–37.
6. Richard Roud, *Jean-Luc Godard* (Bloomington: Indiana University Press, 1970), 67. Godard's inclination to generalize the dynamics of montage is already apparent in his early texts, "Defense and Illustration of Classical Découpage" and "Montage my Fine Care." Written for *Cahiers du Cinéma* in the 1950s, these short essays argued against the normativized opposition between the editing-based, so-called formalist, approaches to filmmaking, and those approaches invested in the realist aesthetic of the long take and deep focus cinematography. See *Godard on Godard*, ed. Tom Milne (New York: Da Capo Press, 1972), 26–30, 39–41. For a brief but perceptive discussion of this issue see also Collin McCabe, *Godard: Images, Sounds, Politics* (Bloomington: Indiana University Press, 1980), 43.
7. Sigmund Freud, *The Interpretation of Dreams* (New York: Avon Books, 1998), 402–403.
8. Jacques Lacan, *Écrits* (New York: W. W. Norton & Co., 2002), 306. See also Slavoj Žižek, *The Sublime Object of Ideology* (London: Verso, 1989), 102–105.
9. Serge Daney, "The Tracking Shot in *Kapo*," *Postcards from the Cinema* (Oxford: Berg, 2007), 21.
10. Jacques-Alain Miller, "Suture (elements of the logic of the signifier)," *Screen* 18, no. 4 (Winter 1977–1978): 26, 32.

11. See the dossier on suture in *Screen* 18, no. 4 (Winter 1977–1978), as well as Joan Copjec's thorough revision of the concept in "Apparatus and Umbra: A Feminist Critique of Film Theory" (PhD diss., New York University, 1986).
12. Gilles Deleuze, *Cinema 2: The Time-Image* (Minneapolis: University of Minnesota Press, 1989), 179–180.
13. The psychoanalytic session in the beginning of *Weekend* explicitly introduces the impossibility of separating reality from fantasy—another notable parallel with Althusser's (Lacan-influenced) critique of ideology.
14. Drawing on the ideas of Roland Barthes, film scholar James Monaco describes *Le Gai Savoir* as "Godard's ultimate effort at 'semioclasm.'" James Monaco, *The New Wave* (New York: Sag Harbor, 2004), 209.
15. During the Dziga-Vertov period, Godard dismissed most of his earlier films—including the overtly political *La Chinoise*—as "Hollywood films because I was a bourgeois artist. They are my dead corpses." He was, however, still willing to attribute some "positive merit" to *Weekend*, *Pierrot le fou*, and "some things in *Two or Three Things*." See Kent E. Carroll, "Film and Revolution: Interview with the Dziga-Vertov Group," in *Focus on Godard*, ed. Royal S. Brown (New Jersey: Prentice Hall, 1972), 61–62.
16. Victor Burgin, *The Remembered Film* (London: Reaktion Books, 2004), 9–10.
17. Daney is quoted in Julia Lesage, *Jean-Luc Godard: A Guide to References and Resources* (Boston: G.K. Hall & Co, 1979), 126.
18. Robert Phillip Kolker, "Angle and Reality: Godard and Gorin in America," *Jean-Luc Godard Interviews*, ed. David Sterritt (Jackson: University Press of Mississippi, 1998), 64.
19. Notably, I borrow Krauss's formulation from her analysis of the films of Paul Sharits. See Rosalind Krauss, "Paul Sharits," *Film Culture* 65–66 (1978): 94.
20. It is useful to evoke Blake Stimson's recent differentiation between the photographic essay and film: "The photographic essay was born of the promise of another kind of truth from that given by the individual photograph or image on its own, a truth available only in the interstices between pictures, in the movement from one picture to the next. At the moment when photography became film, however, a new question opened up that threatened to undermine its promise before it had even really emerged: How best to realize that movement? How best to develop the truth content of the exposition itself? Would it be with the spatialized time of the photographic series or with the retemporalized space of film as a form?" Blake Stimson, "The Pivot of the World: Photography and Its Nation," in *The Cinematic*, ed. David Company (Cambridge, Massachusetts: MIT Press, 2007), 96.

However, the effect achieved in the slide sequence in *Ici et ailleurs*—as well as in a number of other works such as Chris Marker's *La Jetée* (1962), Michael Snow's *One Second in Montreal* (1969), and Hollis Frampton's *(nostalgia)* (1971)—is that of blurring the distinction between serial still images and motion pictures through *concurrent* "spatialization of time" and "temporalization

of space." Referring to Dziga Vertov's own exploration of the relationship between kinesis and stasis in the film *The Man with a Movie Camera*, Laura Mulvey describes this effect as "delayed cinema" and "cinema's variable temporality becoming visible." See: Laura Mulvey, *Death 24x a Second* (London: Reaktion Books, 2006), 182.
21. As Raymond Bellour elegantly put it: "As soon as you stop the film, you begin to find the time to add to the image." See his essay, "The Pensive Spectator," *Wide Angle* 9, no. 1 (1987): 10.
22. Experimentation with fragmented and multiple images also distinguishes *Numéro Deux* (1975), another Godard-Miéville collaboration from this period. Concerned with the impact of visual oversaturation on the spectatorial subject, this film heavily utilizes such formal and structural devices as split-screens, superimpositions, frames within frames, images surrounded by blackness, and even comic strip-like video découpage. Notably, the horizontal alignment of slide-viewers in *Ici et ailleurs* has its equivalent in *Numero Deux*'s vertically stacked television monitors showing a changing selection of audiovisual content (from news reports on May Day celebrations in Paris, to kung fu films and pornography). Godard and Miéville punningly present reification of the mass-media as, literally, a petrified mass of media.
23. Serge Daney, "From Projector to Parade," 37. In 1967, another "difficulty of intervening with images" (he was denied permission to film in Vietnam) had already led Godard to an overtly political experiment in cinema conducted by "other means." "Camera Eye," the segment Godard contributed to the collectively made film *Far From Vietnam* (S.L.O.N/Chris Marker, 1967), explores the *limits* of film and filming and revolves around some tightly framed, noncontextualized footage of the director with a large and heavy 35mm Mitchell camera. Godard looks through the camera's viewfinder, turns various knobs and lights on it, and behaves as if he is filming something or is about to do so. But while the images in "Camera Eye" insistently and reflexively depict some abstracted elements of the technological apparatus and of the labor of shooting a film, the soundtrack—specifically the director's voice—casts the cinema as, in fact, primarily an imaginary activity. For while he may be preoccupied with his camera, Godard is actually (only) *telling* us what he *would have* filmed in Vietnam had he had an opportunity to go there (the "strange show" of planes, bombing raids, machine-gun fire, and astounded peasants; "to show on a woman's body the impact of cluster bombs"; defoliation, contamination of water, and more).
24. Paul Virilio, *The Information Bomb* (London: Verso, 2005), 14–15.
25. Kolker, "Angle and Reality," 64.
26. Philip Rosen, *Change Mummified* (Minneapolis: University of Minnesota Press, 2001), 48. In "Entering History," the second chapter of the book, Rosen extensively analyzes the difference between architectural *restoration* and *preservation*.

27. The official website for the project of the Old Bridge's "rehabilitation" is unequivocal in this respect. One of its stated goals is the "reconstruction of a 'new old bridge' *marked and declared* as a recent intervention" (emphasis added). http://www.gen-eng.florence.it/starimost/00_main/main.htm (accessed August 14, 2007).
28. See Victor Tausk, "On the Origin of the 'Influencing Machine' in Schizophrenia," *Sexuality, War and Schizophrenia* (New Brunswick: Transaction Publishers, 1991), 186–190. Interestingly, Tausk himself must have crossed the Old Bridge many times, for in 1904–1905 he lived and worked in Mostar.
29. Preposterous promises of future restoration of damaged and destroyed architectural objects—sometimes even of entire cities (Dubrovnik, for instance)—in ways that would increase not only their original beauty but also their *age*, were not infrequent during the 1990s Yugoslav wars. They are to be understood as drastic manifestations of a typical nationalist ideological investment in the "invention of tradition" (the term is Eric Hobsbawm's). In the case of the Old Bridge, this historicist obsession acquired a fascinating new dimension in the postwar period as well. The fantasy that the new version of the Bridge would be "older than the original" now grounded itself in the fact that the stones used for its restoration, while brought from the same quarry that had been exploited in the sixteenth century, belonged to an even deeper and therefore *geologically earlier* stratum!
30. *Fatale Beauté*, episode 2B of the serial *Histoire(s) du cinéma* (1988–1998).
31. This section is in part inspired by Branko Vučićević's ideas about montage, developed in his book *Paper Movies* (Zagreb, Belgrade: Arkzin & B-92; 1998), 28–46.
32. Not limited to the cinema, the rapport between violence and (de-)montage has, of course, also prominently figured in the arts and literature of the twentieth century; one thinks of Picasso and Tzara, Artaud and Bataille, Bellmer, Burroughs, and many others.
33. This *coincidentia oppositorum* is also clearly reflected in the name popularly used for one of the essential pieces of film editing equipment: the "guillotine splicer."
34. George Baker, "Reanimations (I)," *October* 104 (Spring 2003): 58.
35. As Thierry Kuntzel argued in the early 1970s, the space between two shots is a "relay," understood "beyond its accepted meaning in cybernetics, in the sense of the gap left in a tapestry at the moment of changing to a different color (a discontinuity of the text) which is filled at a latter moment (après-coup) (a rhetorical pseudo-continuity)." Thierry Kuntzel, "The Film-Work," *Enclitic* 2, no. 1 (Spring 1978): 46.
36. Quoted from Michael Althen, "The Lives of the Images," in Jean-Luc Godard, Anne-Marie Miéville, *Four Short Films* (Munich: ECM Cinema, 2006), 97.

BIBLIOGRAPHY

Abel, Richard, ed. *French Film Theory and Criticism, 1907–1939*, 2 vols. Princeton: Princeton University Press, 1988.
Ades, Dawn. *Dada and Surrealism*. Woodbury: Barron's, 1978.
Aleksić, Dragan. "Tatlin. HP/s + Čovek." *Zenit* 9 (November 1921).
Althusser, Louis. *Philosophy of the Encounter: Later Writings, 1978–1987*. London: Verso, 2006.
Andrew, Dudley. *What Cinema Is!* Malden: Wiley-Blackwell, 2010.
Apollinaire, Guillaume. *Selected Writings of Guillaume Apollinaire*. New York: New Directions Books, 1971.
Apollonio, Umbro, ed. *Futurist Manifestos*. Boston: MFA Publications, 2001.
Aragon, Louis. *Le Payson de Paris*. Paris: Éditions Gallimard, 1926.
Artaud, Antonin. *Collected Works*, vol. 3. London: Calder & Boyars, 1972.
Bachmann, Gideon. "Jancsó Plain." *Sight and Sound* 43 no. 4 (Autumn 1974).
Badiou, Alain. *Theory of the Subject*. London: Continuum, 2009.
Baker, George. "Reanimations (I)." *October* 104 (Spring 2003).
Baker, George. "Entr'acte." *October* 105 (Summer 2003).
Baker, George. *The Artwork Caught by the Tail: Francis Picabia and Dada in Paris*. Cambridge: MIT Press, 2007.
Baldwin, Neil. *Man Ray: American Artist*. New York: Da Capo Press, 2000.
Ball, Hugo. *Flight out of Time*. New York: Viking Press, 1974.
Barnard, Suzanne, and Bruce Fink, eds. *Reading Seminar XX*. Albany: State University of New York Press, 2002.
Bataille, Georges. *Visions of Excess*. Minneapolis: University of Minnesota Press, 1985.

BIBLIOGRAPHY

Bataille, Georges, Michel Leiris, Marcel Griaule, Carl Einstein, Robert Desnos and writers associated with the Acéphale and Surrealist groups. *Encylopaedia Acephalica*. London: Atlas Press, 1995.

Beauvais, Yann, ed. *Paul Sharits*. Dijon: Le presses du reel, 2008.

Bellour, Raymond. "The Pensive Spectator." *Wide Angle* 9 no. 1 (1991).

Benjamin, Walter. *The Work of Art in the Age of Its Technological Reproducibility, and Other Writings on Media*. Cambridge: Belknap Press, 2008.

Benson, Timothy O. *Raoul Hausmann and Berlin Dada*. Ann Arbor: UMI Research Press, 1987.

Bois, Yve-Alain, and Rosalind Krauss. *Formless: A User's Guide*. New York: Zone Books, 1997.

Bolter, Jay David, and Richard Grusin. *Remediation: Understanding New Media*. Cambridge: MIT Press, 2000.

Brčić, Tomislav. "Fenomen i kultura kinoklubova šezdesetih godina." *Zapis* 62 (2008).

Breton, André. *Manifestoes of Surrealism*. Ann Arbor: University of Michigan Press, 1972.

Breton, André. *Mad Love*. Lincoln: University of Nebraska Press, 1987.

Breton, André. *The Lost Steps*. Lincoln: University of Nebraska Press, 1996.

Brinckmann, Christine Noll. "Collective Movements and Solitary Thrusts: German Experimental Film 1920–1990." *Millennium Film Journal* (Fall 1997): 30–31.

Brown, Royal S., ed. *Focus on Godard*. Englewood Cliffs: Prentice Hall, 1972.

Buck-Morss, Susan. *The Dialectics of Seeing*. Cambridge: MIT Press, 1991.

Burgin, Victor. *The Remembered Film*. London: Reaktion Books, 2004.

Burroughs, William S. *The Ticket that Exploded*. New York: Grove Press, 1967.

Campany, David, ed. *The Cinematic*. Cambridge: MIT Press, 2007.

Cassetti, Francesco. *Theories of Cinema, 1945–1995*. Austin: University of Texas Press, 1999.

Cha, Theresa Hak Kyung, ed. *Apparatus*. New York: Tanam Press, 1980.

Copjec, Joan. "Apparatus and Umbra: A Feminist Critique of Film Theory." PhD diss., New York University, 1986.

Collette, Jean. *Jean-Luc Godard*. New York: Crown Publishers, 1970.

Ćosić, Bora. *Vidljivi i nevidljivi čovek*. Zagreb: Stvarnost, 1962.

Daney, Serge. "From Projector to Parade." *Film Comment* 38 no. 4 (July/August 2002).

Daney, Serge. *Postcards from the Cinema*. Oxford: Berg, 2007.

Davičo, Oskar. *Izabrana Srbija*. Belgrade: BIGZ, 1972.

Deák, František. "Blue Blouse (1923–1928)." *The Drama Review: TDR* 17 no.1 (March 1973).

Debord, Guy. *Society of the Spectacle*. New York: Zone Books, 1995.

de Boully, Monny. *Zlatne bube*, Belgrade: Prosveta, 1968.

de Boully, Monny, and Rade Drainac. *Dve avanturističke poeme*. Belgrade: Biblioteka Hipnos, 1926.

Deleuze, Gilles. *Foucault*. Minneapolis: University of Minnesota Press, 1988.

Deleuze, Gilles. *Cinema 2: The Time-Image*. Minneapolis: University of Minnesota Press, 1989.

Deleuze, Gilles. *Negotiations, 1972–1990*. New York: Columbia University Press, 1990.

Denegri, Ješa. *Razlozi za drugu liniju: za novu umetnost sedamdesetih*. Novi Sad: M. Sudac/Muzej savremene umetnosti Vojvodine, 2007.

Dickerman, Leah, and Matthew S. Witovsky, eds. *The Dada Seminars*. Washington: The National Gallery of Art, 2005.

Dimendberg, Edward. "Transfiguring the Urban Gray, László Moholy-Nagy's Film Scenario 'Dynamic of the Metropolis'." In *Camera Obscura, Camera Lucida: Essays in Honor of Annette Michelson*. Amsterdam: Amsterdam University Press, 2002.

Djurić, Dubravka, and Miško Šuvaković, eds. *Impossible Histories: historical avant-gardes, neo-avant-gardes, and post-avant-gardes in Yugoslavia, 1918–1991*. Cambridge: MIT Press, 2003.

Doane, Mary Ann. "The Indexical and the Concept of Medium Specificity." *differences* 18, no. 1 (2007).

Donguy, Jacques. "Machine Head: Raoul Hausmann and the Optophone." *Leonardo* 34 no. 3 (June 2001).

Dufour, Diane, and Serge Toubiana. *The Image to Come, how cinema inspires photographs*. Paris: Magnumsteidl, 2007.

Eisenstein, Sergei. *The Film Sense*. New York: Harcourt, Brace & World, Inc., 1947.

Fédida, Pierre. "The Movement of the Informe." *Qui Parle* X no. 1 (Fall/Winter 1996).

Flaker, Aleksandar. *Ruska avangarda*. Zagreb: SN Liber & Globus, 1984.

Fondane, Benjamin. *Écrits pour le cinema*. Paris: Plasma, 1994.

Foster, Hal. *Compulsive Beauty*. Cambridge: MIT Press, 1993.

Foster, Stephen C., ed. "Lettrisme: Into the Present." Special Issue, *Visible Language* 17 no. 3 (Summer 1983).

Frampton, Hollis. *On the Camera Arts and Consecutive Matters: The Writings of Hollis Frampton*. Cambridge: MIT Press, 2009.

Freud, Sigmund. *The Interpretation of Dreams*. New York: Avon Books, 1998.

Gale, Matthew, Dawn Ades, Montserrat Aguer, and Fèlix Fanés, eds. *Dalí and Film*. London: Tate Publishing, 2007.

Gattin, Marija, ed. *Gorgona*. Zagreb: Muzej suvremene umjetnosti, 2002.

Gidal, Peter, ed. *Structural Film Anthology*. London: BFI, 1976.

Gidal, Peter. *Materialist Film*. New York: Routledge, 1989.

Godard, Jean-Luc. *Godard on Godard*. New York: Da Capo Press, 1972.

Godard, Jean-Luc. *Jean-Luc Godard Interviews*. Jackson: University Press of Mississippi, 1998.

BIBLIOGRAPHY

Godard, Jean-Luc, and Anne-Marie Miéville. *Four Short Films*. Munich: ECM Cinema, 2006.

Golubović, Vida, ed. "Dada u Subotici" (dossier). *Književnost* (1990): 7–8.

Golubović, Vidosava. "*Sobareva metla*: tekst Marka Ristića za baletsku grotesku Miloja Milojevića." *Književna istorija* 28 no. 100 (1996).

Golubović, Vidosava. "Iz prepiske oko časopisa Zenit i češke avangardne skupine Devetsil." *Ljetopis 1997*. Zagreb: Srpsko kulturno društvo Prosvjeta, 1997.

Golubović, Vidosava. "Dva 'dijaloga' Boška Tokina." *Književna kritika* (Spring–Summer 1998).

Golubović, Vidosava. "Prezentizam Raula Hausmana u časopisu Zenit." *Zbornik matice srpske za slavistiku* 69 (2006).

Golubović, Vidosava. *"Zenit i nadrealizam." Nadrealizam u svom i našem vremenu*. Belgrade: Filološki fakultet, Društvo za kulturnu saradnju Srbija-Francuska, 2007.

Golubović, Vidosava, and Irina Subotić, *Zenit 1921–1926*. Belgrade, Zagreb: Narodna biblioteka Srbije, Institut za književnost i umetnost, SKD Prosvjeta, 2008.

Goodwin, James. *Eisenstein, Cinema, and History*. Urbana: University of Illinois Press, 1993.

Greene, Naomi. "Artaud and Film: A Reconsideration." *Cinema Journal* 23 no. 4 (Summer 1984).

Greene, Naomi. *Pier Paolo Pasolini: Cinema As Heresy*. Princeton: Princeton University Press, 1992.

Guattari, Félix. *Soft Subversions*. New York: Semiotext(e), 1996.

Hammond, Paul, ed. *The Shadow and Its Shadow*. San Francisco: City Lights Books, 2000.

Harvey, Sylvia. *May '68 and French Film Culture*. London: BFI, 1980.

Hausmann, Raoul. *Sieg Triumph Tabak mit Bohnen: Texte bis 1933*, vol. 2. Mucich: Edition Text + Kritik, 1982.

Heath, Stephen. *Questions of Cinema*. Bloomington: Indiana University Press, 1981.

Hein, Birgit. *Film im Underground*. Frankfurt: Verlag Ullstein, 1971.

Hollier, Denis. *Against Architecture: The Writings of George Bataille*. Cambridge: MIT Press, 1989.

Hollier, Denis. *Absent Without Leave*. Cambridge: Harvard University Press, 1997.

Ilić, Aleksandar Battista, and Diana Nenadić, eds. *Tomislav Gotovac*. Zagreb: Hrvatski filmski savez, Muzej suvremene umjetnosti, 2003.

IRWIN, ed. *East Art Map: Contemporary Art and Eastern Europe*. London: Afterall, 2006.

Isou, Jean Isidore. *Esthétique du cinéma*. Paris: Ur, 1953.

Isou, Jean Isidore. *Amos, ou Introduction à la Métagraphologie*. Paris: Arcanes, 1958.

James, David E. *Allegories of Cinema: American Film in the Sixties*. Princeton: Princeton University Press, 1989.
Janicot, Christian. *Anthologie du cinéma invisible*. Paris: Éditions Jean-Michel Place/ARTE Éditions, 1995.
Jocić, Ljubiša. *Mesečina u tetrapaku*. Belgrade: Prosveta, 1975.
Jocić, Ljubiša. *Ogledi o signalizmu*. Beograd: Miroslav, 1994.
Jovanov, Jasna. *Demistifikacija apokrifa*. Novi Sad: Apostrof, 1999.
Kenez, Peter. *Cinema and Soviet Society from the Revolution to the Death of Stalin*. London: I. B. Tauris, 2001.
Khlebnikov, Velimir. *Letters and Theoretical Writings, Collected Works*, vol. 1. Edited by Charlotte Douglas. Cambridge: Harvard University Press, 1987.
Kittler, Friedrich A. *Discourse Networks*. Stanford: Stanford University Press, 1990.
Kluge, Alexander. "On Film and the Public Sphere." *New German Critique* 24/25 (Fall/Winter 1981–1982).
Kluge, Alexander. *Cinema Stories*. New York: New Directions, 2007.
Krauss, Rosalind. "Reinventing the Medium." *Critical Inquiry* 25 no. 2 (Winter 1999).
Krauss, Rosalind. *A Voyage on the North Sea: Art in the Age of the Post-Medium Condition*. London: Thames & Hudson, 2000.
Kuenzli, Rudolf E., ed. *Dada and Surrealist Film*. Cambridge: MIT Press, 1996.
Kuleshov, Lev. *Kuleshov on Film: Writings of Lev Kuleshov*. Berkeley: University of California Press, 1974.
Kuntzel, Thierry. "The Film-Work." *Enclitic* 2 no. 1 (Spring 1978).
Lacan, Jacques. *The Seminar of Jacques Lacan, Book VII: The Ethics of Psychoanalysis, 1959–1960*. New York: Norton, 1992.
Lacan, Jacques. *The Seminar of Jacques Lacan, Book XX: On Feminine Sexuality, the Limits of Love and Knowledge, 1972–1973 (Encore)*. New York: Norton, 1998.
Lacan, Jacques. *Écrits*. New York: W. W. Norton & Co., 2002.
Layton, Edwin T., Jr. "Technology as Knowledge." *Technology and Culture* 15 no. 1 (January 1974).
Le Grice, Malcolm. *Abstract Film and Beyond*. Cambridge: MIT Press, 1977.
Lemaître, Maurice. *Le film est déjà commencé? Séance de cinema*. Paris: A. Bonne, 1952.
Lemaître, Maurice. *Le Cinéma Lettriste*. Paris: Centre de créativité, 1991.
Lesage, Julia. *Jean-Luc Godard: A Guide to References and Resources*. Boston: G. K. Hall, 1979.
Levy-Bruhl, Lucien. *How Natives Think*. Princeton: Princeton University Press, 1985.
Leyda, Jay. *Kino: A History of the Russian and Soviet Film*. Princeton: Princeton University Press, 1983.
Liebman, Stuart. *Paul Sharits*. St. Paul: Film in the Cities, 1981.
Lissitzky, El. *El Lissitzky: Life, Letters, Texts*. Greenwich: New York Graphic Society, 1968.

Lottman, Yuri. *Semiosfera*. Beograd: Svetovi, 2004.
Lyotard, Jean-François. *Libidinal Economy*. Bloomington: Indiana University Press, 1974.
MacBean, James Roy. *Film and Revolution*. Bloomington: Indiana University Press, 1975.
MacCabe, Colin. *Godard: Images, Sounds, Politics*. Bloomington: Indiana University Press, 1980.
Malevich, Kazimir. *The White Rectangle: Writings on Film*. Berlin: Potemkin Press, 2003.
Man Ray. *Self Portrait*. Boston: Little, Brown and Company, 1963.
Mannoni, Laurent. *The Great Art of Light and Shadow: Archaeology of the Cinema*. Exeter: University of Exeter Press, 2000.
Manovich, Lev. *The Language of New Media*. Cambridge: MIT Press, 2001.
Marc'O. "Numéro special sur le cinéma." Special Issue, *Ion*. Paris: Jean-Paul Rocher, 1999.
McLuhan, Marshall. *Understanding Media: The Extensions of Man*. Cambridge: MIT Press, 1994.
Metz, Christian. *The Imaginary Signifier*. Bloomington: Indiana University Press, 1982.
Michelson, Annette. "Camera Lucida /Camera Obscura." *Artforum* 11 no. 5 (January 1973).
Michelson, Annette. "De Stijl, Its Other Face: Abstraction and Cacaphony, or What Was the Matter with Hegel?." *October* 22 (Autumn 1982).
Michelson, Annette. "The Kinetic Icon and the Work of Mourning: Prolegomena to the Analysis of a Textual System." *October* 52 (Spring 1990).
Micić, Ljubomir. "Reči u prostoru 15." *Zenit* 9 (November 1921).
Micić, Ljubomir. *Antievropa*. Belgrade: Zenit, 1926.
Micić, Ljubomir. *Zenitizam*. Belgrade: DOV, 1991.
Milutis, Joe. *Ether, the nothing that connects everything*. Minneapolis: University of Minnesota Press, 2006.
Miller, Jacque-Alain, Jean-Pierre Oudart, and Stephen Heath. "Dossier on Suture." *Screen* 18 no. 4 (Winter 1977–1978).
Milošević, Miodrag, ed. *Alternative film 1982*. Belgrade: Dom kulture "Studentski grad," 1983.
Miltojević, Branislav. *Celuloidni zalogaji Bojana Jovanovića*. Belgrade: Dom kulture "Studentski grad," 2008.
Moholy-Nagy, László. *Painting, Photography, Film*. Cambridge: MIT Press, 1969.
Monaco, James. *The New Wave*. New York: Sag Harbor, 2004.
Morin, Edgar. *The Cinema, or the Imaginary Man*. Minneapolis: University of Minnesota Press, 2005.
Motherwell, Robert, ed. *Dada Painters and Poets: An Anthology*, 2nd ed. Cambridge: Belknap Press of Harvard University Press, 1981.

Mulvey, Laura. *Death 24x a Second*. London: Reaktion Books, 2006.
Munitić, Ranko. *Alisa na putu kroz podzemlje i kroz svemir*. Belgrade: Dečje Novine, 1986.
Munitić, Ranko, ed. *Beogradski filmski kritičarski krug*, vols. 1 and 2 *(1896–1960)*. Niš: NKC Art Press, 2002, 2005.
Murray, Timothy. *Like a Film*. New York: Routledge, 1993.
Nedić, Marko, ed. *Pisci kao kritičari posle prvog svetskog rata*. Novi Sad: Matica srpska, 1975.
Pansini, Mihovil et al., eds. *Knjiga Geffa 63*. Organizacioni komitet geffa, 1967
Pasolini, Pier Paolo. *Heretical Empiricism*. Washington: New Academic Publishing, 2005.
Peters, John Durham. *Speaking into the Air: A History of the Idea of Communication*. Chicago: University of Chicago Press, 1999.
Petrie, Graham. *History Must Answer to Man: The Contemporary Hungarian Cinema*. Budapest: Corvina Kiadó, 1978.
Petrie, Graham. *Red Psalm*. Wiltshire: Flicks Books, 1998.
Petro, Patrice, ed. *Fugitive Images: From Photography to Video*. Bloomington: Indiana University Press, 1995.
Picabia, Francis. *I am a Beautiful Monster: Poetry, Prose, and Provocation*. Cambridge: MIT Press, 2007.
Picabia, Francis, and Michel Sanouillet. *391 revue publiée de 1917 à 1924 par Francis Picabia*. Paris: Le Terrain Vague, 1960.
Piškur, Bojana, and Tamara Soban. *Catalogue for the exhibition This is all Film! Experimental Film in Yugoslavia 1951–1991*. Ljubljana: Museum of Modern Art, 2010.
Popović, Duško, ed. *Kinoklub Zagreb, 1928–2003*. Zagreb: Hrvatski filmski savez, 2003.
Popović, Koča. *Nadrealizam i postnadrealizam*. Belgrade: Prosveta, 1985.
Popović, Koča, and Marko Ristić. *Nacrt za jednu fenomenologiju iracionalnog*. Belgrade: Prosveta, 1985.
Posner, Bruce, ed. *Unseen Cinema*. New York: Anthology Film Archives, 2005.
Powrie, Phil. "Film-Form-Mind: The Hegelian Follies of Roger Gilbert-Lecomte." *Quarterly Review of Film and Video* 12 no. 4 (1991).
Radovanović, Vladan. *Pustolina*. Belgrade: Nolit, 1968.
Radovanović, Vladan. *Vokovizuel*. Belgrade: Nolit, 1987.
Ristić, Marko, et. al. *Nemoguće*. Belgrade: Nadrealistička izdanja, 1930.
Ristić, Marko. *Uoči Nadrealizma*. Belgrade: Nolit, 1985.
Rodowick, D. N. *The Crisis of Political Modernism*, 2nd ed. Berkeley: University of California Press, 1994.
Rodowick, D. N. *Reading the Figural, or Philosophy after the New Media*. Durham: Duke University Press, 2001.
Rodowick, D. N. *The Virtual Life of Film*. Cambridge: Harvard University Press, 2007.

Rohdie, Sam. *The Passion of Pier Paolo Pasolini*. Bloomington: Indiana University Press, 1996.
Rose, Barbara. "Kinetic Solutions to Pictorial Problems: The Films of Man Ray and Moholy-Nagy." *Artforum* 10 no. 1 (September 1971).
Rosen, Philip. *Change Mummified*. Minneapolis: University of Minnesota Press, 2001.
Rumble, Patrick, and Bart Testa, eds. *Pier Paolo Pasolini: Contemporary Perspectives*. Toronto: University of Toronto Press, 1994.
Sandqvist, Tom. *Dada East, the Romanians of Cabaret Voltaire*. Cambridge: MIT Pres, 2006.
Sanouillet, Michel, and Elmer Peterson, eds. *The Writings of Marcel Duchamp*. New York: Da Capo Press, 2005.
Saveski, Zoran. *Avangarda, alternativa, film*. Belgrade: Dom kulture "Studentski grad," 2006.
Šejka, Leonid. *Traktat o slikarstvu*. Sombor: Zlatna grana, 1995.
Sharits, Paul, et al. "Paul Sharits." Special Issue, *Film Culture* no. 65–66 (1978).
Šijan, Slobodan. *Vrtoglavica*. Belgrade: Artget, 2005.
Šijan, Slobodan. *Filmski letak*. Belgrade: Glasnik, 2009.
Sitney, P. Adams. *Visionary Film, the American Avant-Garde, 1943–2000*. New York: Oxford University Press, 2002.
Spies, Werner. *Max Ernst Collages: The Invention of the Surrealist Universe*. New York: Harry N. Abrams, Inc., 1988.
Sretenović, Dejan, ed. *Video umetnost u Srbiji*. Belgrade: Centar za savremenu umetnost, 1999.
Sretenović, Dejan, ed. *Slobodan Šijan: oko filma*. Belgrade: Muzej savremene umetnosti, 2008.
Sudac, Marinko, ed. *Rubne posebnosti: avangardna umjetnost u regiji*. Rijeka: Muzej moderne i suvremene umjetnosti, 2007.
Susovski, Marijan, ed. *The New Art Practice in Yugoslavia*. Zagreb: Gallery of Contemporary Art, 1978.
Susovski, Marijan, and Fjodor Fatičić, eds. *Exat 51 & New Tendencies: Avant-Garde and International Events in Croatian Art in the 1950s and 1960s*. Zagreb: Muzej suvremene umjetnosti, 2003.
Šuvaković, Miško. "Neoavangarda, konceptualna umetnost i krize socijalističkog modernizma." *Republika* (June 2008): 430–431.
Tausk, Viktor. *Sexuality, War and Schizophrenia*. New Brunswick: Transaction Publishers, 1991.
Taylor, Richard. *The Politics of the Soviet Cinema, 1917–1929*. Cambridge: Cambridge University Press, 1979.
Taylor, Richard, and Ian Christie, eds. *Inside the Film Factory: New Approaches to Russian and Soviet cinema*. London: Routledge, 1991.
Teitelbaum, Matthew, ed. *Montage and Modern Life, 1919–1942*. Cambridge: MIT Press, 1992.

Temple, Michael, and James S. Williams, eds. *The Cinema Alone: Essays on the Work of Jean-Luc Godard, 1985–2000*. Amsterdam: Amsterdam University Press, 2000.
Temple, Michael, James S. Williams, and Michael Witt, eds. *For Ever Godard*. London: Black Dog Publishing, 2004.
Tešić, Gojko, ed. *Antologija srpske avangardne književnosti*. Novi Sad: Bratstvo jedinstvo, 1989.
Tešić, Gojko, ed. *Antologija pesništva srpske avangarde, 1902–1934*. Novi Sad: Svetovi, 1993.
Tešić, Gojko. *Srpska književna avangarda*. Belgrade: Institut za književnost i umetnost, Službeni glasnik, 2009.
Todić, Milanka. *Nemoguće: Umetnost nadrealizma*. Belgrade: Muzej primenjene umetnosti, 2002.
Todorović, Miroljub. *Signalizam*. Niš: Gradina, 1979.
Todorović, Miroljub. *Čorba od mozga*. Belgrade: Zapis, 1982.
Todorović, Predrag. "Prilozi za biografiju Dragana Dade Aleksića." In *Književna istorija* 39, no. 131–132 (2007): 341–368.
Tokin, Boško. "Evropski Pesnik Ivan Goll." *Zenit* 1 (February 1921).
Tokin, Boško. *Terazije*. Belgrade: Narodna biblioteka Srbije, 1988.
Tupitsyn, Margarita. *El Lissitzky: Beyond the Abstract Cabinet*. New Haven: Yale University Press, 1999.
Turković, Hrvoje. "Filmski modernizam u ideološkom i populističkom okruženju." *Hrvatski filmski ljetopis* 59 (2009).
Vertov, Dziga. *The Writings of Dziga Vertov*. Berkeley: University of California Press, 1984.
Virilio, Paul. *The Information Bomb*. London: Verso, 2005.
Virmoux, Alain, and Odette. *Le Grand Jeu et le cinema*. Paris: Paris Experimental, 1996.
Vučićević, Branko, ed. *Splav meduze*. Ljubljana: Viba film, 1980.
Vučićević, Branko, ed. *Avangardni film 1895–1939*. Belgrade: Radionica SIC, 1984.
Vučićević, Branko, ed. *Avangardni film 1895–1935*, vol. 2. Belgrade: Dom Kulture-Studentski Grad, 1990.
Vučićević, Branko, *Paper Movies*. Zagreb, Belgrade: Arkzin & B92, 1998.
Vučo, Aleksandar, "Ljuskari na prsima." *Nemoguće* (May 1930).
Vučo, Aleksandar. *Podvizi družine 'Pet Petlića'*. Belgrade: Globus, 1933.
Walley, Jonathan. "The Material of Film and The Idea of Cinema: Contrasting Practices in Sixties and Seventies Avant-Garrde Film." *October* 103 (Winter 2003).
Weiss, Allen S. *Shattered Forms: Art Brut, Phantasms, Modernism*. Albany: SUNY Press, 1992.
Weiss, Allen S. *Perverse Desire and the Ambiguous Icon*. Albany: SUNY Press, 1994.

Weiss, Allen S. *Breathless: Sound Recording, Disembodiment, and the Transformation of Lyrical Nostalgia*. Middletown: Wesleyan University Press, 2002.
Williams, Raymond. *Television*. London: Routledge, 2003.
Wollen, Peter. *Readings and Writings: Semiotic Counter-Strategies*. London: Verso, 1982.
Wollen, Peter. *Paris/Hollywood: Writings on Film*. London: Verso, 2002.
Yoon, Soyoung. Review of The Cinema, or the Imaginary Man by Edgar Morin. *Film Quarterly* 60, no. 3 (Spring 2007).
Youngblood, Gene. *Expanded Cinema*. New York: E. P. Dutton & Co., Inc., 1970.
Žižek, Slavoj. *The Sublime Object of Ideology*. London: Verso, 1989.

INDEX

"A.B.C.D. . . .", 75–76
Abel, Richard, 72
acting, cinematograph controlling, 78
Admiration of the Orchestelle for the Cinematograph, 38–40
Aesthetics of Cinema (Isou), 86
"The Alchemy of the Eye: Cinema as a Form of Mind," 74
Aleksić, Dragan, 23
    cinema endorsement of, 21
    influences and inspirations of, 20–21, 162n24
    on language as phonetic body, 18
    Outlaws in Topčider, or God Be With Us, 21
    "TABA CIKLON II," 17–18, 23
Amos, 87
Anatomies, 6
antifilm
    GEFF debates on, 114
    object of, 116
    Pansini on, 115–16
Antonioni, Michelangelo, 105
Apollinaire, Guillaume, 72
Aragon, Louis, 26
Arp, Hans, 7
art. *See also* Dada movement
    cinema by other means represented in, 27–28
    conceptual-materialist, 40
    demand and technological realization of, 43–44
    fidelity to medium specificity in, 29–30
    medium's dual nature in, 44–45
    psychoanalysis and libidinal apparatuses of, 8–9
    Signalism and, 98–99
Artaud, Antonin, 73
    on film as definitive, 74–75
    "The Precocious Old Age of Cinema," 74
audience. *See* spectatorship
automatism
    Breton defining, 14
    de Boully and, 54
    The Pulse and, 15–16, 16f
    Surrealism and, 14, 62
    Vučo and, 67–68
    written film and, 55–57
Avramović, Milenko, xv

Bachmann, Gideon, 96
Badiou, Alain, 110, 122
Baker, George, 41–42, 157
"Barbarogenius," 11
Baron, Jacques, 61
Bataille, Georges, 61, 169n36

INDEX

Bazin, Andre, 28, 32
beauty, convulsive, 58, 60
Belgrade Film Academy (FDU), 127–28
Belgrade Surrealist Group, 53, 83. *See also* Ristić, Marko
Can You Recognize Her?, 65, 66f
Benjamin, Walter, 43–44, 166n38
  on cinematic technology and reality, 81–83
  "The Work of Art in the Age of Its Technological Reproducibility," 81
Benson, Timothy O., 33
Black Wave, 128–29
Blink-Film, xv
Blink-O-Scope, xv–xvi
"Body Film Essay," 126f, 127
Bolter, Jay, 42, 166n35
Bor, Vane Živadinović, 70–71, 71f
Bresson, Robert, 125
Breton, André, 17, 26, 53, 168n22
  on automatism, 14
  "Essay on the Simulation of the Cinematic Delirium," 25
  "The Mediums Enter," 54
  on Surrealism, 54–55
The Bride Stripped Bare by Her Bachelors, Even, 9, 9f
Buñuel, Luis, 61, 69
Burgin, Victor, 147
Burroughs, William S., 171n13

The Cabinet of Doctor Caligari, 11, 36
"Camera Eye" segment, *Far From Vietnam*, 179n23
cameraless film, 5–6
camera obscura, 69, 70f
cameras. *See* film cameras
Can You Recognize Her?, 65, 66f
Carrive, Jean, 73
Casetti, Francesco, 94
Les Cashiers jaunes, 74
Castle 1, 111–12
Un Chien andalou, 61, 69
La Chinoise, 146–47
cine-clubs, Yugoslav culture and, 175n14
cine-desire, xii–xiii
cinefication. *See* general cinefication

cinema
  Aleksić's endorsement of, 21
  cinematograph transforming, 32
  Dada movement and, 5, 21–23, 44
  de Boully on metaphysical quality of, 56–57
  defilement of, 175n11
  as design, 38
  ethereal, 65–66
  exhibition dependence of, xv–xvi
  film separation from, xiii, 28–29, 31
  Godard on history of, 156
  Gotovac on omniscience of, 124, 127
  as illusionist medium, 108
  imagination and experience of, 107–8, 111
  "inferential current" of, 118
  interstice as imagination in, 159
  interstice as structure of, 145
  Lemaitre's innovations in, 91–92
  Lettrism and time in, 90
  Man Ray abandoning, 25–26
  Man Ray on reality and, 65
  Man Ray's beginnings in, 5
  meaning in, 118–19
  as metalanguage, 92, 94–95, 172n26
  meta-reality of, 81
  paracinema and, 28–29
  Pasolini on film and, 94
  as performative act, 31
  Picabia's hybridized, 41–42
  as praxis, xiv–xv
  process, 109
  psychological potential of, 84
  relational indeterminacy of, 95
  as religion, 11–13
  Sharits on conceptual material of, 121–22
  Šijan's work on decay of, 134–35
  still photography in, 77, 148, 149f, 151f
  suture process in, 143–44
  technological limitations of, 74
  theater influenced by, 78
  Zenithism and, 21
The Cinema, or the Imaginary Man (Morin), 84–86, 164n15
cinema by other means
  art representative of, 27–28
  dematerialization in, 31
  dialectal reversal of, 31–32

INDEX

The Frenzied Marble as, 27
Moholy-Nagy on, 29–30
remediation of, 42–43
"cinematics," of Sharits, 123
cinematic technology
Benjamin on reality and, 81–83
film as concept and, 38
language replacing, 104
Morin on imagination and, 84–86
philosophy and, 38, 40
reality's connection to, 35–38
rematerialization of, 38–40
cinematograph, xii
acting controlled by, 78
cinema transformed by, 32
re-materialization of, xiii, 103–4
Tokin on capabilities of, 13
Clair, Rene, 41
Entr'acte, 56–57
close-ups, in *Return to Reason*, 6
Code of Cinema, Pasolini's, 95–96
comic strip, 140–43
conceptual-materialist art, 40
convulsive beauty, 58, 60
Ćosić, Bora, 83–84
Crustaceans on the Chest, 62, 63f, 67f
structural dynamic of, 66–68
Surrealism and narrative structure of, 61
Curtay, Jean-Paul, 88
Cutrofello, Andrew, 172n26

The Dada Machine, 104
Dada movement
cinema and, 5, 21–23, 44
montage and, 7
negation of negation in, 3
nose art and, 58
sound poetry of, 17–18, 20
Tzara on poetry of, 7
Yugoslav, 58
Dali, Salvador, 58
Un Chien andalou, 61, 69
The Dancer, 23
Daney, Serge, 138, 143
on *Ici et ailleurs*, 152
Daumal, René, 73–74

Davičo, Oskar, 83–84
Debord, Guy, 93
de Boully, Monny
"A.B.C.D....", 75–76
artistic ideals of, 58
automatism and, 54
on cinema's metaphysical quality, 56–57
"Doctor Hypnison, or the Technique of Living," xiii, 46–47, 52–54, 59–61
on film's limitations, 75
on film's psychological impact, 57–58
Le Grand Jeu and, 73
libidinal apparatus of, 9–10, 10f
"Radio-Cinematographic Poem: Shadows of the Heart," 52, 52f
radio-film of, 52–53
Surrealism and, 55–56, 58–59
on Zenithism, 52
Deleuze, Gilles, 84
on diagrams, 40
on interstice, 144–45
Demaria, Jules, xii
Denegri, Ješa, 124–25
de Saint-Point, Valentine, 8–9
design, 165n24
cinema as, 38
"Destiny Sold," 69
Devaux, Frederique, 87, 91
Discontinuité, 73–74
Djurić, Nikola, 174n9
Remembrance, 110, 111f
Djurović, Žarko, 98
"Doctor Hypnison, or the Technique of Living," xiii, 46–47, 52–54
Surrealism in, 59–61
as written film, 61
Drainac, Rade, 47
Dubois, Philippe, xvi
Duchamp, Marcel, 3
The Bride Stripped Bare by Her Bachelors, Even, 9, 9f
"dumb poetry," 17, 19f, 20, 22–23
duration. *See* time
Dziga Vertov Group
Ici et ailleurs (Here and Elsewhere), 145–52, 149f, 151f
objective of, 147

INDEX

editing. *See also* montage
    Godard's techniques with, 146, 149–50
    "gutter" between frames in, 139–40
    in-camera, 35
    limitations of, 143
    as "meaningful nonexistent," 95
    necessity of, 138
    time and, 150
Eisenstein, Sergei, 28
    on montage, 138–39
    on spectatorship, 139
Electra, My Love, 96
Elsaesser, Thomas, 44
Eluard, Paul, 25
Emak Bakia, 65
Encyclopedia Acephalica (Bataille), 61
Entr'acte (Clair and Picabia film), 41, 56–57
Entrac'te (Sabatier film), 89–90
Epstein, Jean, 174n44
Ernst, Max, 14
    The Failed Immaculate Conception, 35, 36f
    La femme 100 tetes, 69, 70f
"Essay on the Simulation of the Cinematic Delirium," 25
ethereal cinema, 65–66
Evidence, 89, 89f, 106, 110
"An Example," 57
The Exorcist, 102
Expressionism, Zenithism and influence of, 11
eye
    of human aligned with film camera, 82
    Surrealism and displacement of, 69–71, 70f
    Surrealism and violation of, 68–69

The Failed Immaculate Conception, 35, 36f
"The False Messiah, Amphion or The Stories and Adventures of the Baron of Ormesan," 72
Far From Vietnam, 179n23
FDU. *See* Belgrade Film Academy
La femme 100 tetes, 69, 70f
film. *See also* cinema
    Artaud on definitive nature of, 74–75
    cameraless, 5–6
    cinema separation from, xiii, 28–29, 31
    cinematic technology and concept of, 38
    de Boully on limitations of, 75
    de Boully on psychological impact of, 57–58
    dematerialization of, 29
    Hausmann on life and, 32
    infinitesimal, 88–89, 106
    Isou on chiseling, 105–6
    Lettrism and matter of, 105–6
    Morin on consciousness and, 33
    nonrepresentational, 109–11, 111f
    Pasolini on cinema and, 94
    photographic essay compared to, 178n20
    pure, 113–14
    reality's connection to camera-based, 35
    Ristić re-materializing, 66, 67f
    Sharits on duality of, 120
    Sharits on time and, 119–20
    spectatorship proximity to, 163n6
    structural-materialist cinema material concerns with, 106–7
film cameras. *See also* cinematograph
    human eye aligned with, 82
    Jancsó's technique with, 96–97
    Latham Loop in, xi–xii, xif
filmic reflexivity, of *Return to Reason*, 16–17
Film Leaflet, 131
film projection
    as execution, 117–18
    experiments getting jammed in, 113
    Latham Loop in, xi–xii, xif
    material over imagination in, 113
    redefining, 109, 112–13
    Sharits liberating, 118
    structural-materialist cinema and, 107–8
film technology. *See* cinematic technology
Filmus. *See* Tokin, Boško
Flaker, Aleksandar, 50
Fondane, Benjamin, 46
    on written film and unfilmable scenarios, 73
Foster, Hal, 55
Frampton, Hollis, 77
    Information, 165n29

INDEX

"A French Nurse's Dream," 140, 141*f*, 142–43
The Frenzied Marble, 26–27, 26*f*, 45
   as cinema by other means, 27
Freud, Sigmund, 140, 143
Friedkin, William, 102
Frozen Film Frames, 120–21

Le Gai Savoir, 147
GEFF. *See* Genre Film Festival
general cinefication
   idealism of, 93
   Isou on, 86–87
   Jocić on, 101–2
   Kuleshov's Film Wokshop and, 78
   Lettrism and, 86
   of reality, 77, 83
   terminology of, 170*n*1
   world understood through, 84
Genre Film Festival (GEFF)
   antifilm debates at, 114
   formal and stylistic reduction at, 116
   influences on, 114–15
   programmatic statement of, 117
   Šijan influenced by, 124
Gidal, Peter, 107–8
Gift, 3, 4*f*, 7
Gilbert-Lecomte, Roger, 73–74
   "The Alchemy of the Eye: Cinema as a Form of Mind," 74
Godard, Jean Luc, 139–40
   La Chinoise, 146–47
   on cinema history, 156
   editing techniques of, 146, 149–50
   Far From Vietnam, "Camera Eye" segment, 179*n*23
   Ici et ailleurs (*Here and Elsewhere*), 145–52, 149*f*, 151*f*
   on identity construction, 152–53
   Notre Musique, 153, 154*f*, 155–59, 158*f*
   Numéro Deux, 179*n*22
   self-conscious style of, 150
   on shot and counter-shot, 158
   Weekend, 146–47
Gorin, Jean-Pierre, 145–52, 149*f*, 151*f*
Gotovac, Tomislav
   "Body Film Essay," 126*f*, 127
   on cinema's omniscience, 124, 127
   Heads, 124–25
   in "It's all a movie," 125, 126*f*
   The Morning of a Faun, 124, 125*f*
   Šijan's relationship with, 124
Le Grand Jeu
   de Boully joining, 73
   principles of, 73–74
   Surrealism's relationship with, 74
"The Great Lalula," 18
Grimoin-Sanson, Raoul, xii
Grusin, Richard, 42, 166*n*35
Guattari, Felix, 176*n*22
Gurk, 33, 34*f*

Hajdler, Zlatko, 117–18
Has the Film Started Yet?, 91
Hausmann, Raoul, 164*n*17, 168*n*24
   on film as form of life, 32
   Gurk, 33, 34*f*
   optophonetics and, 30–31
   Self-Portrait of the Dadasoph, 33
Heads, 124–25
Heath, Stephen, 35
Hein, Birgit, 112–13
Hein, Wilhelm, 112–13
Here and Elsewhere. *See Ici et ailleurs*
Hitchcock, Alfred
   Šijan's work on, 131–33
   Vertigo, 131
Horror is a Bestseller, 102–4
Hypnism
   influences of, 47
   Surrealism in, 53
Hypnos, 47, 48*f*, 49*f*

Ici et ailleurs (*Here and Elsewhere*), 145–50
   Daney on politics of, 152
   interstice in, 150
   slide insertion sequence in, 148, 149*f*, 151*f*
   time in, 151–52
Ilić, Aleksandar Battista, 126*f*, 127
imaginary aesthetics, 88–89

INDEX

imagination
  cinematic experience and, 107–8, 111
  film projection with material over, 113
  interstice as cinematic, 159
  Morin on cinematic technology and, 84–86
  in reality, 85
in-camera editing, 35
Indestructible Object, 7
"inferential current," of cinema, 118
infinitesimal film, 88–89, 106
Information, 165n29
informe, 15, 20
interstice. *See also* editing
  cinematic imaginary and, 159
  cinematic structure of, 145
  Deleuze on, 144–45
  in *Ici et ailleurs*, 150
"In the Name of Hundred Gods!", 35–37, 37f
Iskra projector, 113
Isou, Isidore, 45, 86
  Amos, 87
  on film chiseling, 105–6
  on general cinefication, 86–87
  imaginary aesthetics of, 88–89
  media inventions of, 88–89
  "supertemporal films" of, 90
  Sup Film or The Idiots Hall, 90
  Treatise on Drool and Eternity, 105
"It's all a movie," 125, 126f
Ixion (de Boully), 9–10, 10f

Jancsó, Miklós
  Electra, My Love, 96
  film camera technique of, 96–97
  history in work of, 97–98
Jocić, Ljubiša
  on abstract painting, 174n45
  The Dada Machine, 104
  on general cinefication, 101–2
  Horror is a Bestseller, 102–4
  on language transparency, 100–101
  poetry of, 99–100
  Signalism and, 98
  on technology and communication, 101

Jovanović, Miša, xv
Jusqu'à la victoire. *See Ici et ailleurs*

K-3, 115–16, 116f
Kariokinesis, 117–18
Kessler, Ivana, "Body Film Essay," 126f, 127
Khlebnikov, Velimir, 50, 164n11, 168n24
The Kingdom of Ghosts (Tokin), 47
Kino-Eye method, of Vertov, 79
Kinofon, 21, 22f
Kitsch-sequences, 129
Kittler, Friedrich, 18
Kluge, Alexander, 163n6
Kovács, Stephen, 4–5, 26
Krauss, Rosalind, 150, 165n27
Kuleshov's Film Wokshop, 78
Kuntzel, Thierry, 175n11, 180n35

Lacan, Jacques, 18, 172n26
lalangue, 18
The Landscape, 70–71, 71f
Langlois, Henry, 174n9
language. *See also* written films
  Aleksić on phonetic body of, 18
  cinematic technology replaced by, 104
  Jocić on transparency of, 100–101
  Lettrism reconceptualizations of, 101
  meta, 92, 94–95, 172n26
The Language Machine, 99
Latham Loop, xi–xii, xif
The Law of Accommodation among the One-Eyed (*La Loi d'accomodation chez les borgnes*), 42
Layton, Edwin T., Jr., 165n24
Le Grice, Malcolm, 109
  Castle 1, 111–12
Lemaitre, Maurice
  cinematic innovations of, 91–92
  Has the Film Started Yet?, 91
L'Etoile de mer, 61–62
Lettrism, 45
  cinema and time in, 90
  film matter and, 105–6
  general cinefication and, 86
  idealism of, 93, 106

INDEX

language reconceptualizations of, 101
"medium free media" of, 92–93
metagraphology and, 87
retrograde remediation and discrepancy in, 87
screen relocation by, 92
Levy-Bruhl, Lucien, 173n42
libidinal apparatus
of de Boully, 9–10, 10f
psychoanalysis on art and, 8–9
Lissitzky, El, 50, 78–79
London Filmmakers' Cooperative, 109
loop, film, xi–xii
Lottman, Yuri, 86
Lyotard, Jean-Francois, 8

magic lantern, xii
Malevich, Kazimir, 78
A Man Escaped, 125
"Manifesto of the Film Garbage-Man," 134, 135f
Man Ray
Admiration of the Orchestelle for the Cinematograph, 38–40
Anatomies, 6
cinema abandoned by, 25–26
on cinema and reality, 65
cinema beginnings of, 5
The Dancer, 23
"dumb poetry" of, 17, 19f, 20, 22–23
Emak Bakia, 65
"Essay on the Simulation of the Cinematic Delirium," 25
Gift, 3, 4f, 7
Indestructible Object, 7
L'Etoile de mer, 61–62
rayography discovery of, 4–5
Return to Reason, 4–7, 6f, 15–17, 19f, 22–24, 105, 118–19
Ristić influenced by, 62
The Man With a Movie Camera, 105
The Marathon Family, 134–35
Marinetti, Filippo Tommaso, 38
Masson, André, 14–15
Matić, Dušan, 3, 54
The Frenzied Marble, 26–27, 26f, 45

McLuhan, Marshall, 42, 162n23
"Media Suicide," 176n36
"medium free media," of Lettrism, 92–93
"The Mediums Enter," 54
metagraphology, 87
metalanguage, cinema as, 92, 94–95, 172n26
Metz, Christian, 108
Michelson, Annette, 25, 79–80, 106
Micić, Ljubomir, 10
"In the Name of Hundred Gods!", 35–37, 37f
radio-film of, 50, 52
"Shimmy at the Graveyard in the Latin Quarter," 49–50, 52
"Words in Space" poem of, 11–13
on Zenithism, 11, 14
Miéville, Anne-Marie
Ici et ailleurs (*Here and Elsewhere*), 145–52, 149f, 151f
Numero Deux, 179n22
Miller, Jacques-Alain, 143
The Mirror, 33, 35
Moholy-Nagy, László, 6
on cinema by other means, 29–30
montage, xiv. *See also* editing
as butchery, 156
Dada movement and, 7
Eisenstein on, 138–39
in *Notre Musique*, 156–59
in *Return to Reason*, 7
Vertov on reality of, 79–81
Monument, 50, 52
Moonshine in a Tetra Pack (Jocić), 99–100, 102
Morgenstern, Christian, 18
Morin, Edgar, 32, 164n15, 172n17
on cinematic technology and imagination, 84–86
on film and consciousness, 33
le mouvement flou, 53
Murray, Timothy, 81
Music Biennale Zagreb, 115
My Adventures at the Cinematheque, 129, 130f

New American Cinema, 123
Noe, Radojica Živanović, 15, 16f

INDEX

nonrepresentational film, 109–11, 111f
nose art, 168n24
    Yugoslav Dada movement and, 58
Notre Musique, 158f
    black screen intervals used in, 157
    montage in, 156–59
    rebuilding bridge in, 153, 154f, 155
    retrograde remediation and, 153
The Nova Express (Burroughs), 171n13
Numéro Deux, 179n22

100 Headless Woman (Ernst), 35, 36f
Optophone, 30–31
opto-phonetic poetry, 19–20
optophonetics, 30–31
Outlaws in Topčider, or God Be With Us, 21
"The Outline for a Phenomenology of the Irrational," 169n38

Painleve, Jean, 61
Painting, Photography, Film (Moholy-Nagy), 29–30
Pal, George, 127
Pansini, Mihovil, 114
    on antifilm, 115–16
    K-3, 115–16, 116f
    spectatorship redefined by, 115
paracinema, 28–29
Pasolini, Pier Paolo, 93
    Code of Cinema of, 95–96
    on film and cinema, 94
Pavlović, Živojin, 127–28
Petrović, Miroslav Bata, 113
photo-chemical process, structural-materialist cinema and, 107
photograms, of Ristić, 62, 64f, 65
photography. *See* still photography
Picabia, Francis, 55
    Entr'acte, 41
    hybridized cinema of, 41–42
    The Law of Accommodation among the One-Eyed, 42
    mechanical period of, 40–41
    Portrait of Max Jacob, 41
    written film of, 42

Plastic Jesus, 128
poetry
    "dumb poetry," 17, 19f, 20, 22–23
    of Jocić, 99–100
    opto-phonetic, 19–20
    of Šijan, 136–37
    sound, 17–18, 19f, 20
    Tzara on Dada movement and, 7
    of Zenithism, 49
Popović, Koča
    "Destiny Sold," 69
    "The Outline for a Phenomenology of the Irrational," 169n38
Portrait of Max Jacob, 41
Posavec, Ivan, 125, 126f
"The Precocious Old Age of Cinema," 74
process cinema, 109
projection. *See* film projection
The Pulse, 15–16, 16f
pure film, 113–14

Raban, William, 109
"Radio-Cinematographic Poem: Shadows of the Heart," 52–53, 52f
radio-film
    of de Boully, 52–53
    of Micić, 50, 52
"The Radio of the Future," 50
rayography
    immediacy of, 5–6
    Man Ray discovery of, 4–5
    in *Return to Reason*, 4–6, 6f
reality
    Benjamin on cinematic technology and, 81–83
    camera-based film's connection to, 35
    cinematic technology's connection to, 35–38
    general cinefication of, 77, 83
    imagination in, 85
    Man Ray on cinema and, 65
    remediation of, 88
    Vertov on montage as, 79–81
    written film and, 76
religion, cinema as, 11–13
remediation
    of cinema by other means, 42–43

of reality, 88
retrograde, 42–43, 47, 87, 101, 153
Remembrance, 110, 111f
retrograde remediation, 42–43
 Lettrism dynamic of discrepancy and, 87
 media relocation in, 101
 Notre Musique and, 153
 written film as, 47
Return to Reason, 15, 105, 118
 close-ups in, 6
 "dumb poetry" in, 17, 19f, 22–23
 filmic reflexivity of, 16–17
 materialist content discovered in, 118
 meaning and abstraction in, 23–24
 montage in, 7
 rayography in, 4–6, 6f
 stylistic techniques in, 4
La Révolution Surréaliste, 54
In the Rhythm of Howard Hawks, 131, 133f
In the Rhythm of John Ford, 131, 132f
Ristić, Marko, 53
 Crustaceans on the Chest, 61–62, 63f, 66–68, 67f
 ethereal cinema of, 65–66
 "An Example," 57
 film re-materialized in work of, 66, 67f
 Man Ray influencing work of, 62
 "The Outline for a Phenomenology of the Irrational," 169n38
 photograms of, 62, 64f, 65
Rohfilm, 112–13
Rose, Barbara, 7, 39
Rosen, Philip, 155

Sabatier, Roland
 Entrac'te, 89–90
 Evidence, 89, 89f, 106, 110
Šamec, Milan, 117
Schwitters, Kurt, 7
Self-Portrait of the Dadasoph, 33
sense of smell. *See* nose art
Sharits, Paul
 on cinema as conceptual material, 121–22
 "cinematics" of, 123
 on film and time, 119–20
 film projection liberated by, 118

on film's duality, 120
Frozen Film Frames, 120–21
Šijan compared to, 122–23
structural-materialist cinema and, 122
"Shimmy at the Graveyard in the Latin Quarter," 49–50, 52
Shots (Davičo), 83
Signalism, 28, 102–4
 art forms of, 98–99
 Jocić and, 98
Šijan, Slobodan
 on Black Wave, 128–29
 cinematic decay in work of, 134–35
 diverse tastes of, 123–24
 FDU education of, 127–28
 Film Leaflet, 131
 garbage depot footage of, 176n35
 GEFF influencing, 124
 Gotovac's relationship with, 124
 Hitchcock in work of, 131–33
 Kitsch-sequences, 129
 "Manifesto of the Film Garbage-Man," 134, 135f
 The Marathon Family, 134–35
 "Media Suicide," 176n36
 My Adventures at the Cinematheque, 129, 130f
 Plastic Jesus, 128
 poetry of, 136–37
 In the Rhythm of Howard Hawks, 131, 133f
 In the Rhythm of John Ford, 131, 132f
 Sharits compared to, 122–23
 written film and, 132–33
Sitney, P. Adams, 174n9
Škerović, Slobodan, 103–4
The Sketch for a Feature Length Fiction Film, 113
The Society of the Spectacle (Debord), 93
sound poetry
 of Dada movement, 17–18, 20
 writing, 18, 19f
spectatorship
 Eisenstein on, 139
 film proximity in, 163n6
 Pansini redefining, 115
 suture and, 144
 in written film, 65, 72

INDEX

still photography, in cinema, 77, 148, 149f, 151f
Stimson, Blake, 178n20
Story of Two Squares (Lissitzky), 78–79
structural-materialist cinema, 105
  film material concerns of, 106–7
  film projection as basis of, 107–8
  photo-chemical process and, 107
  Sharits and, 122
"supertemporal films," 90
Sup Film or The Idiots Hall, 90
Suprematism, 78–79
Surrealism
  automatism and, 14, 62
  Breton on, 54–55
  Crustaceans on the Chest narrative structure and, 61
  de Boully and, 55–56, 58–59
  in "Doctor Hypnison, or the Technique of Living," 59–61
  eye displacement in, 69–71, 70f
  eye violation in, 68–69
  Le Grand Jeu's relationship with, 74
  in Hypnism, 53
  written film and, 58–61
suture
  cinema and process of, 143–44
  Miller on, 143
  spectatorship and, 144

"TABA CIKLON II," 17–18, 23
Take Measure, 109
Tatlin, Vladimir, 50, 52
Tausk, Viktor, 167n41
technology. *See also* cinematic technology
  cinema and limitations of, 74
  demand for art and realization of, 43–44
  dual nature of, 44–45
  Jocić on communication and, 101
  reversal of influence of, 45
  universal mediation of, 83, 87
  written film's dependence on, 68
Termites, 117
theater, cinema influencing, 78
The Ticket That Exploded (Burroughs), 171n13

time
  editing and, 150
  in *Ici et ailleurs*, 151–52
  Lettrism cinema and, 90
  Sharits on film and, 119–20
Todorović, Miroljub, 98
  The Language Machine, 99
Tokin, Boško
  on cinematograph capabilities, 13
  Outlaws in Topčider, or God Be With Us, 21
  poems of, 13–14
  written films of, 47–48
Treatise on Drool and Eternity, 105
Tsivian, Yuri, 77–78
Turković, Hrvoje, 114–15
Tzara, Tristan, 5
  on Dadaist poetry, 7

unfilmable scenarios, 73
universal mediation, of technology, 83, 87
Untitled (Vučo, Nikola), 56

Ve Poljanski, Branko, 21
Vertigo (Šijan book), 132–33, 136–37
Vertigo (Hitchcock film of 1958), 131
Vertov, Dziga, 32. *See also* Dziga Vertov Group
  on "intervals," 80–81
  Kino-Eye method of, 79
  The Man With a Movie Camera, 105
  on montage as reality, 79–81
  The Visible and the Invisible Man: A Subjective History of Film (Ćosić), 83
Vladimir et Rosa, 147
Vučo, Aleksandar
  automatism and, 67–68
  Crustaceans on the Chest, 61–62, 63f, 66–68, 67f
  The Frenzied Marble, 26–27, 26f, 45
  The Mirror, 33, 35
Vučo, Nikola, 56

Walley, Jonathan, 28–29
Weekend, 146–47

INDEX

Weiss, Allen S., 60–61
Wiene, Robert, 11, 36
"the winker," 111–12
Wollen, Peter, 107–8
"Words in Space," 11–13
"The Work of Art in the Age of Its Technological Reproducibility," 81
written films. *See also* radio-film
    automatism and, 55–57
    "Doctor Hypnison, or the Technique of Living" as, 61
    Fondane on unfilmable scenarios in, 73
    Picabia and, 42
    reality and, 76
    as retrograde remediation, 47
    Šijan and, 132–33
    spectatorship in, 65, 72
    Surrealism and, 58–61
    technological dependence of, 68
    of Tokin, 47–48

Yugoslav Dada movement. *See* Dada movement

Zaitseva-Selivanova, Anna, 78
Zenit, 11, 12f, 50, 51f
Zenithism
    ambitions of, 10
    cinema and, 21
    de Boully on, 52
    Expressionism's influence on, 11
    Micić on, 11, 14
    poetry of, 49
"Zenith-Man," 11

www.ingramcontent.com/pod-product-compliance
Ingram Content Group UK Ltd.
Pitfield, Milton Keynes, MK11 3LW, UK
UKHW022211230426
12048UKWH00016BA/784